QUANTRILL'S WAR

DUANE SCHULTZ

QUANTRILL'S WAR

THE LIFE AND TIMES OF
WILLIAM CLARKE QUANTRILL
1837–1865

ST. MARTIN'S GRIFFIN ❧ NEW YORK

A THOMAS DUNNE BOOK.
An imprint of St. Martin's Press.

Title page photo of William Clarke Quantrill is used courtesy
of the State Historical Society of Missouri, Columbia.

Maps pages 22 and 148 © 1996 by Mark Stern Studios

Photo insert by Barbara M. Bachman

Design by Pei Koay

Library of Congress Cataloging-in-Publication Data

Schultz, Duane P.
    Quantrill's war : the life and times of William Clarke
Quantrill (1837–1865) / by Duane Schultz.
        p.   cm.
    "A Thomas Dunne book."
    Includes bibliographical references and index.
    ISBN 0-312-16972-8
    1. Quantrill, William Clarke, 1837–1865.   2. Guerrillas—
Missouri—Biography.   3. Guerrillas—Kansas—Biography.
4. United States—History—Civil War, 1861–1865—Underground movements.   5. Kansas—History—Civil War,
1861–1865.   6. Missouri—History—Civil War, 1861–1865.
I. Title.
E470.45.Q3S38   1996
973.7'42'092—dc20
    [B]   96-23709
                                                                  CIP

10   9   8   7   6   5   4

To the memory of
Anita Diamant,
literary agent

CONTENTS

Lawrence should be thoroughly cleansed, and the only way to cleanse it is to kill! Kill!

—WILLIAM CLARKE QUANTRILL

Because of [Quantrill], widows wailed, orphans cried, maidens wept.

—WILLIAM ELSEY CONNELLEY

Quantrill's massacre at Lawrence is almost enough to curdle the blood with horror. We find it impossible to believe that men who have ever borne the name of Americans can have been transformed into such fiends incarnate.

—THE NEW YORK TIMES

1

HE BORE MALICE

HE SAID HIS NAME was Charley Hart, but that was a lie. He claimed to be a detective for the Delaware Indian tribe, but that, too, was a lie.

He said he was pro-Southern—in favor of states' rights and slavery, opposed to the attempt to make Kansas a free state. That wasn't true, either. He was no more in favor of the South's cause than he was of the North's. All he believed in was what was best for Charley Hart, whatever was likely to bring in a dollar. That was what he cared about—that, and revenge. Always revenge.

Throughout the spring and summer of 1860, Charley Hart lived like an outlaw, a common thief. He stole horses and cattle, then called on their owners, offering to retrieve the livestock for so much a head. He crossed the border into Missouri and stole slaves, reselling them to their owners for the reward. He kidnapped free blacks in Kansas and sold them into slavery across the line in Missouri.

He led three Quaker abolitionists into Missouri, promising the do-gooders they would steal the slaves of a wealthy landowner and set them free. When they reached the farm, Charley Hart betrayed his new friends and shot one in the head. His reward was fifty dollars, a saddle, and a purebred Kentucky horse. Hart also bedded the landowner's daughter.

He told everyone who would listen his tale of revenge. He claimed that while he and his brother were camped outside Lawrence on their way to California, some Kansans had murdered his older brother and left him for dead. Nursed back to health by an Indian, Charley Hart vowed to track down and kill his assailants.

And he said he had done it—killed more than twenty, shot them between the eyes. The Quaker abolitionists he had lured to the Missouri farm were the last of his brother's killers, he said. Not a word of Hart's story was true—he did not even have an older brother—but it was a good tale, well told, and it got him invited into the county's best homes. He became what he had always dreamed of becoming: a hero.

To the people of Lawrence, Kansas, however, Hart remained a common thief, and in late November of 1860, the last year of peace for the nation, a warrant was issued for Hart's arrest. The charges were kidnapping, horse stealing, burglary, larceny, and arson. Hart eluded the sheriff, and by the time he returned to Lawrence three years later to take revenge against the town he believed had wronged him, he was using his true name—William Clarke Quantrill—a name soon to be linked with the greatest atrocity of the Civil War.

By then, Quantrill was more than a thief. He was a cold-blooded killer, gunning down Union soldiers and civilians, showing no mercy or remorse. Plundering, burning, murdering, Quantrill earned a reputation as the "bloodiest man in American history," waging his personal war under the protection of the Confederate flag. It was a war against the world, driven by hatred and a desire to avenge himself against everyone he imagined had maligned him. He vowed to get them all. He wasn't lying about that.

William Clarke Quantrill did not look like a killer. There was no feral mask of madness, no savage sneer, no half-demented stare. At age twenty-three, when he rode into Lawrence for the first time in the spring of 1860, he had retained his boyish good looks. He stood a little shy of six feet tall, though he appeared shorter because of his slouch. He weighed about 160 pounds, slender but well-built.

Some people remember him as handsome, with a Roman nose, a deeply tanned face, and blond, almost yellow, hair. He was smooth-shaven, with a firm jaw and a smile that could be as faint and beguiling as the Mona Lisa's. His eyes were his most memorable feature, either gray or blue, depending on who was doing the telling, and hooded by deeply drooping lids. He looked perpetually tired, even weary, some said. But to others, the hooded lids made him seem dangerous, even cruel. If there was any hint of a killer, it was in those eyes. Boyhood friends recall the strange gleam in his eyes whenever his father, the school's principal, whipped his son for making trouble in the classroom. The boy would return to the room trembling, his murderous eyes glittering. But he never cried.

As a child, Bill Quantrill was a monster, as cruel and merciless with animals as he would later be with people, and equally without pity or remorse. He liked to torture animals, delighting in their cries of pain as they died. He nailed snakes to trees and shot pigs through the tips of their ears, laughing as the creatures squealed and ran berserk. He tied cats together by their tails and threw them over a clothesline, watching, transfixed, as they clawed each other to death. While walking through a farmer's field, he had been known to slice open the side of a cow casually, or to stab a horse.

He used to keep small snakes in his pocket and toss them at his sister and the other girls at school, enjoying their horror. He locked the teenaged housekeeper of the Catholic church in the belfry and threw away the key. The child spent a terrifying twenty-four hours imprisoned without food or water until she was found. Quantrill thought it was a pretty good joke.

Mostly, though, he led a solitary life, wandering in the woods with a rifle to shoot small game. Other children considered him peculiar, but if the lack of friends bothered him, he never let on.

He never got along with his father. There was none of the

closeness between them that the boy had with his mother. He was her favorite child. To her, little Bill could do no wrong. She saw him as intelligent, quick and alert, clever enough to escape punishment for his misdeeds. He could be charming, even eloquent, when he set his mind to it. But most of the time he was stubborn, obstinate, and deceitful.

As he grew up, he showed he was lazy, too, not willing to work for the money and property he thought was his due. He plotted, manipulated, and lied, convinced that some stroke of luck would bring him his rightful fortune. Others could toil and plod; that was not for him. And certainly he would not work for someone else to make his way in the world. The few times he tried, he rebelled at the restraint, at the power and authority of his bosses. He bucked authority every chance he got, insisting on doing things his way. And why not? He knew he was better than everybody else, above their rules and laws. He'd do as he pleased, and the devil with them all!

And Quantrill was superior in at least a few ways. He could plan and scheme better than most, which was why so many men were eager to follow when he organized his band of outlaws. He would devote hours to devising the details of a guerrilla raid, giving careful consideration to the route of retreat, should the operation not go well. He was brave and daring in battle, time and again demonstrating his courage. Calm in the most ferocious of fights, he betrayed no weakness, doubt, or fear.

Combat excited him, and he was often seen laughing aloud, the way he used to when tormenting some animal as a child. His laughter was remembered as "a sort of gay, nervous chuckle. Sometimes this strange giggle would be heard right after he had killed a man. The guerrillas themselves found it rather eerie and even a little frightening." But the outlaws continued to ride with him, at least for a time, until the slaughter at Lawrence sickened them; until Quantrill's laugh became too eerie, too frightening, even for those hard-bitten men.

By then, most of these men knew firsthand what was driving him. They realized he was not fighting to save the Confederacy. Quantrill stood for no principles; he had no personal convictions. He killed for the love of killing, and the War Between the States merely provided an opportunity to pursue his chosen career of theft, murder, and destruction disguised and sanctioned as a fight for a nobler cause. From his childhood until his early death at the age of twenty-eight, William Clarke Quantrill fought for only one cause: personal vengeance. "He brooded over imagined insults and suspected any kindness shown him. He bore malice, cherishing it, waiting until he could wreak his venom. He was coldly calculating and had the patience to wait silently for the right time for his vengeance."

The war afforded him the right time and circumstances, and his own twisted mind gave him the perfect target. It was Lawrence, Kansas, the center of Unionism and abolitionism, the *symbol* of all that the Yankees stood for. More important, it was the town that had humiliated him by swearing out a warrant for his arrest and forcing him to flee through the back alleys and to hide. The town had run off the outlaw Charley Hart, but Quantrill the guerrilla leader would return to exact revenge.

2

I ALONE AM MISERABLE

ONE OF Quantrill's uncles was a pirate, another tried to murder his ex-wife, and his father attempted to kill a man who exposed his misuse of public funds. The pirate, whose name is lost to history, sailed the Gulf of Mexico off the Texas coast. More is known about Uncle Jesse Quantrill, a charming, dashing rogue. He married Mary Lane, seized her inheritance through trickery, and quickly squandered it all. He embarked on a career of larceny, fraud, and swindle, moving from city to city and jail to jail, with his loyal wife following. For several months, she lived with him in his cell.

After skipping bail, which his wife had posted, Jesse left her, got in trouble again, and was sentenced to three years in a Pennsylvania jail. She finally divorced him and remarried, but she was not to be rid of him yet. Once out of prison, he appeared at her house in Cumberland, Maryland, and threatened to kill her. He threw her to the floor, aimed a pistol at her face, and pulled the trigger. The gun misfired. Jesse pulled a knife, but her screams brought help, and Jesse Quantrill went back to jail. In due course, between prison terms, he married six more women and deserted them all.

Thomas Quantrill, William's father, was a handsome, outgoing man who settled in Canal Dover, Ohio. A tinsmith by trade, or tinner, as they were called then, he wrote a book about his craft, showing how various household items could be fashioned out of tin. To pay for the printing of the book, he took money from the local school fund, of which he was a trustee. A neighbor, Harmon V. Beeson, questioned this use of public money and exposed the culprit. Thomas Quantrill was outraged.

He went to Beeson's home, armed with a loaded derringer. He found Beeson heating the tip of an iron poker, about to plunge it into a cup of cider. When Beeson saw Quantrill's gun, he decided there was a better use for the hot poker, and he struck Quantrill on the head, knocking him unconscious. Quantrill survived, although the incident left him with a large, ugly gash. He did not threaten Beeson again, but he did not manage to stay clear of trouble.

He made disparaging remarks about the wife of Mr. Roscoe, a local resident of French descent, repeating his comments frequently. Mr. Roscoe did not respond, but Mrs. Roscoe did, which brought much excitement and delight to the residents of peaceable Canal Dover. Mrs. Roscoe, equipped with a bullwhip, went looking for Thomas Quantrill. When she found him on the street, talking to his cronies, she flexed her arm and proceeded to administer a good lashing.

Despite this background, when the local school district was established, Thomas Quantrill was named assistant principal. There may have been a dearth of qualified applicants, but in his favor was the fact that he had received more schooling than most of the town's residents. After two years, he was promoted to principal, and it appears he never again made a spectacle of himself.

Little is known of William Clarke Quantrill's mother, Caroline. She seems to have been a good wife and mother, at least for a time. However, when neighbors were questioned by reporters after her son became famous, they described her as treacherous and cruel. While her children were young, she preferred to be alone, rarely venturing outside the house, not even to church, which inspired considerable gossip. A biographer of Quantrill wrote, "Her temperament was brooding and full of jealousy and malice." The couple had eight children, but four died young.

Daughter Mary was a cripple, born with curvature of the spine. Like her mother, she rarely left the house, but she became a skilled seamstress and helped support the family. Son Franklin was disabled by a severe swelling in one knee. He went into the fur business and apparently led an uneventful life. Thomas became a bum, a hobo, "a vile, base, worthless, despicable but petty scoundrel." Little has been recorded about the other children or about Bill's relationships with them.

Young Bill seemed smart, and he performed well enough in school to become a teacher at the age of sixteen, in the same school where he had been a pupil. It was not unusual in those days for a bright pupil to "keep school." He might have continued in the job had his father not died the following year, leaving the family in financial difficulty. Mrs. Quantrill took in boarders, which made Bill angry and resentful, embarrassed by their reduced circumstances and status. He felt that at home he was just an extra mouth to feed. His teacher's salary did not go far in providing for his brothers and sister.

Like so many young men of his time, the solution to his problem seemed to lie farther west. There, perhaps, he would find his fortune. When one of the teachers at Quantrill's school announced plans to join her family in Mendota, Illinois, Quantrill's mother persuaded the woman to take her beloved eighteen-year-old firstborn son along, so he might make his way in the world.

But there was no fortune to be found in Mendota for William Clarke Quantrill. He taught school, hawked his father's book about the tinsmith trade, although he sold not a one, and hunted game birds. He sold prairie chickens for $1.50 a dozen and ducks for a quarter each. Geese brought fifty cents. Whatever enthusiasm he had had when he headed out west quickly faded. Three months after leaving Canal Dover, he wrote to his mother that the trip had been a mistake.

Well I must tell you one thing & that is that I am tired of the west al-
ready, and I do not think I shall stay in it very much longer than I
can help. . . . You may expect me home early in the spring, for I was
a dunce to go away for I could have done just as well at home as out
here and then I would have been at home. I have learned one good les-
son that I would never have learned at home & when I get there again
(which will not be long) I will turn over a new leaf entirely. . . . This
is the last winter you will ever have to keep boarders if I keep my health.
I feel that I have done wrong in going from home & hope you will for-
give me for it. I must bring my letter to a close.

> *Yours with respect*
> *Your son*
> *William C. Quantrill*

Quantrill wrote this letter in November 1855, but his mother heard nothing more from him for three months.

It remains unclear what his activities were that winter. His teaching job ended for some reason, but instead of going home, he went to work for a Mendota lumber company, unloading timber from railroad cars. He did not write his mother about that, nor did he tell her that he may have committed his first murder.

The story is a vague one, without substantiation, but enough people told tales of a killing by the Quantrill boy to take it beyond the realm of gossip and rumor. Although the details may not be known, the essence of the story is that he shot a man to death at the lumberyard. He was arrested and charged with murder. In one version, Quantrill shot in self-defense when someone tried to rob him. Another version has Quantrill killing a man who attacked him while he was sleeping in the lumberyard office. The man was a stranger in town, and since there were no witnesses and no one to contradict Quantrill's story, he was freed. However, the sheriff strongly suggested that Quantrill leave Mendota.

When he next wrote to his mother, in February 1856, he was living in Fort Wayne, Indiana.

I suppose you think that something has happened to me, and
you think right; for if it had not been so you would have heard
from me before this. I think I will not tell you in this letter what
it was as this is the first one I have wrote since it happened. The
last letter I wrote you was then. You will not think so hard of
me when you know all.

. . . The next time I will tell you all about what has happened. But I want you to never tell any body else, whoever it
may be for my sake.

He never explained the events that caused him to leave Mendota. In Fort Wayne, he taught school and wrote to his mother
that he was the best teacher the district had ever had. He also
said he was definitely returning home in the spring because he
could make as much money in Canal Dover as anywhere else. He
apologized for leaving her to rear the other children on her
own. He was studying bookkeeping, he wrote, so he would be able
to earn a decent living when he returned.

Quantrill did not go home in the spring, nor did he write again
until July. He was upset that he had not heard from his mother.
"Well, mother, I am going to write one more letter to you, and
it is the last letter until I receive an answer. This is the fourth one
without an answer yet and the last one." He told her that he was
still in Fort Wayne, and he claimed to be taking courses in chem-
istry, physiology, Latin, and trigonometry. He finally returned in
the fall, back where he had started, back to the same school-
house. Little had changed.

[His] venture into the world in quest of wealth and success had
failed. His mother still took boarders, his sister continued to
sew other people's clothes, they all remained poor. As the
bleak winter days passed, he sat in his little backwoods school-
house bored and restless, and filled with a spirit of longing.

In February 1857, Quantrill, not yet twenty, left for Kansas Territory to make another new beginning. Thousands of Ohioans

were migrating there because of the promise of cheap land, good soil, and pleasant climate—or so the advertising lures said—and the chance to start anew. Here was the American dream that drew generations westward to conquer and settle the continent.

Two Canal Dover men, Col. Henry Torrey, whose title came from service in the Mexican War, and Harmon V. Beeson, whom Quantrill's father had tried to shoot, decided to try their luck in Kansas. Both were having financial problems and looking for fresh opportunities. Beeson's seventeen-year-old son, Richard, a friend of Quantrill's, planned to accompany them. The rest of their families would follow later, once the men were established in the new promised land.

Bill Quantrill wanted to go with them. His venture to Indiana had not brought riches, and he had no prospects at home. Surely, he could make his fortune, or at least work a farm, in a new territory. He asked Beeson and Torrey if he could accompany them, but they were not eager to have him. There was something unsavory about Quantrill, always had been. They did not trust him. But when Mrs. Quantrill pleaded his case, they gave in. If only her son could get himself a farm, she explained, then the whole family could move to Kansas and escape the poverty that bound them to Ohio.

Beeson and Torrey reluctantly agreed to pay Quantrill's way to Kansas. In return, he would work for them for several months. The two men bought claims to adjoining parcels of land on the Marais des Cygnes and purchased a third claim in Quantrill's name, which was illegal, since he was a minor. It was a common practice, however, and Torrey paid Quantrill sixty dollars for the deed to the land.

For two months, the men worked all through the daylight hours, clearing the land and breaking the soil. It was hard work under primitive conditions, but Quantrill thought the land held promise. In May 1857, he wrote to his mother, encouraging her to sell the place in Canal Dover and send him the proceeds so he could buy 160 acres for a farm, a new home for the whole family.

If you can do this by any possible means do so and we can move
here this fall & be much more comfortably situated than in
Dover, or any place else east of Kansas. . . . Then we will all be
square with the world & be able to say our soul is our own without being contradicted. Is not this worth sacrificing something
for?

Apparently, it was not worth the sacrifice of sustained effort
on Quantrill's part. He was failing to do his share of the work
carving farms out of wilderness, not living up to his agreement
with Beeson and Torrey to repay the money for his passage to
Kansas through his sweat and labor. He preferred hunting and
took to wandering through the woods with a rifle. The only reason Beeson and Torrey did not send him packing was in defer-
ence to Mrs. Quantrill. They knew how much she was counting
on this chance to start a new life and how dependent she was on
Quantrill to bring that about.

But Quantrill continued his aimless days, roaming the woods
with a new friend, John Bennings, a shiftless, idle sort of person
who eked out a living hunting and trapping. Quantrill admired
Bennings's free and easy life—no hard work and no responsi-
bilities.

Quantrill lived with the Beesons, father and son, and Colonel
Torrey in a hardscrabble cabin with only one proper bed, and
that was no more than a shelf built into a wall. Quantrill and
Richard Beeson slept on the floor, where Quantrill wrapped
himself in the only blankets, leaving young Beeson to fend for
himself in the freezing Kansas winter. The two older men warned
Quantrill he was not behaving fairly—he should share the two
blankets—but the criticism only made him angry. He would stalk
out of the cabin and complain to John Bennings that they were
interfering in his life. Bennings was a sympathetic listener; his approval fed Quantrill's discontent.

One night, the elder Beeson awoke, to see Quantrill hovering
over him, holding the Mexican dagger Colonel Torrey kept in
his trunk. Beeson shouted at Torrey, who lunged from his cot

and disarmed Quantrill. Beeson seized a hickory switch and beat Quantrill until he begged for mercy.

"Bill," Beeson said to Quantrill, "I hated to give you such a thrashing, but I hope it will make you think. Your good mother would be terribly grieved if she knew of your bad conduct out here. She confided in me that she hoped your coming out here would make a man of you. But it seems to me you are in league with the devil himself. I am sorry for the day I first laid eyes on you."

Quantrill backed away from Beeson and his hickory switch. He'd had enough. He told them he was leaving.

"I'm glad to be rid of you and your damned orders," he said. "On my own I'll be able to get somewhere. You can go straight to hell, all of you! And let me tell you something before I go: you'll hear aplenty about me before I pass off this no-good earth!"

Quantrill went to live with John Bennings, and the two skulked around the countryside, Quantrill whining to anyone who would listen that Beeson and Torrey were cheating him out of his land. With Bennings's encouragement, Quantrill confronted Colonel Torrey and demanded ninety dollars for his claim. Torrey had little choice, because it was against the law to assign land to a minor. He submitted the matter to arbitration in squatter's court, and they ruled he had to pay Quantrill sixty-three dollars, in two installments. Torrey could not afford even the first payment, so Quantrill would have to wait until he could scrape up the money.

But patience was not part of Quantrill's personality. He stole a blanket and two pistols from Torrey, as well as a pair of oxen from Beeson, considering them his due. Beeson immediately suspected Quantrill and he set out to track him. He found him at sunup a few days later out on the prairie. Quantrill started to run, but Beeson got the drop on him with his rifle.

"Bill, stop!" Beeson shouted. "I want to see you."

Quantrill turned toward him.

"Lay your gun down in the grass!" Beeson ordered. "You must bring my oxen back by three o'clock this afternoon, or I shall shoot you on sight!"

Quantrill returned the oxen and Torrey's pistols but not the blanket, which was later found rotting in a hollow log. The oxen were in poor condition; Quantrill had not given them food or water. It was several days before they were strong enough for Beeson to take them home. He was furious.

"Bill Quantrill," he thundered, "you're even worse than I thought. Mark my words! You'll come to no good end!"

A bit later, Quantrill sat by a stream and wrote gentle, soothing words to his mother.

> I have but one wish, and that is that you were here, for I cannot be happy here all alone; and it seems that I am the only person or thing that is not happy along this beautiful stream. But I must close my letter, or I will make you sad; and in caring for three helpless children you have cares enough, without my adding to them.

Harmon Beeson returned to Canal Dover toward the end of the summer of 1857 to move his family and the Torrey family to Kansas. His enthusiasm for his new home persuaded other Canal Dover townsfolk to emigrate, among them several of Quantrill's former schoolmates. A few families bought adjoining claims and named their community Tuscarora Lake, after the Ohio county they had come from. Quantrill joined them, and because he had by then turned twenty-one, he took up a land claim himself.

In January 1858, he wrote to a friend in Ohio, urging him to come to Kansas. He extolled the virtues of Tuscarora Lake, the climate, the availability of land, the abundance of game and women.

> About the girls . . . a man can have his choice for we have all kinds & colors here Black White & Red. But to tell you which I like the best is a mixture of the two latter colors if properly brought up for they are both rich and good looking & I think go ahead of your Dover gals far enough. . . . You and the rest of the boys there must attend to the girls well while we are here

in Kansas, & tell them we are all going to marry squaws & when they die we are coming to old Dover for our second wives so that they must not despair.

Even with land of his own, friends his own age nearby, and his repeated promise to his mother to work a farm so they could live together again, Quantrill was unable to give up his idle, irresponsible ways. Instead of settling down and working his claim, he became more dissolute as the winter of 1858 turned to spring.

His cronies from home began to notice that some of their possessions went missing—blankets, clothing, food, and other items. Somebody was stealing from them. Quantrill was vocal in denouncing the thefts. He said he had done some detective work and had discovered the thieves: a bunch of settlers from a neighboring community. Nobody believed him. Given his reputation, everyone was sure he was the culprit.

They took turns watching him, until they finally caught him taking things out of one cabin. They made inquiries in nearby settlements and learned that Quantrill had been selling the stolen goods. Stealing from hometown friends was too despicable to forgive, and they banished him from Tuscarora Lake. No one would have anything to do with him, except the reprobate Bennings.

Quantrill loitered around for a few weeks and decided to make a clean break—with both Kansas and his own identity. It was time for another new start. He went to Fort Leavenworth and signed on as a teamster with a U.S. Army expedition leaving for Utah. He gave his name as Charley Hart.

Little is known about the time he spent out west, other than what he chose to reveal in three letters to his mother and what was fancifully described in 1907 by a soldier at Fort Bridger, ninety miles northeast of Salt Lake City, Utah. The post was rife with gamblers, and one of the notorious cardsharps the soldier heard about—a fellow who won a lot of money from the soldiers—was a Charley Hart. The soldier, R. M. Peck, described Hart as dressed in new clothes, having struck it rich.

A pair of high-heeled calf-skin boots of small size; bottoms of trousers tucked into boot-tops; a navy pistol swinging from his waist belt; a fancy blue flannel shirt; no coat; a colored silk handkerchief tied loosely around his neck; yellow hair hanging nearly to his shoulders; topped out by the inevitable cowboy hat. This is the picture of Charley Hart as my memory presents him now.

The soldier followed Hart into one of the gambling tents and watched him unwrap a silk handkerchief, revealing a substantial pile of gold coins, which he proceeded to bet. Hart placed his revolver on the table, to ensure fair play, he told the dealer, whose own revolver was also on the table. When Hart won the hand, he grabbed his pistol, shoved it in the dealer's face, and told him to back away while he raked in his winnings. With a cavalier gesture, he tipped the dealer a twenty-dollar gold piece and tossed some smaller silver coins in the air for the crowd to fight over. The soldier went on to report that the following day Hart lost every cent and left camp dead broke.

Quantrill's letters to his mother make no mention of gambling. He wrote from Salt Lake City on October 15, 1858, to tell her he planned to apply for a job teaching school, which he apparently did not do. He talked about going to Canada to prospect for gold, but he didn't do that, either. He was still a dreamer.

"You need not expect me home till you see me there, but bear in mind that I will do what is right, take care of myself, try to make a fortune honestly, which I think I can do in a year or two," he wrote.

Two months later, he wrote his mother again, saying he had been ill with what he described as mountain fever. He reported that he was going to work as an army clerk for fifty dollars a month. He swore he would not return home until he had made some money. Whether he took the army job is not known, but a month later he wrote his mother that he had been fired and that it was his fault, a rare admission that he might have done something wrong—if it was true. He said he was working as a cook until something better turned up.

Quantrill abruptly left Salt Lake City with a party of nineteen, heading for the gold fields of Colorado. It was a fiasco, he wrote to his mother in July of 1859. All the talk of gold had been just so much humbug. He worked forty-seven days prospecting for the yellow metal and earned only $64.34, which barely covered living expenses. He reported that his camp had been set upon by Indians and a friend had been shot in three places but survived. Quantrill escaped, he said, only because he was out hunting when the Indians struck.

His mother must have been surprised when she saw that the letter had been written from Lawrence, Kansas. As far as she knew, her son remained as aimless and shiftless as when he had first left home four years earlier. He had failed again, and there seemed to be no prospects for his future. He was a thief, a vagrant, and possibly a murderer, for there were rumors he had shot a man or two in Colorado. He wrote:

> I hardly know what to do at present, nor where to go. . . . You would hardly know me if you were to see me I am so weather beaten & rough looking that every body says I am about 25 years of age. I expect every body thinks & talks hard about [me] but I cannot help it now; it will be all straight before another winter passes.

He did not stay long in Lawrence. By the end of the summer of 1859, he was back in the Tuscarora Lake area, near the old Ohio friends who had banished him for stealing. He moved in with John Bennings in Stanton, forty-five miles south of Lawrence, and abandoned his Charley Hart identity to become Bill Quantrill once more. And again he became a schoolteacher, at least for one term. It was the last peaceful and stable period in his life, before he turned outlaw and guerrilla.

Quantrill was described by those who knew him then (they were interviewed in 1907) as a good teacher. They all agreed about that, and they said he hadn't caused any trouble that winter. He talked against slavery but took no part in the brutal border war with the slave state of Missouri. People remembered him as quiet and particular about his clothes, careful always to dress neatly. Even forty-seven years later, some recalled his strange eyes, which were like no other eyes they had seen. The more perceptive said he carried his passivity to the point of being secretive, even peculiar; they never knew how to take him. But at least he behaved amiably and gave no cause for anyone to turn against him or to fear him.

In letters to his mother and sister, he reminisced about his days out west, about the hardships and the beauty of the land. He confessed to being homesick and asked his mother to write him about Canal Dover. He said he dreamt about home and wished he could be there. He admitted to behaving foolishly over the last three or four years. "Still," he added, "I have been taught many a good lesson by them and think I shall not regret it in after life so much as I do now, for it is now that I feel it the keenest."

It almost sounded as though he was maturing and trying to change his ways. Yet, in that same letter, dated January 26, 1860, he revealed himself at his most duplicitous. To the people of Stanton, he condemned slavery as it was practiced across the border in Missouri, and he argued for Kansas remaining a free state. Writing to his mother, he took the opposite position, in favor of Missouri and slavery, referring to Kansans as the most lawless people anywhere.

A few weeks later, on February eighth, he wrote about how happy he had been in Canal Dover and how unhappy since leaving. He said he wanted to change, if only he could keep firm his resolve.

> I can now see more clearly than ever in my life before, that I have been striving and working really without any end in view. And now since I am satisfied that such a course must end in nothing, it must be changed, and that soon or it will be too late. . . . I am done roving around seeking a fortune, for I have found where it may be obtained by being steady and industrious. And now that I have sown wild oats so long, I think it is

time to begin harvesting; which will only be accomplished by putting in a different crop in a different soil.

Mrs. Quantrill had long been waiting to read such words from her firstborn child. What hope they must have given her. But it was false hope, an empty dream, as it had so often been with Bill.

He continued to write about wanting to be home again, to revisit the scenes of his past, now remembered with such joy. He promised to return soon, but not before midsummer. He wrote to his sister, Mary, about needing to see his family again, wanting them all to be together.

Overall, Quantrill's letters speak of sadness, as though he knew things would never be the same and realized that those happy days in his memory could never be repeated. He seemed to know there was no happiness in store for him and no way he could alter his fate. "I have not enjoyed myself much or felt very happy since I left home," he wrote to Mary, "for happiness depends on contentment, and that has not fell to my lot, and it seems to me never will."

He wrote of the songs of "merry little birds [that] make one wish he were as happy as all around him; but that cannot be; as this earth is not a heaven for man; for we at the happiest day feel a burden of sorrow which we cannot throw off here."

This morbid strain continues in another letter to his mother: "I think every thing and every body around me is happy and I alone am miserable; it seems that man is doomed to aspire after happiness; but never in reality to obtain it, for God intended *the earth* and not *heaven* for mortal man."

He asked his mother to write to him in Lawrence. As soon as the school term ended in March 1860, Quantrill, once again calling himself Charley Hart, left Stanton for Lawrence, a rabid center of abolitionism. It was there that he changed from petty thief to outlaw and killer. There were no shadowy rumors about murders; this time, the stories were true. As Charley Hart, Quantrill reverted to the viciousness and cruelty he had practiced as a child, once again becoming as lawless, aimless, and deceitful as he had been most of his life, save for the last few months in Stanton, the quiet time when he had yearned for and abandoned his chances for decency, happiness, and redemption.

In ordinary times, Charley Hart would have ended up swinging from a hangman's noose tightened around his neck by a posse of vigilantes, or shot down by the sheriff in the middle of some dusty street, and no one would have known his name. But these were not ordinary times. And Kansas in 1860, poor "bleeding Kansas," was no ordinary place. It was locked in a deadly war over the issue of slavery, a controversy that would soon divide the nation in two. Because of that war, men like Quantrill found an outlet for their hatred and sickness, an arena in which they could indulge their passion for murder, thievery, and destruction. Soon they would be celebrated as heroes.

It was that accident of time and geography, together with his own nature, that propelled William Clarke Quantrill from obscurity to infamy and enabled him to carry out on a national scale his personal battle for revenge. Quantrill's war was about to begin in earnest, and Kansas was its crucible.

3

A RIFLE IN ONE HAND
AND A BIBLE IN THE OTHER

THE CONFLAGRATION IN Kansas, which was to change
the life of William Clarke Quantrill, began three years before he first set foot there. In 1854, the year Quantrill's father died, the U.S. Congress passed the Kansas-Nebraska Act,
which one historian described as the "most important single
event pushing the nation toward civil war."

The Kansas-Nebraska Act opened up two huge territories for
homesteading, one further step in America's manifest destiny.
As territories, Kansas and Nebraska would begin to undertake the
process of self-government as a preliminary stage to inevitable
statehood. Two new states, then, lay in embryo, but what kind of
states would they be? Nebraska, by virtue of its geography, would
become a free state, because it shared no border with any slave
state.

The danger lay with Kansas, which had a 270-mile border with
Missouri, a slave state. At first glance, therefore, it appeared that
the futures of these incipient states were already determined: Nebraska free, and Kansas a slave state. But this was not set forth ex-
plicitly in the new law. Instead, the matter was to be resolved by

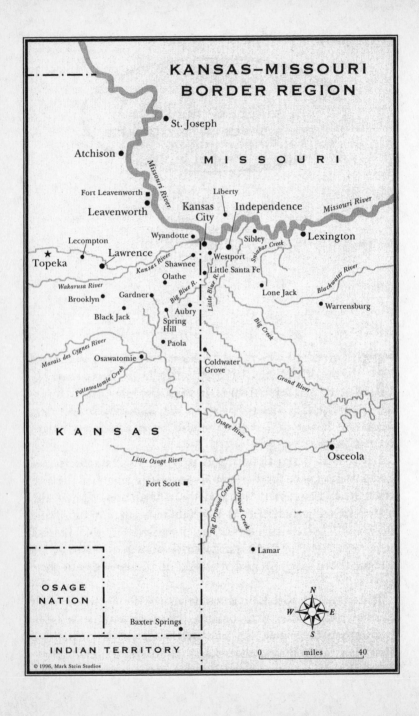

KANSAS–MISSOURI BORDER REGION

MISSOURI

St. Joseph

Atchison

Missouri River

Fort Leavenworth

Leavenworth

Liberty

Kansas City

Independence

Missouri River

Wyandotte

Sibley

Lexington

Lecompton

Lawrence

Kansas River

Westport

Little Santa Fe

Smabar Creek

Topeka

Shawnee

Olathe

Wakarusa River

Big Blue R.

Little Blue R.

Lone Jack

Blackwater River

Brooklyn

Gardner

Warrensburg

Black Jack

Aubry

Spring Hill

Big Creek

Paola

Osawatomie

Coldwater Grove

Grand River

Marais des Cygnes River

Pottawatomie Creek

Osage River

KANSAS

Little Osage River

Osceola

Fort Scott

Big Drywood Creek

Drywood Creek

Lamar

OSAGE NATION

Baxter Springs

N

W E

S

INDIAN TERRITORY

© 1996, Mark Stein Studios

0   miles   40

the doctrine of "squatter sovereignty." The residents of each territory would decide for themselves. In effect, "the side that got there first with the most settlers would win—or should."

For people who opposed slavery, the line had to be drawn in Kansas, which, they felt, could not be allowed to join other Southern states in perpetuating, indeed, expanding, that odious institution. The gauntlet was thrown to the South on the floor of the U.S. Senate by William Seward of New York, who declared, "Come on, then, gentlemen of the slave states. Since there is no escaping your challenge, I accept it in behalf of the cause of freedom. We will engage in competition for the virgin soil of Kansas, and God give the victory to the side which is stronger in numbers as it is in right."

Southerners, led by a vocal advocate of the Southern way of life, David Atchison of Missouri, were hell-bent on turning Kansas into another slave state. The institution of slavery, Atchison thundered, must be extended into the new territory "at whatever sacrifice of blood or treasure." The fight was on, with Kansas a symbol of the souls of North and South. It would be a fight to the death. "The storm that is rising," Senator Seward warned, "is such a one that this country has never yet seen."

The rush was on to populate the new Kansas Territory with sufficient numbers of people who would vote the right way. It would be a holy crusade on both sides.

In Massachusetts, the center of the movement to abolish slavery, Amos Lawrence, a textile millionaire, financed the New England Emigrant Aid Society. His mission was to help antislavery families move to Kansas to make sure abolitionists would rapidly outnumber proslavery settlers.

Rallies were held throughout Northern cities to raise money and recruits for Kansas. New words were set to old hymns and sung lustily, none with more fervor than poet John Greenleaf Whittier's "Song of the Kansas Emigrant," set to the tune of "Auld Lang Syne."

> *We cross the prairie as of old*
> *The fathers crossed the sea,*

To make the West, as they the East,
The homestead of the free.
We go to rear a wall of men
On Freedom's southern line,
And plant beside the cotton tree
The rugged northern pine.
We're flowing from our native hills
As our free rivers flow,
The blessing of our mother land
Is on us as we go.
We go to plant the common school
On distant prairie swells,
And give the Sabbaths of the wilds
The music of her bells.
Upbearing, like the ark of God,
The Bible in our van,
We go to test the truth of God
Against the fraud of man.

The settlers were sent off with a Bible in one hand and a rifle in the other, the newest and best Sharps rifle money could buy. A breechloader that could fire at the astonishing rate of ten shots per minute, it could strike a target with greater accuracy and at a greater range than any other. Throughout the North, there was scarcely a church worthy of the name that did not raise funds for rifles. In Brooklyn, New York, the Reverend Henry Ward Beecher raised so much money for them that some wag called his congregation "the Church of the Holy Rifles." The weapons became known in Kansas as "Beecher's Bibles." Beecher preached that this was a period in history when self-defense was a religious duty.

The New England Emigrant Aid Society sent out its first contingent for the cause in July 1854. Hundreds of settlers from other Northern states joined in this Kansas crusade. One of the first communities to be established, some thirty-five miles from the Missouri border, was Lawrence, named after Amos Lawrence, its patron. To Southerners, the town would become a reviled symbol of the abolitionist movement and all they hated with such a righteous passion. Lawrence was marked from the day it was founded.

Among Missouri's residents, tempers mounted as more and more wagon trains carrying Yankees with their Beecher's Bibles passed through on their way to Kansas. Missourians believed that Kansas Territory was rightfully theirs; some already had staked out their claims. They were in no mood to allow abolitionists to grab all that valuable land and threaten their way of life. A Liberty, Missouri, newspaper echoed these thoughts: "Shall we allow the cutthroats of Massachusetts to settle in the territory adjoining our own state? No! We are in favor of making Kansas a 'Slave State' if it should require half the citizens of Missouri, musket in hand, to emigrate there, and even sacrifice their lives in accomplishing so desirable an end!"

The firebrand Missouri senator David Atchison wrote to his friend Jefferson Davis: "We are organizing. We will be compelled to shoot, burn & hang, but the thing will soon be over."

Atchison spent the summer of 1854 visiting settlements and towns along the western Missouri border, haranguing crowds about the threats they faced from Northern intruders traipsing through their fair state. Missouri's citizens had a duty to go to Kansas, too, to stake out claims and prepare to fight for them. Hundreds of Missourians answered his plea, swarming over the border to settle towns where no free-staters were welcome: Fort Scott, Lecompton, Leavenworth, and the inevitable Atchison.

They formed a secret brotherhood, known variously as the Blue Lodge, the Social Band, Sons of the South, and the Self-Defensives. Their purpose was to extend slavery into Kansas and to expel the abolitionists, those who were not, as they phrased it, "sound on the goose." Even fellow slave-staters were judged as not sound on the goose if they voiced objections to the use of violence to make Kansas a slave state. You were either for them or against them; there was no middle ground.

It was easy for Blue Lodge members throughout Kansas to recognize one another. They wore a small piece of hemp rope in

their buttonholes. Hemp, as they were fond of reminding anyone who would listen—but particularly those who were not sound
on the goose—was used for making nooses. And nothing pleased
them more than the idea of nooses around the necks of no-good
Yankee abolitionists with their Beecher's Bibles.

Free-staters also had a secret organization. It was known as the
Kansas Regulators or Kansas Legion. The members held secret
meetings and recognized each other by a special sign, the thumb
placed under the chin while the forefinger scratched the nose.
The countersign was given by rubbing the lower lip with the left
thumb and forefinger. The Kansas Regulators were organized,
armed, and ready, but so were the Missourians.

An election was scheduled for March 1855, for Kansans to vote
for their first representatives to the territorial legislature. Missourians vowed to ensure that only proslavery men were voted in.
Senator Atchison led the campaign. At a rally in St. Joseph, Missouri, one of Atchison's henchmen fired up the crowd: "Mark
every scoundrel among you that is the least tainted with free-
soilism, or abolitionism, and exterminate him. . . . Enter every
election district in Kansas . . . and vote at the point of a Bowie
knife or revolver!"

Atchison himself, with a revolver and a knife stuck in his belt,
led a contingent of eight hundred Missourians directly to the
town of Lawrence. The ferries across the Missouri River were so
full that other boats had to be pressed into service, and the great
California Road heading west from Missouri was jammed with
men.

Men on horses, men on mules, men in a hundred wagons; men
with guns across the knees of their butternut breeches, red
shirts flaming beneath their sky-blue mackinaws. Border men,
bearded giants, they came with banners flying, to the music of
fifes and fiddles. They came singing, with guffaws ringing,
passing the jug from man to man, toasting the strength of
their arms, their delight in their two cannons, loaded with
musket balls.

They went to every district not already populated by slave-staters and terrorized voters and election officials, threatening death to all who opposed them. Flourishing their guns and knives to show their intent, they broke windows, fired weapons in the air, and stole ballot boxes, which they returned overflowing with fraudulent ballots. It was not uncommon for more votes to be cast than the number of people living there.

The Missourians won. A census showed that 2,905 Kansas residents were eligible to vote. The final tally was 6,307 ballots, more than twice the number of legal voters. Thirty-nine legislators were elected, thirty-six of whom were proslavery. Northerners were outraged. Free-Soilers in Kansas refused to recognize the new legislature. They formed their own government and named Charles Robinson, an agent of the New England Emigrant Aid Society, as governor. The men of Lawrence surrounded their town with trenches and forts and requested more Sharps rifles from their supporters in the cities of the East.

Atchison, furious that his rigged election results were being challenged, managed to get his proslavery candidates seated in the new legislature anyway. He prevailed on President Franklin Pierce to appoint a governor sympathetic to the Southern cause. Wilson Shannon was his name, and the first problem he faced was a slave law passed by Atchison's legislature that made it illegal to express an opinion against slavery. The law imposed the death penalty for helping slaves escape, required Kansas voters to swear to uphold the law, and legalized the bogus Missouri ballots. Although tension was high on both sides, no one had yet been killed. That was about to change.

In November 1855, a Missouri squatter in Kansas killed a free-state man over a land dispute, which had nothing to do with the slavery issue. Sam Jones, the Missouri sheriff with jurisdiction over that portion of Kansas Territory, refused to arrest the killer. After all, it was only an abolitionist who got himself killed. The Kansas Regulators decided to try to capture the killer, but he escaped. In retaliation, the Regulators set fire to several cabins belonging to proslavery men.

Sheriff Jones arrested the leader of the Regulators, but before he could get him to jail, a posse of Kansans from Lawrence confronted him and took the prisoner by force. An angry and embarrassed Jones rode across the border to Missouri and gathered an army of fifteen hundred armed men. They vowed to wipe the abolitionist hotbed of Lawrence, Kansas, clear off the map. Senator Atchison himself took command.

The men of Lawrence, one thousand strong, had dug in and were waiting. On December third, Atchison, Jones, and the Missourians made camp along the Wakarusa River, six miles outside Lawrence. "We mean to have Kansas," one man told a newspaper reporter, "and we are going to have it, if we have to wade through blood to our knees to get it." Atchison sent a message to Charles Robinson, the governor appointed by the Free-Soilers, demanding the surrender of the men who had kidnapped the sheriff's prisoner. In addition, the town would have to turn over all the Sharps rifles.

When Robinson refused Atchison's demands, newspaper headlines across the country trumpeted the beginning of civil war in Kansas. Robinson claimed that the men who had taken the leader of the Kansas Regulators were no longer in town. Further, the Sharps rifles were private property; the town did not have the authority to surrender them. Both stories were untrue, but they caused the Missourians to hold back. Even Senator Atchison felt the need for legal justification before proceeding.

Undecided about whether to attack, the Missourians sat by the riverbank for nearly a week. Finally, Kansas governor Wilson Shannon, the official appointed by President Pierce, drew up an agreement that denounced the freeing of the sheriff's prisoner by the Kansas Regulators' posse and promised not to interfere with the enforcement of the law in the future.

Jones and his Missourians clamored to raze Lawrence, but Atchison persuaded them that if they acted without legal sanction, they would do their cause more harm than good in the eyes of the nation. He cautioned them to wait. "You cannot now destroy these people without losing more than you would gain." Frustrated, but consoled by the thought that there would surely be another chance to burn Lawrence to the ground, the Missouri contingent dispersed.

Atchison continued to preach war against the Kansans, but he was not the only demagogue to take advantage of the situation for personal gain. The Free-Soilers had their own firebrand, who arrived in the spring of 1855. His name was James H. Lane, and he came to be called the Grim Chieftain. The forty-one-year-old Lane was an unprincipled, unscrupulous, selfish opportunist with a consuming drive for power and prestige.

He came from Indiana, the son of a politician. He had served in the Mexican War as a colonel and had been the state's lieutenant governor and U.S. congressman. But he was so volatile a liar, schemer, grandstander, and back-stabber that he was thrown out of his own party. Since his political career in Indiana was finished, Lane sought a place where his skills and cunning might restore his power—a place where chaos, fear, anger, and uncertainty led men to look for a strong leader who would tell them what they wanted to hear and rile them up so much, they might proclaim him king, or any damned thing he wanted to be. Senator from Kansas, when Kansas became a state, would do nicely for Jim Lane—for a start. And so he came to Kansas with no love for slaves and no desire to free them, commenting that he would "just as soon buy a nigger as a mule," but once there, he joined the cause of the Free-Soilers, sensing the path to a bright future.

Having decided which side to join, Lane quickly identified his main rival, the leader of the Free-Soilers, Charles Robinson. Lane took Robinson's measure and realized he could easily outclass him. Robinson was quiet, not a crowd-pleaser, not a jingoist. He counseled reason, patience, and peace. Lane knew that men really wanted action; they wanted war.

Lane was a magnetic, charismatic, imposing figure, six feet tall, slim and wiry, full of nervous energy. He had restless, darting coal black eyes. He wore overalls, like a man of the people, with a calfskin vest and black bearskin overcoat. One admirer gushed, "He burst with vitality—his voice was hypnotic. His hair was long and reckless, and above his ears black locks curled like horns. . . . He had a wide, loose mouth, as mobile as that of a Shakespearean 'ham' actor. He was indeed an actor, an artist—perhaps a great artist."

Lane could work a crowd like few other speakers. "He talked like none of the others," a historian wrote. "None of the rest had his husky, rasping, blood-curdling whisper or that menacing forefinger, or could shriek 'Great God!' on the same day with him."

Jim Lane had only to rise and slouch forward on the platform, close his eyes, take a deep chaw on his tobacco, and spit, preparatory to speaking, to cause an outbreak of stomping and applause. His audiences always knew they were in for a show when Jim Lane uncoiled his thin, wiry length—a show of shout and whisper, of spellbinding, if unreportable, oratory.

The Free-Soilers had found their messiah. Before he was finished, he would build, as a monument to his success and his ego, the finest mansion in Lawrence. William Clarke Quantrill would call Lane "as good a man as we have."

By 1856, Lane was a hero to the Free-Soilers in Kansas and to the abolitionist groups he spoke to back east, pleading so successfully for money and recruits. Of course, he did not wear his overalls or spit tobacco or shout and scream in the parlors of the eastern gentry. He sat demurely, sipping tea, dressed in impeccable black broadcloth, telling sad tales of the poor black slaves he loved like little children. A man of the people was James H. Lane.

Lane and others like him in the North and the South were effective spokesmen for their causes, and emigration to Kansas from both camps increased markedly. In the Southern states, David Atchison's appeals were bringing record numbers of proslavery settlers to Kansas. In Alabama, for example, Col. Jefferson Buford heeded the call and raised a band of three hundred men. He spent twenty thousand dollars of his own money and sold some of his slaves to raise more. The recruits were given Bibles and were blessed by a Methodist preacher before departing by boat for Kansas. Others joined the cause when the boat stopped at Mobile and New Orleans.

One southern county raised $100,000 to help Missouri residents cross the border and lay claim to Kansas land. Southern women donated jewelry, railroads gave free rides to people heading for Missouri and Kansas, and aid societies in every town raised money for the sacred crusade. In South Carolina, the Kansas Association of Charleston sent twenty-eight volunteers west. Marietta, Georgia, sent a dozen; Atlanta, twenty more. And so it went, until the roads and railways and rivers were full of young, zealous men ready to fight and to die, if that was what it took. No sacrifice was too great in the struggle to preserve their way of life.

That same fervor and fanaticism rang throughout the North for their equally holy crusade, to keep Kansas soil free from slavery. New Haven, Connecticut, sent more than a hundred men, including a clergyman, a doctor, and a group of eager young Yale University graduates. When a community could not find enough of its own men to enlist, it raised funds to help others to go.

Throughout the North and the South, preachers intoned, hymns were sung, and prayers chanted. Bibles were handed out to all emigrants—along with pistols and rifles. The holy Scriptures might inspire a man, keep him going against any hardship, and tell him how righteous was his cause, but it took guns to kill the heathen enemy.

Not all those who flocked to Kansas from the North went for such idealistic reasons; not all were abolitionists. Many residents opposed slavery in the abstract, as a social institution, and would vote to make Kansas a free state, but they were also prejudiced against Negroes. They may not have wanted them to be slaves, but neither did they want them as neighbors or competing with them for jobs. Also, not all settlers came from Massachusetts or New York or other Northern states noted for their virulent stand against slavery. Most came from midwestern states such as Ohio—Quantrill's home—or Indiana, and they came for a basic economic reason: the chance to acquire low-cost land and to start life over in a new part of the country.

* * *

The influx of Northerners worried the proslavery men of Kansas and Missouri. They knew the presence of all those Yankees and all those weapons had to lead, inevitably, to violence. It started in the early months of 1856, near the town of Leavenworth. A Free-Soiler by the name of E.P. Brown was waylaid by a bunch of proslavery men. They were half-drunk, but they had sense enough to know that Brown was against slavery; he was not sound on the goose. That was all they needed to know. They set upon him with knives and a hatchet and took him, barely alive, back to his cabin. When his wife opened the door, they tossed him to the ground. "Here's Brown," one shouted, and they rode off happy as could be. Brown died from his wounds; Mrs. Brown, distraught with grief, spent the rest of her days in a lunatic asylum.

In April 1856, Sam Jones, the Missouri sheriff, came to Lawrence hunting for the men who had taken away his prisoner the previous fall, or so he said. In reality, he was out to stir up trouble. The sight of him made folks angry. One man grabbed him by the collar; another punched him in the face. Jones got out of town as fast as he could and complained about his treatment to Governor Shannon. Shannon ordered a squad of ten soldiers to back him up. Even that proved to be little protection. He wasn't back in Lawrence long when a bullet whizzed past his head. "I believe that was intended for me," he observed shrewdly. Another shot rang out; the sheriff found a hole in his pants. "That *was* intended for me!" he yelled. He ran into a tent to take shelter, where a third bullet wounded him. The rumor spread quickly that Jones had been killed, but he survived his wound. Irate crowds of Jones's Missouri supporters stood ready to take their revenge against the abolitionists.

This time, they were determined to do it legally. A hastily convened grand jury indicted Charles Robinson and some other leaders among the Free-Soilers on the charge of treason. They also indicted the newspapers in Lawrence—the *Herald of Freedom* and the *Free State*—for publishing inflammatory and seditious articles. They condemned Lawrence's Free State Hotel because it had parapets and portholes from which weapons could be fired. Armed with these warrants, the U.S. marshal of Kansas Territory, a Missourian, called for a posse to march on Lawrence.

Hundreds of Missourians assembled on the border. David Atchison, who always managed to be where trouble was brewing, was ready to harangue them onward. On May twenty-first, they headed over the border, carrying banners and colorful flags. SOUTHERN RIGHTS was embroidered on one, THE SUPREMACY OF THE WHITE RACE on another, SOUTH CAROLINA emblazoned on a third. But the men brought more than slogans; they had a battery of artillery.

They called themselves the Border Ruffians, a phrase first used by Northern newspapers as a term of derision for what their reporters saw as bands of outlaws and brigands. The Missourians adopted the label with pride. A Northern observer wrote:

> Imagine a man standing in a pair of long boots, covered with dust and drawn over his trousers, the latter made of coarse, fancy-colored cloth, well-soiled; the handle of a large Bowie knife projecting from one of the boot tops; a leathern belt buckled around his waist, on each side of which is fastened a large revolver; a red or blue shirt, with a heart, anchor, eagle, or some other favorite device braided on the breast and back, over which is swung a rifle or carbine; a sword dangling by his side; an old slouched hat, with a cockade or brass star on the front or side, and a chicken, turkey, or goose feather sticking in the top; hair uncut and uncombed, covering his neck and shoulders; an unshaven face and unwashed hands. Imagine such a picture of humanity . . . and you will have a pretty fair conception of the border ruffian.

Envision several hundred of them appearing at the edge of town. The people of Lawrence offered no opposition. It would have been pointless. There were too many Missourians, and they were too well armed. This time, the Missourians had the law on their side and the artillery in place overlooking the town. The townspeople could do nothing but watch.

The invaders ransacked the offices of the two newspapers, smashing the presses with sledgehammers. They tossed the blocks of type into wagons, which were driven to the river's edge and dumped. All the newspapers' files and more than three hundred books from their libraries were pitched out the windows and ripped to pieces.

Three cannons were wheeled into the square in front of the Free State Hotel. The owner begged for time to remove the furnishings; he was given two hours. Some of the Missourians pitched in to help, but most of them focused on the wine cellar, which they emptied in record time.

At the end of two hours, Atchison's army gathered around the cannons in the square. Atchison, who appeared to be intoxicated—though whether from wine or excitement, no one knew—claimed the honor of firing the first shot. "This day we have entered Lawrence," he shouted, "with 'Southern Rights' inscribed upon our banner. . . . If one man or woman dare stand before you, blow them to hell with a chunk of cold lead." He aimed a cannon at the massive building, three stories tall and eighty feet wide, and lit the fuse. The crowd watched as the cannonball flew harmlessly over the hotel roof and buried itself in a faraway hillside. Other men took their turns, firing a total of thirty shots from the three cannons, but the building remained standing. Its thick, solid concrete walls repelled all hits.

The Border Ruffians rolled two kegs of powder into the lobby, lit the fuses, and ran like hell. After the noise and smoke from the explosion cleared, the hotel looked pretty much as it had before. Finally, the men set fires throughout the building, cheering at last as flames leapt from every window and the interior structure came crashing down.

Emboldened by their success, the Missourians embarked on a spree of looting, stealing whatever they could carry from homes and shops—canned goods, clothing, silk curtains. They torched the home of Charles Robinson, destroying everything, including his large collection of books.

Most of the Ruffians camped out that night on Mount Oread, overlooking the town. In the morning, Atchison—now calling

himself General Atchison—sent a messenger into town request-
ing permission to parade his men down the main street, the
shortest route to the ferry that would carry them across the river
to Missouri. Nobody dared object. The people of Lawrence
"watched from windows and sidewalks as the 'army' passed,
solemnly as a funeral procession, cannon rumbling ahead and
in the rear. Atchison, on his big horse, seemed to be dejected."
Was it a hangover, or did Atchison have forebodings about the
forces of retribution he might have unleashed?

Two horrible events occurred within the next three days—one
in broad daylight in the halls of Congress in Washington, the
other in the dark of night only thirty miles from Lawrence. Their
brutality and savagery shocked the nation.

Shortly after midday on May twenty-second, Congressman
Preston Brooks of South Carolina entered the U.S. Senate chamber, taking a seat in the back row. In one hand, he gripped an
eleven-and-a-half-ounce gutta-percha walking stick with a heavy
gold head, which he had chosen specifically for his purpose. It
measured one inch in thickness at the top, tapering to three-
quarters of an inch at the bottom. Congressman Brooks was
about to make history, to become a hero to his beloved South
and a blackguard to the hated abolitionists of the North.

He was thirty-seven years old and, until that day, few people
outside his native South Carolina had heard of him. Six feet tall,
with an erect military bearing, a holdover from his service in the
Mexican War, Brooks weighed 170 pounds. He was a proud man
and handsome, with black hair and fashionable clothes, a Southern gentleman to the core. And he was mightily offended.

The man who had offended him, and the entire South, Senator Charles Sumner of Massachusetts, sat three seats away across
a narrow aisle, hunched over his desk, writing letters. Sumner was
two inches taller than Brooks, broad across the chest, and
weighed 185 pounds. At forty-five, he was one of the most imposing and dignified men in all of Washington. And he was as
ardent an abolitionist as Massachusetts had ever produced.

Three days before, he had delivered a speech on the Senate floor that lasted all of two days. He called his lengthy oration "The Crime Against Kansas." "My soul is wrung by this outrage," he had told a friend, "and I shall pour it forth." And he did, mincing no words, holding back no accusations, repressing no venom. He spoke to a gallery packed to the doorways. The chamber had not held a crowd of such size since the days of Daniel Webster. "A crime has been committed," he thundered, "which is without example . . . It is the rape of a virgin territory, compelling it to the hateful embrace of slavery."

Sumner roared against the murderous robbers from Missouri, "hirelings, picked from the drunken spew and vomit of an uneasy civilization." Protesters shouted at him, objecting to the inflammatory language, but Sumner would not be silenced. He turned his wrath on a fellow senator—elderly Andrew Pickens Butler of South Carolina—who was not present to defend himself. Senator Butler had spoken in favor of confiscating the guns of the Free-Soilers in Kansas, and that made him an enemy of the abolitionists.

"The senator from South Carolina," Sumner said sarcastically, "has read many books of chivalry, and believes himself a chivalrous knight, with sentiments of honor and courage. Of course he has chosen a mistress to whom he has made vows, and who, though ugly to others, is always lovely to him; though polluted in the sight of the world, is chaste in his sight. I mean the harlot Slavery."

There was more. "The senator touches nothing which he does not disfigure. . . . He shows an incapacity of accuracy." Rarely had such a personal assault been made on the Senate floor. Finally, Sumner demeaned Butler's home state. "Were the whole history of South Carolina blotted out of existence . . . civilization might lose—I do not say how little, but surely less than it has already gained by the example of Kansas, in its valiant struggle against oppression." When Sumner was finished, one senator was heard to say that some damned fool just might kill that damned fool. The mood was ugly.

Congressman Brooks did not intend to kill Sumner, or so he said afterward. He just wanted to teach him a lesson. No one impugned the honor of the South, or South Carolina, or his cousin, Senator Butler, and got away with it. Butler was old and frail; Brooks took it on himself to avenge the slurs.

He had considered challenging Sumner to a duel, the time-honored way of settling such matters among gentlemen. But Yankees did not duel, and Sumner would simply refuse the challenge. Of course, dueling was only possible between social equals, which Sumner would never be. To Brooks, then, there was left only one right and proper way to deal with a social inferior: horsewhipping or caning. Brooks thought about a cowhide whip, but Sumner outweighed him and might grab the lash end and wrest it away. That left the option of caning.

The chamber was emptying. Brooks became impatient, waiting for a lady to leave the adjacent lobby; gentlemen did not take such action in a lady's presence. Finally, he strode over to Sumner's desk, where the senator was still writing letters.

"Mr. Sumner," he said, politely, formally.

The senator looked up, but being nearsighted and too vain to wear spectacles, he could not distinguish the features of the tall man looming over him. Not that glasses would have helped; he did not know Congressman Brooks.

"I have read your speech twice over carefully," Brooks said quietly. "It is a libel on South Carolina, and Mr. Butler, who is a relative of mine."

Brooks raised his cane and brought it crashing down on Sumner's head. The senator raised his arms to protect himself. Brooks struck him again and again, each blow feeding his rage. Gone was the intent to teach Sumner a lesson. Now he was out for blood. A murderous fury took control. As fast and hard as he could, Brooks battered Sumner's head and shoulders.

The senator tried to get up from his desk. His eyes were clouded with blood. His weight trapped him at the desk, which was bolted to an iron plate in the floor. Blinded, howling in pain, he lunged with such force that the pressure of his thighs against the underside of the desk tore it from its fastenings.

Brooks hit him again, so hard that the cane he had chosen for its exceptional toughness split and broke. Sumner lurched away, reeling against the other desks, slipping in his own blood. Brooks pursued him, stabbing him with the splintered end of the cane. When Sumner started to fall, Brooks grabbed him by the lapels and punched him. Finally, other senators were able to come to Sumner's aid and pull the raving Brooks away.

Brooks later said that he "gave [Sumner] about thirty first rate stripes. Towards the last he bellowed like a calf. I wore my cane out completely but saved the Head which is gold." It was more than three years before the severely injured Sumner was able to return to work.

Northerners were irate, outraged at such bestial behavior on the Senate floor. Rallies were held to protest the assault and to urge swift and appropriate punishment for the perpetrator. Nonetheless, Brooks became a hero. Arrested and freed on five hundred dollars' bail, he was later fined three hundred dollars. Dozens of people sent him gold-headed canes; one, from Charleston, was inscribed "Hit him again." South Carolina's governor arranged a subscription list of admirers to buy Brooks a commemorative silver pitcher and goblet. Students at the University of Virginia sent him a stick bearing a replica of a cracked head. "Every Southern man sustains me," Brooks wrote to his brother. "The fragments of the stick are begged for as *sacred relicts.*"

The U.S. Senate took no action; Brooks was, after all, not one of theirs. The House of Representatives, after much bitter debate, voted three months later on a measure to expel him. The vote was 121 to 95, short of the two-thirds majority needed. Brooks resigned as a matter of honor and went home, where he was promptly reelected by an overwhelming majority. He returned to Washington in triumph.

But the impact of his deed was far from over when the dazed and bloody Sumner was led off the Senate floor. Brooks's action unleashed an event of greater savagery two days later, in Kansas. The telegraph wire had compressed time and altered people's lives. A thousand miles away from Washington, they learned about the beating within hours of the event.

South of Lawrence, the news reached a fifty-six-year-old abolitionist who saw himself as God's messenger on earth. As fierce-looking and possessed as any Old Testament prophet, he wore soiled clothes, a black cravat, and a wide-brimmed straw hat. His reddish brown hair was streaked with gray. His face was unshaven and craggy as a bald mountain. His smoldering, intense blue eyes could send chills down a man's back. He stood five feet ten and weighed 150 pounds, with taut muscles and the gaunt weather-beaten look of a hardscrabble farmer, a man who had known hard times.

It was said there was insanity in his family. His mother, grandmother, an aunt, and three uncles on his mother's side had all died insane. There were those who felt he carried the seed in him, too, and that one day it would flourish. Most people were wary of him, some genuinely afraid, and many did not like him. One historian wrote, "He was ignorant, narrow-minded, frantically prejudiced on many issues, highly tenacious, a thoroughly selfish egotist, ready to commit acts that others would term unscrupulous. . . . a man with a vein of hard cruelty."

He had tried many ways to earn a living to support his twenty children by two wives. A farmer, tanner, land speculator, sheep and wool broker, he had failed at every endeavor. Accused of dishonest practices, even embezzlement, he was dogged by allegations and lawsuits. But he clung to the dream that his big break was just around the corner, maybe with the next deal, the next speculation. He did not have the temperament to work hard and relentlessly at any one enterprise. Like William Clarke Quantrill, he jumped restlessly from one to another, looking for an easy success, for his main chance. His only commitment was to the abolitionist cause; on this he was rabid, zealous, fanatical, convinced he was doing God's work. It was his one true calling, the only thing at which he ever succeeded. His name was John Brown.

On May twenty-fourth, when Brown heard about the caning of Senator Sumner, he went berserk, ranting about the incident to his audience—four of his sons and three other men. "Something must be done to show these barbarians that we, too, have rights!" he shouted. Determined to create an example the world would not soon forget, he told them: "It has been ordained by the Almighty God, ordained from eternity." He named five proslavery men who lived in his neighborhood along Pottawatomie Creek and told his followers to sharpen their broadswords to a razor's keenness. He was about to smite his enemies with a terrible swift sword.

Shortly after 11:00 P.M., Old Brown, as he was called, knocked on the door of Mr. and Mrs. James Doyle's cabin and asked for directions to a neighbor's house. Doyle opened the door, little suspecting any trouble. Brown shoved Doyle inside and demanded that he and his sons—ages twenty-two, twenty, and sixteen—surrender to his so-called Army of the North. Brown's apostles, with pistols in their belts and swords drawn, crowded into the tiny cabin.

Doyle and his boys were unarmed and only partially dressed, but Brown ordered them out into the night. Mrs. Doyle, in tears, begged Old Brown to spare the youngest child. Brown agreed, then led the other men away. Mahala Doyle knew she would never see her husband and sons alive again.

John Brown and his followers led the Doyles about a hundred yards down the road and set to work methodically, hacking the sons to death. One of the boys had his head sliced open and both arms cut off, and the bodies were pierced in the sides. When that task was done, Brown walked over to the elder Doyle and shot him square in the forehead.

The next cabin belonged to Allen Wilkinson, who was up late nursing his wife, who was sick with measles. He heard the insistent pounding at the door, the shouted request for directions, the thunderous voice announcing that Wilkinson was now a prisoner of the Army of the North. The eight wild men forced their way into the cabin. Louisa Wilkinson lay in one bed, too weak to rise; two little girls were in a second bed, too terrified to move.

John Brown ordered Wilkinson outside in his stocking feet, not allowing him to put on his boots.

> "I begged them to let Mr. Wilkinson stay with me," Louisa testified. "My husband also asked them to let him stay until he could get someone to stay with me, told them he would be around the next day." But the old man, tall and stern, who was the leader, said, "You have neighbors." Louisa said they could not get them that late at night. "It matters not," said the old man.

Louisa Wilkinson waited, afraid and trembling. After a few minutes, she thought she heard her husband's voice, but she was not sure. She went to the door and peered out into the darkness, but she heard nothing. She gathered her children in her arms and cried through the night. A neighbor found Allen Wilkinson the next morning. His head had been hacked by broadswords and mutilated, his side pierced, his throat slit.

It was after midnight now, and Saturday had turned to Sunday, the Sabbath, the Lord's day, but that did not deter John Brown. His mission was to kill five proslavery men, and nothing would stand in his way. The final victim was William Sherman; he was not on Brown's list, but he happened to be an overnight guest at the home of James Harris, one of three men staying overnight, travelers who had picked the wrong house on the wrong night to ask for hospitality.

One by one, the men were taken outside and questioned. Were they Free-Soilers or were they proslavery? All but Sherman gave the right answer. Brown and his men seized Sherman and led him to the Pottawatomie Creek. They bashed his skull with such force, his brains spilled out into the water. They pierced him in the side and cut off his hands, pausing to rinse their swords in the cool, clear water.

After the killings, Brown returned to his cabin to ask God's blessing on his night's work. Then he sat down calmly to his breakfast. "I believe that I did God service in having them killed," he later told a friend. Brown's victims deserved to die, he said, because they had "committed murder in their hearts already, according to the Big Book." If there had ever been a chance for peace in Kansas, it was gone after that bloody night. What Brown had sown, others would reap, for many years to come.

Through the remaining months of 1856, the border counties of Kansas and Missouri became, as one account stated, a " 'seething hell.' Proslavery spokesmen called for a war of extermination against the Free-Soilers: 'Let our motto be written in blood on our flags, "Death to all Yankees and traitors in Kansas!" ' Free staters replied with the slogan, 'War! War to the knife and the knife to the hilt!' "

There was much fighting to report after Old Brown's savagery at Pottawatomie Creek. Eastern newspapers described it as a "civil war." Every week saw another attack, an ambush, a bloody skirmish between the two sides. Many Free-Soilers, expecting a full-scale invasion from Missouri, left their farms to form militias. They practiced close-order drills and established picket lines around their towns. In the thirty-mile stretch, north to south, between Lawrence and the Pottawatomie, armed farmers banded together in groups of six or more to till their fields, always on the alert.

Strangers on the Kansas roads approached one another with guns in hand. Their greeting was not "Hello," but "Free-state or proslave?" Depending on the answer, the next sound was often a pistol shot. Every day men were wounded and killed, houses and barns torched, cattle and horses stolen. Terrified, innocent people packed up their belongings and fled for safety.

Missourians sealed the border with Kansas, intercepting shipments of weapons, demanding of everyone who sought passage whether they were sound on the goose—for slavery or against it. Newspapers that described a reign of terror in Kansas were not exaggerating, and their stories of horror, repeated in city after city, fueled mass meetings to raise funds to send more free-state settlers to Kansas.

On May thirty-first, Jim Lane addressed a crowd in Chicago,

describing the plight of his fellow Kansans at his hypnotizing and hysterical best. When he finished, pledges were called for, and the vast sum of fifteen thousand dollars was raised in minutes. Of course, similar rallies took place in the South. The result was more money, more recruits for the cause, more weapons, more violence.

David Atchison led an army of three hundred Missourians over the border in August to hunt for John Brown and his men. When they found them, they killed one of Brown's sons, but Old Brown and about forty followers were able to hold them off for a considerable time. The Missourians organized a massive charge, forcing Brown and his group to flee—another day, another battle, another twelve men dead, another twenty or so wounded.

Missourians patrolled their border, stopping riverboats, wagon trains, and lone men on horseback. Guns were confiscated, and many emigrants were turned back under threat of death. Travelers to Kansas forged a new route, the Lane Trail, named for Jim Lane, through Iowa and south from Nebraska. It soon became well rutted from the passage of so many wagons. Before the year 1856 was out, the population of Kansas included four Northerners for every Southerner.

The violence was not one-sided, particularly by the time Free-Soilers were in the majority. Organized bands of fanatical Kansans embarked on their own campaigns of destruction and murder. They came to be called Jayhawkers, and their most famous and savage leaders were James Montgomery and Charles Jennison.

Montgomery came from Ohio and was a dangerous combination of abolitionist and evangelical preacher. His eyes held a strange, haunted gleam, and his laugh struck many as demented. He and Jennison, a New Yorker, whose face was described as having a satanic cast, led the Jayhawkers on raids to kill and burn and steal, matching each attack and atrocity committed by the Border Ruffians with an outrage of their own.

The violence, which had become commonplace, came to a halt in March 1857, and a strange and unfamiliar peace settled over the border regions. No one was quite sure why it happened. Perhaps the men simply grew tired of the killing, or even disgusted. As one Kansan put it, the territory was "weary of war and worn out of the conflict." But it was during this lull that Quantrill went to Kansas with Beeson and Torrey. It is well to recall why they went: They were not part of the tide of emigrant Free-Soilers, not part of that holy crusade. They went in search of land, hoping for the chance to start over. Opportunity, not ideology, drove them to Kansas.

Although their land was in Stanton, close by Pottawatomie Creek, there is no indication that they were involved in the civil war raging around them. They were occupied with scratching a living out of the farm, with trying to survive. Quantrill's mother claimed she reared him as an abolitionist, and he praised Jim Lane in letters home, although he never joined forces with Lane or any other fanatic Free-Soiler. Quantrill was too busy scheming and plotting and stealing for his own advantage. And because 1857 was mostly a time of peace, he was not forced to choose sides. When he did choose, four years later, he sided with the Border Ruffians, acting for personal gain rather than out of loyalty to a cause. William Clarke Quantrill was never one for slogans or crusades or ideology. Whatever suited his malice and need for revenge was what drove him, nothing else.

The peace did not last. Toward the end of 1857, a band of Missouri Border Ruffians swept into Kansas, burning houses and crops, stealing horses and cattle, taking "'everything they wanted, and I think they took things they didn't want, to keep their hands in,' reported one victim, who while losing his property at least retained his sense of humor."

Enraged at this action, James Montgomery, the abolitionist preacher, traveled throughout Missouri to find out who had participated in the raid. He identified them all by name and came after them with a small army of Kansas Jayhawkers. The Jayhawkers pursued each man, stealing from their homes every item that could be carried. They transported their loot back to Kansas, to distribute it to the people who had been burned out by the Missourians.

Of course, Missouri could not let that deed go unpunished. Revenge came on May nineteenth. Charles Hamilton, a Georgia native whose house had been ransacked by Montgomery's Jayhawkers, led a gang across the border. They headed for the settlements of the Free-Soilers along the Marais des Cygnes River, about ten miles from Pottawatomie Creek. They captured nine men, lined them up against a dirt embankment, and formed a firing squad, rifles at the ready.

"Gentlemen," said one of the prisoners, "if you are going to shoot, take good aim."

The Missourians fired, but their aim was poor. Four Kansans survived to tell the story to a nation once again shocked by such blatant savagery. John Greenleaf Whittier, the abolitionist movement's poet laureate, wrote about the event.

> *A blush of roses,*
> *Where roses never grew!*
> *Great drops on the bunch grass,*
> *But not of the dew!*

The violence continued into the early months of 1858, but by summer a shaky truce was being maintained. In May, Quantrill had left Kansas for Utah and did not return for over a year. The truce held through the fall, but in December, John Brown returned to Kansas after a speaking tour of New England. A crowd-pleaser, especially popular with society ladies, Old Brown held forth to enthusiastic audiences of abolitionists.

By now, he was back to raiding and killing, and he joined forces with Jayhawker leaders Montgomery and Jennison. They rode into Missouri, shot up a couple of settlements, plundered stores and homes, killed two men, and freed eleven slaves. And so it was, raid after raid, month after month, an eye for an eye, the cycle broken only when fierce arctic winds blasted across the flat plains. Only nature was powerful enough to stop the violence.

In 1859, nature added to the problem of survival. A drought

soon destroyed the crops. For two years, hardly a drop of rain fell, and in the winter of 1859, it did not snow, a condition hitherto unheard of in a region where horse and rider could disappear in a snowdrift within minutes.

By July of 1861, rains were falling again, the crops were growing, and poor "bleeding Kansas" became a state. Jim Lane was elected senator.

During the statehood debate in Washington, Senator Charles Sumner of Massachusetts spoke for four hours to a packed Senate gallery. He was wearing full evening dress and white gloves. He had lost none of his passion during his three years of recovery from his caning, and he attacked the Southern institution of slavery with undiminished vigor. He said slavery was "barbarous in origin; barbarous in its law; barbarous in all its pretensions; barbarous in the instruments it employs; barbarous in consequences; barbarous in spirit; barbarous wherever it shows itself; Slavery must breed Barbarians."

As for himself, he had "no personal griefs to utter . . . no personal wrongs to avenge; only a barbarous nature could attempt to wield that vengeance which belongs to the Lord."

In Kansas and Missouri, there were many on both sides with barbarous natures who stood ready to wield vengeance. William Clarke Quantrill was one of them, and he was destined to take the greatest vengeance of all.

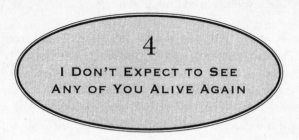

4

I Don't Expect to See
Any of You Alive Again

QUANTRILL WAS Charley Hart again in the spring of 1860 when he left his teaching job in Stanton to return to Lawrence. He reverted to his role as outlaw, as cold-blooded killer, and he would remain such until the day he died. He went to live with the Delaware Indians on Mud Creek, four miles from Lawrence, telling people he was a detective for the tribe, but in reality his only work was to pursue a life of crime.

Every morning at nine o'clock, he rode into Lawrence on an Indian pony and spent the day loitering at the Kansas River ferry landing, where he remained until nightfall. The landing was a dangerous place, a hangout for thieves and murderers, for restless, aimless men like himself. Some were Border Ruffians from Missouri, yet they made a living from raids into Missouri to rob shops and homes and steal slaves and cattle. They had no loyalty—they would just as easily steal from one side as the other—and it bothered them no more to kill a Kansan than a Missourian.

Jake Herd was the worst of the lot, "a holy terror, violent, quick and deadly with the revolver, fearless and daring, and a man who would risk his life to capture a negro." Charley Hart admired Herd, even idolized him, and he desperately wanted to be like him.

Charley Hart quickly fit in with this rough crowd. He joined their daily pursuits—wrestling, gambling, footraces, drinking, lolling about in thickets with so-called fallen women. They came to be his greatest weakness, and pleasure, and he was frequently seen in their company. It was not long before he joined Jake Herd and the gang on their raids, robberies, and kidnappings.

Like the others, he showed no qualms about attacking either side in the civil war that raged along the border. One day would find him a Border Ruffian, terrorizing and stealing from Free-Soilers. Another day, he would attack Missourians as fanatically as the most ardent abolitionist in Kansas. As Jake Herd put it, Quantrill was always willing to go into anything that had a dollar in it for Charley Hart. A biographer phrased it more formally. "He could not be true to any cause, for, of moral character . . . he was devoid. Being false at heart and governed by self-interest solely, it was natural that he should be two-faced, untrue to every-thing and everybody, governed entirely by what he believed would make him the most money."

When Charley Hart had money to spend, he would check into Lawrence's City Hotel, which was owned by Nathan Stone. Hart was remembered as dressing in an old slouch hat, a woolen shirt, and corduroy pants tucked into his boot tops. People at the hotel also recalled his drooping eyelids and the malice in his eyes. He signed the register as Charley Hart, but he and Stone got along well enough that soon he confided his real name. Three years later, Stone's acts of friendship would save his own life. Hart usu-ally took the same hotel room, sharing it with Holland Wheeler. On hot nights, the men slept on the roof. Wheeler recalled that he would borrow a pistol and keep it under his pillow whenever Hart was in town. When asked why, he said he wasn't sure, but something about Hart bothered him.

When Charley Hart's funds ran out, or he got bored, or an op-portunity for easy money presented itself, he pursued his life of crime. One day, an escaped slave showed up at the ferry landing, asking for Jim Lane, whose name was well known to those in the

Underground Railroad, which provided a means for escaped slaves to reach safety in the North. Unfortunately for this young black man, the person he asked was Jake Herd, who took him across the river and introduced him to Charley Hart and Frank Baldwin.

Hart and Baldwin volunteered to escort the man to Lane's home. The former slave told them how he had escaped, giving the name and address of his owner in Missouri. Hart and Baldwin easily overpowered the man, tied him to a horse, and took him back to his owner. She was so grateful for the return of her property that she gave Hart and Baldwin five hundred dollars in new twenty-dollar bills. They, in turn, gave Jake Herd one hundred dollars for his good deed in delivering the black man to them.

Charley Hart disappeared from Lawrence and the Delaware Indian tribe for several weeks. He returned riding a sleek racehorse named White Stockings. He said he had bought the horse in Paola, a town thirty miles southeast of Lawrence, and planned to get rich racing it. Sure enough, in a Westport, Missouri, race he made $150. He had brought White Stockings out covered with mud, looking unkempt and so unimpressive, he thought nobody would bet on her. That may have been his only race, for he returned to Lawrence without the horse or any explanation of its whereabouts.

About this time, Hart befriended John Stewart, a preacher turned abolitionist from Salem, New Hampshire. Stewart had ridden on raids with James Montgomery, the Jayhawker leader, and with John Brown, though Stewart did not participate in Old Brown's killing spree along Pottawatomie Creek. Stewart built a fort on his land, about four miles from Lawrence, for use as a way station on the Underground Railroad. Many runaway slaves passed through the fort on their way north, and Stewart himself had brought some of them over from Missouri. It was said he was not averse to liberating horses and cattle, too, providing they belonged to Missourians. There was a price on Stewart's head in Missouri, sufficient inducement for Charley Hart to want to betray him, but Stewart proved too wily to let himself be trapped.

Hart and a buddy stole eighty head of cattle from proslavery settlers near Atchison and Leavenworth. It was not the first time Hart had delivered stolen cattle to Stewart's fort for selling south of Lawrence. As they herded the cows across the Kansas River and through Lawrence early one morning, they were spotted by Sam Walker, the new sheriff.

A small man, crippled with a hip disorder, Walker was another convert to the abolitionist cause, though not for ideological reasons. His motivation was personal. Five years earlier, when he brought his family to Kansas, they were caught in a vicious sleet storm. His nine-year-old daughter was hurt, her leg broken in two places. He bundled her in a blanket and carried her through howling winds and rain to the first house he saw, the residence of a proslavery Baptist preacher. When the preacher heard that Walker was from Ohio, he assumed this was another no-good abolitionist come where he had no business, and he refused shelter to Walker and the injured child. Walker had hated slavery with a passion ever since.

Walker had his eye on Charley Hart and the group at the ferry landing, suspecting them of mischief, and worse, but unable to prove it. He had been particularly suspicious of Hart since their first meeting. "I was Badly impressed with him then & never got over it," he said. "He did not deceive me one bit. . . . he was a Monster of the worst kind." When Walker saw Charley Hart with eighty head of cattle, he wondered just where Hart had gotten hold of them.

Later that day, a citizens' posse from the Leavenworth area rode into Lawrence and told Sheriff Walker they were on the trail of their stolen cattle. Walker knew exactly where to find them—at John Stewart's fort. Sure enough, all the animals were there, save two that had been butchered for eating. Charley Hart was there, too, unconcerned about Walker and the posse.

Stewart told Sheriff Walker he had bought two cows from a couple of strangers, who had left the rest of the herd with him for safekeeping, assuring him they would be back. Walker knew Stewart was lying to protect himself and Hart, but there was no way he could prove it. He allowed the owners to reclaim their cattle. In his mind, he placed another mark against Charley Hart.

Not long after that incident, Hart went to see the sheriff to report two murders, professing to be doing his duty as a good citizen. He said two men from Missouri had been staying at the City Hotel. They had come to Lawrence with money in their pockets, looking to buy back runaway slaves. According to Hart, two local men—prominent, respected members of the community—took the visitors down to the river, murdered them, and then tied the bodies together and tossed them in the water. To prove his story, he told Walker he would show him where the killers had left the Missourians' horses.

The sheriff went along with Hart and found two horses that looked as if they had been neglected for a couple of days, exactly where Charley said they would be. When the sheriff confronted the men Hart had accused, they laughed, and Walker was sure they were innocent. He was not even convinced a crime had been committed until nearly two weeks later, when the bodies of two men, tied together, were found floating a few miles downriver, just where the current would have taken them if they had been thrown in where Hart had said they were.

As with the theft of the cattle, Walker believed Charley Hart had committed the crime, but he had no evidence. No one ever accused Charley Hart of lacking in nerve.

Toward the end of the summer of 1860, Hart showed again how capable he was of betraying anyone when it was to his advantage financially, or just to show he could get away with it. The first instance involved John Stewart, who had lied to Sheriff Walker about the cattle to protect Hart and himself. A group of Missouri slave owners turned up at the ferry landing looking for escaped slaves and willing to pay rewards for their recapture. Charley Hart, Jake Herd, and most of the other regulars heard the announcement. They were always happy to return slaves to their masters and be paid for it, even if they had stolen the slaves themselves.

In this case, they had not stolen the missing slaves, but Hart knew where they were—at Stewart's fort, waiting to move on to the next station along the Underground Railroad. Hart led Herd and his cronies there. Hart stayed out of sight, not wanting to be recognized by Stewart, while the others approached the fort and demanded the slaves be turned over to them. Stewart refused. He armed the Negroes with guns, and when Hart's men attacked the fort, a vicious battle ensued, during which they were sent packing, having captured only one of the former slaves. Hart told the slave owners that the other slaves had all been wounded so badly that they would not be worth anything. In truth, which he could not admit, he had failed. All the other slaves were uninjured and able to proceed north to freedom. Charley had made no money from this endeavor.

Hart's next venture was more successful. He gathered a group of men and led them on a raid into Missouri to steal horses and cattle. He had scouted the territory and knew where to find the best pickings. They quickly gathered a large amount of livestock, which they began driving north, back to Kansas. Before they reached the border, Hart disappeared. He had doubled back to the farms from which he had stolen the horses and cattle and had informed the owners that he knew what had happened to their stolen livestock. He said he would lead the farmers to the animals and help recover them for so much per head. Hart and the farmers caught up with his band before they had reached the Kansas line. While the farmers attacked them, Hart remained out of sight to avoid being recognized by the men he had double-crossed, and to reduce the chance they would take their anger out on him.

The raiders got away with most of the cattle, which they sold to farmers in the settlements on the way back to Lawrence. Charley Hart followed, leading the Missouri farmers to the men he knew from experience were most likely to buy the stolen stock. The Missourians recovered most of their horses and cattle, and Hart was paid for retrieving what he had stolen.

When he caught up with his cronies in Lawrence, he concocted a story about how he had gotten lost. He said he had been attacked by the owners of the stolen livestock and had barely escaped with his life. He demanded his portion of the proceeds from the sale of the stolen goods—since he had been the one to organize the raid—which the others reluctantly gave him, the second time Hart profited from the same deal. But some of the men doubted his story and refused to ride with him again. People were beginning to catch on to his deceptions; his days in Lawrence were numbered.

Hart wrote to his mother on June 23, 1860, telling lies, as he had done so many times before. He told her he had enclosed money in his last two letters—five dollars in one, ten in the other—and would send more when he was sure she had received it. Of course, he had not sent any money, yet he promised to forward enough for a new roof, perhaps as much as fifty dollars, as soon as she answered his letter. He claimed he had the money in his pocket and that it would be hers just as soon as she wrote back.

He did have money in his pocket, but it was not for his mother. He had never sent even a dollar in all the years since he had left home, and he never would. He closed the letter with the hope that he would see her and his brothers and sister soon. He expected to be home no later than September first, he said, and probably sooner. Mrs. Quantrill never heard from her son again.

During the late summer and fall of 1860, Charley Hart committed three acts that put an end to his career of crime in Kansas. First, he stole ponies from the Delaware Indians, the people he had lived among for months. White Turkey, a young Delaware Indian warrior, and a half dozen of his friends rode into town and told everyone who gathered round that they had trailed their stolen ponies to Lawrence and seen Charley Hart nearby. Hart overheard them. He pushed forward through the crowd and announced that he did not much like that kind of talk. Nobody accused him of being a thief and got away with it.

Hart reached for his gun. White Turkey was faster. Hart did not even attempt to raise his gun, because the Indian's pistol was already pointing at his head. As White Turkey moved toward him, Hart backed away, keeping his gun pointed at the ground, until he disappeared in the crowd. The Delaware Indians did not press charges against Charley Hart for the stolen ponies, but he was no longer welcome on the reservation.

Hart stole a large amount of explosive powder from a Lawrence general store. Somehow, Sheriff Walker connected him to the theft. Some time later, Hart, Jake Herd, and a few other drifters rode up toward Lecompton, about ten miles north-east of Lawrence, to find a runaway slave. Knowing Herd took pride in being a Border Ruffian and was therefore proslavery, some foolish abolitionist had boasted to him that he had hidden a Negro man where Herd would never find him. Herd and Hart decided to accept the challenge.

They had a stroke of luck. A group of children had happened to see the runaway slave hiding under a pile of hay in an unfin-ished house. They told Jake Herd, who led Hart and the gang to the house. Sure enough, they found the man and decided to smoke him out. They set fire to the building's timbers and joists. The flames attracted the attention of abolitionist neighbors, who tried to rescue the unfortunate black man. Shots were fired, but no one was hit, and Hart and Herd took their captive across the border to Missouri, where they sold him back into slavery.

This time, there were witnesses, people who recognized Hart and identified him as having been present at the fire. The county attorney drew up an indictment charging Charley Hart with kid-napping, burglary, larceny, and arson. A federal warrant was is-sued against him for horse stealing. Now it was up to Sheriff Sam Walker to bring him in. When Hart found out about the indict-ment, he decided to remain in town, bragging that Walker would never get him. The sheriff would be a dead man if he tried, Hart declared.

Walker spotted Hart walking down Massachusetts Street, but instead of fighting, Hart ran, heading for John Dean's wagon shop, with Walker close on his heels. Hart burst through the door, and Dean slammed and locked it behind him.

Dean, an abolitionist from Iowa, was known to be a self-important bigot, braggart, and coward. Charley Hart had met him in the spring of 1860, shortly after Hart arrived in Lawrence.

Hart had offered to help Dean steal slaves from Missouri and send them north on the Underground Railroad. Initially, Dean was suspicious of the offer, but Hart proved himself on raids with Dean and other Jayhawkers and earned their trust. When he was not bunking at the City Hotel, Hart lived in Dean's house.

But Dean was puzzled. How could Hart be antislavery, a Jayhawker, as he claimed, and yet spend so much time with Jake Herd and the other Border Ruffians? Hart claimed he only hung around to spy on them so he could disrupt their plans. He was acting as a detective, he said, a role he enjoyed playing in his mind. John Dean believed him and was willing to hide him from the sheriff.

While Walker pounded on Dean's door, Hart ran out the back and down the alley to the house of another friend. The sheriff forced the door open, searched the wagon shop, and went on to the City Hotel and other of Hart's known haunts. He never found Charley Hart, but the outstanding warrants kept Hart from returning to Lawrence for three years.

Hart had been playing to both sides in the great struggle, to the Free-Soilers and the proslavery crowd, riding with Jayhawkers *and* with Border Ruffians and telling each side he was spying on the other. Now that he had to leave Lawrence, he probably would not be safe anywhere in Kansas. He was a wanted man, and, sooner or later, some sheriff would track him down.

He realized that his best chance for the future lay across the border in Missouri with the Border Ruffians and the free-staters, but he would need to make his mark quickly. He wanted to be hailed in Missouri as a hero for the cause, and, as usual, he did not want to wait too long or work too hard for the acclaim.

The day after Charley Hart fled from Sheriff Walker, he took refuge in the woods some three miles northwest of Lawrence. John Dean had given him food and a bottle of whiskey, and Hart spent the day by himself, building a small fire, drinking, and contemplating his next move. As luck would have it, a plan was already in motion that would give him everything he wanted. All he had to do was wait by the fire and it would come to him.

In the settlement of Pardee, north of Lawrence, lived four idealistic abolitionists, young men in their early twenties: Charles Ball, Chalkey Lipsey, Edwin Morrison, and Albert Southwick. Quakers all, they had come from Iowa determined to do good for the cause of the black man. They lived in a cabin measuring only twelve feet by fourteen and made frequent forays into Missouri to rescue slaves and start them on the path to freedom in the North. They knew John Dean to be like-minded, and it was to him they turned for help with their latest scheme.

Three escaped slaves had asked the Quakers to help rescue their families, who were being kept as slaves by the Cherokees in Indian Territory, what is now Oklahoma. This would be a much larger raid than any of their previous ones and would cover a greater distance. They knew it was too big for the four of them to undertake, so they asked John Dean for assistance. Dean rode out into the woods to find Charley Hart and to ask if he wanted to go along. Hart agreed.

Dean recruited another Jayhawker, John Jones, but felt they still needed more men, so they rode south to Osawatomie, forty-five miles from Lawrence, to see Eli Snyder. Leader of a large band of Jayhawkers, Snyder was famous for having burned to death four Border Ruffians on a raid into Missouri. Snyder listened to the plan to travel to the Cherokee Nation, a distance of more than 250 miles, and advised them not to go. It was impractical, he said, and he refused to commit any of his men.

Charley Hart offered an alternative, a plan that would get him out of Kansas and hand him three Negroes to sell in Missouri, and maybe a couple of abolitionists for Missourians to kill. That would give him a good start in his new life.

He told the men about Morgan Walker, a wealthy farmer in Blue Springs, Missouri, some twenty-five miles from the border. Walker had a nine-room house, two thousand acres of land, more than one hundred horses and mules, and thirty-five slaves. It was rumored that Walker kept gold hidden in the house. Hart proposed they steal the slaves and whatever else that took their fancy.

Snyder said he didn't trust Hart. He warned the others that they were in for a lot of trouble if they followed him. John Jones agreed, and so did the three escaped slaves. Hart argued with them, trying to persuade them to come along, but they would not budge.

A few days later, Charley Hart led three of the Quakers—Ball, Lipsey, and Morrison—out of Osawatomie and east toward the Missouri border. John Dean and the other Quaker, Albert Southwick, were to follow in the wagon they would need to haul the loot from Morgan Walker's farm. Eli Snyder kept telling them they were foolish to go with Hart, but he was unable to convince them.

"I don't expect to see any of you alive again," Snyder told them.

Hart and the Quakers traveled on foot, armed with knives and pistols. In Missouri, strangers with rifles aroused suspicion. It was best, Hart cautioned, to leave those weapons behind. If anybody stopped them to ask where they were headed, they were to say it was to work on the Missouri Pacific railroad line.

Two days after leaving Osawatomie, the men made camp in the woods about a mile from Morgan Walker's home. Dean and Southwick arrived in the wagon. Everyone was ready. Charley Hart set his plan in motion.

"Boys," he said, "you lay low here while I take a look-see at Walker's place. I'll be back soon."

Morgan Walker was not at home. Hart went on to Walker's son's house, a quarter of a mile away. Andrew Walker greeted him coldly. Strangers were unwelcome in those parts, certainly one unshaven and unkempt, telling such a tale.

"My name's Charles Quantrill," Charley Hart said, reclaiming part of his real name. "I'm part of a gang of Kansas abolitionists who plan to kill your father and run off his slaves tonight. Three others besides me are camped out in the woods."

"If you're one of them, why are you here telling me this?" Andrew Walker asked.

Quantrill said he did not have time to explain, but he assured Walker that he would never regret putting his trust in him and following his instructions.

"Set a trap at your father's place," Quantrill said. "When it gets dark we'll be coming up on the porch. As soon as I get away from the others, shoot 'em down—that's what they plan to do to your father! Just don't shoot me, that's all I ask."

"I'll get together some of the boys and get things ready," Walker said. "And I'll see to it that you don't get hurt none. But you better be telling the truth."

"I am—you'll see. Just don't shoot me. Now I got to go or the others'll get suspicious."

Andrew Walker rounded up four of his neighbors, armed with double-barreled shotguns. He and another man hid behind a loom on the front porch; the other three waited in a small room at the end of the porch, where harnesses were kept. About ten minutes before the abolitionists were expected, Morgan Walker returned home. Andrew quickly explained the situation. Morgan was irate. He insisted that he would kill all the Kansans, but Andrew persuaded him to honor his agreement and spare Quantrill.

At seven o'clock, Quantrill led Ball, Lipsey, and Morrison up the steps of the Walker house and onto the porch. Dean and Southwick waited with the wagon a short distance away. Quantrill assigned Morrison to stand guard on the porch. Ball would do the talking when they got inside. Quantrill knocked on the door. When Morgan Walker opened it, Quantrill shoved him back into the house. The three men stormed inside, pistols drawn.

"We're here to take your slaves," Ball said, "and also your horses, mules, and any money you got."

"Have you talked to my slaves," Walker said, "and do they want to go with you?"

"Yes," Ball lied, "and they all are anxious to go. So don't give us no trouble."

Quantrill gestured to Ball and Lipsey.

"Boys," he said, "you go take care of the niggers and horses. I'll stay here and keep an eye on the old man."

As soon as Ball and Lipsey joined Morrison on the porch, a shotgun blast shattered the air, its flash illuminating the porch like a bolt of lightning. Morrison died instantly. Lipsey and Ball started to run. Buckshot tore into Lipsey's thigh and groin. He yelled for Ball not to leave him there. Ball, unhurt, came back to help his friend. They headed first for the wagon, but it was already gone, so they fled in the darkness through the underbrush.

John Dean had been hit in the foot by a wild shot and had decided not to wait for anyone. Even Southwick, standing beside the wagon when the firing started, had to run for it when Dean took off. They reached Lawrence a few days later. Dean, "badly lamed in the foot," supported himself with a crutch. He claimed he had frozen his foot, but when newspaper articles appeared about the gun battle at Morgan Walker's place, some people suspected Dean had been involved. He left Lawrence soon after and never returned. No one knows what happened to Southwick.

While Walker and his neighbors went about the business of laying out Morrison's corpse in the harness room, Quantrill told them what a ferocious killer the Quaker had been. Soon neighbors came by to see what a dead abolitionist looked like, and people began to wonder what had happened to the others. Two days later, a neighbor's slave hunting pigs in the woods spied Ball and Lipsey. Ball was cooking a pig over a fire. Lipsey, in considerable pain, lay on the ground. Ball had been able to remove some of the buckshot close to the surface and had applied heated leaves and water to the wounds, but it was obvious Lipsey needed medical treatment.

They begged the slave to help them get across the border, promising him freedom and passage north if he accompanied them to Kansas. All he had to do was bring them a wagon and a team of horses, and soon he would be free. The slave agreed.

Instead, however, he went straight to his master and told him about the fugitives. The slave owner informed Walker, and they gathered a posse to take care of the abolitionists. Charley Quantrill went along with them, even more eager than the others to kill the two Quakers to keep them from informing on him and saying he had been with them. The posse surprised the men at their campsite. Ball reached for his gun, but he was too slow. Morgan Walker cut him down with a blast from his shotgun. Lipsey lay helpless on the ground. Quantrill ran to him and shot him in the head. They buried the men where they fell, without coffins. A couple of days later, the bodies were dug up by local doctors to be used for dissection.

That left only Dean and Southwick as possible threats to Quantrill, but he decided he was safe enough. He knew they had been with the wagon when the shooting started at Walker's house and had had the chance to get away. If Border Ruffians caught them on their way back to Lawrence, they would kill them. But even if Dean and Southwick made it back to Lawrence, it would be a long time before they ventured into Missouri again. The threat to Quantrill now came from the Missourians.

The county sheriff was deeply suspicious of Quantrill, a stranger from Kansas who was involved with abolitionists. Placing Quantrill under arrest, he took him to Independence for questioning. Andrew Walker rode along and eventually persuaded the sheriff to let Quantrill go. But there were a lot of angry people who believed all Jayhawkers should be exterminated. They did not understand why this one was still alive, spending the night in comfort in an Independence hotel with Andrew Walker, son of the man the Kansans had tried to rob. That night, there was a lot of drinking and rough talk. Tempers rose, along with a call for revenge.

By noon the next day, a hostile crowd filled the street, calling for death to the Jayhawker Quantrill. Andrew Walker picked up his horse at the livery stable, intending to get Quantrill out of town and take him back to Blue Springs. When Walker and Quantrill reached the town square, their way was blocked by a group of men erecting a gallows. They were ready for a hanging.

Walker confronted the mob; he warned that the only way they would get Quantrill was over his dead body. The threat worked, and the men let them pass.

Walker took Quantrill to a store in Independence and bought him a suit of blue denim. When they returned to Blue Springs, Morgan Walker showed his gratitude by giving Quantrill a fast purebred Kentucky mare named Black Bess, a saddle, and fifty dollars in cash. A neighbor gave him ten dollars. The locals were eager to hear him tell and retell the story of how he had saved Walker from the Jayhawkers, and Quantrill became exactly what he had aspired to be: a hero, a celebrity. He happily spent several weeks as the honored guest in the homes of Walker's neighbors.

"He seemed to be a very pleasant sort of fellow," one man remarked. "He was laughing and joking with the men in the store and his appearance was any other than that of a killer."

Quantrill also acquired a mistress. Her name was Nannie, and she was Morgan Walker's daughter. Attractive and sexy, Nannie Walker had once been married, but her husband had divorced her after he found her in bed with another man. She had had several lovers and was thought to match Quantrill in her capacity for hypocrisy and double-dealing.

Quantrill continued to tell his sad tale of the events at Morgan Walker's place. He embellished the story each time, enlarging his role as a martyr seeking revenge against the abolitionists. He claimed he was from Maryland, a safe thing to say in Missouri, because Maryland was considered to be Southern in its sympathies. To have admitted he was a native of Ohio or any Northern state would have aroused suspicion; Missourians believed that anybody who went to Kansas from "up there," did so only to challenge slavery and undermine the Southern way of life.

That was not true of Charley Quantrill. He did not have anything to do with trying to end slavery, he assured his listeners. The only reason he had gone to Kansas was because his older brother lived there and wanted them to go to California together. This was all part of the story, of course; Quantrill had no older brother. Off they went, Quantrill explained, with two wagons, good mules, a fine array of provisions, and a freed Negro to cook and do chores.

According to his story, they got as far as Cottonwood, seventy miles west of Lawrence, when a band of thirty Kansas Jayhawkers attacked their defenseless camp. Led by the notorious James Montgomery, the outlaws showed no mercy to the Quantrill brothers, innocent young men, no more than boys, really. They shot Charley Quantrill in the chest and leg, killed his brother, and stole the wagons, mules, food, the Negro, even the clothes off their backs. They left Charley naked, freezing, starving, dying, out on the open prairie.

He forced himself to stay awake day and night, he recounted to his spellbound audience, to keep the buzzards and coyotes from chewing on his brother's body. Then, when all seemed lost, an old Indian named Golightly Spiebuck appeared and nursed him back to health. As soon as he could sit a horse and carry a gun, he went hunting for the men who had killed his brother. To do that, he had to pretend to become a Jayhawker himself. He tracked them one by one, then shot each man between the eyes. The last three of the thirty gunmen were the ones he had led into the trap at Morgan Walker's place. Now all of them were dead and his brother could rest in peace.

Quantrill stayed in the Blue Springs area throughout the winter of 1861, living off his glory and the hospitality of those to whom he was a hero, even though, by then, they had heard his yarn a few too many times. By the end of the winter months, he was growing restless. The story had grown stale for him, too. He longed for action, for new raids and adventures, new legends with him as the hero.

He tried to organize raids into Kansas—desiring the money, the adventure, and the chance to satisfy his need for revenge—but no one seemed interested. Blue Springs was too far from the state line to be home to Border Ruffians he could recruit for a raiding party. Also, since Kansas had become a state, many Missourians saw no reason to continue the six-year civil war. There was nothing to gain, no possibility of making Kansas a slave state, and no point in trying to kick out the Free-Soilers. The issue had been decided and had to be accepted.

Quantrill went on long solitary night rides on Black Bess, his Kentucky mare. Three times he ventured into Kansas, careful to stay away from Lawrence, looking for a main chance, a way to make money, to rob, or deceive, or kill. Toward the end of March 1861, he left for Kansas again, telling Andrew Walker he would be gone only a few days. He rode due west toward Stanton, where he had lived with Colonel Torrey and Harmon Beeson when he arrived in Kansas four years earlier.

He was no safer—nor any more welcome—in Stanton than he would have been in Lawrence. Some would say he might have been safer in Lawrence; there, it was only Sheriff Sam Walker and his warrant waiting for him, a matter of law and justice. In Stanton, it was Eli Snyder, who stood ready to gun down Quantrill on the spot—no arrest, no trial, only the frontier's summary justice. Snyder wanted revenge for the Morgan Walker raid and the deaths of the three men Quantrill had led there.

On March twenty-fifth, Quantrill rode into Stanton. Singing to himself as he ambled along the street in his blue denim suit, he passed Harmon Beeson's house, where he went around the back to the kitchen door. Beeson was not home, but his son-in-law was. Quantrill sneered at him and made some insulting comment, as though he was deliberately looking for trouble, daring anybody to challenge him.

Beeson's son-in-law did not accept the challenge, but a neighbor saddled up his horse the instant he recognized Quantrill. He headed for Osawatomie, just a few miles away, to warn Eli Snyder.

Quantrill rode to the cabin of John Bennings. Still a shiftless hunter and trapper and as proslavery as ever, Bennings was just the person Quantrill wanted to see.

When Snyder learned Quantrill was back, he made up his mind to kill him, but he intended to do it legally. He secured a warrant for Quantrill's arrest from a justice of the peace in Stanton. The warrant charged Quantrill with the crimes committed in Lawrence, the ones for which Sheriff Walker had tried to arrest him. Snyder proposed to get Quantrill for resisting arrest, whether he resisted or not. The justice of the peace, knowing Snyder's feelings about Quantrill, gave the warrant to a constable and cautioned that the law officer, not Snyder, was to make the arrest, although Snyder and his men would be permitted to accompany the constable.

Snyder and his party reached Bennings's cabin at dawn. The constable pounded on the door, waking Quantrill, Bennings, and Bennings's son, Adolphus. The lawman demanded Quantrill's surrender. Quantrill shouted that he would fight to the death rather than surrender. Finally, Quantrill agreed to let the constable enter. After a lengthy discussion and the constable's assurance that he would protect Quantrill from Snyder's posse, Quantrill agreed to turn over his pistol and accompany the man to the justice of the peace in Stanton.

Just before they left, Bennings slipped Quantrill another pistol, which he concealed beneath his jacket. As the constable led his prisoner out the front door, Adolphus ran out the back, saddled Black Bess, and raced off for Paola, the county seat. Paola, a center of the proslavery movement and home to many Border Ruffians, was where Colonel Torrey ran a hotel. Despite Quantrill's attempts to rob and cheat him four years before, the proslavery Torrey stood ready to help anyone who was against the Jayhawkers, as Quantrill was believed to be in those parts.

The ride into Stanton was tense for Quantrill, who expected at any moment a bullet from Snyder's gun. Snyder tried to taunt him into running, so he would have reason to kill him, but Quantrill did not accept the dare. Frustrated, Snyder decided he could not wait any longer, and he raised his gun and took aim at Quantrill's chest. Before he could pull the trigger, someone deflected the barrel of his gun.

When the party reached Stanton, they crowded into a store where the justice of the peace was holding court. The judge told Quantrill he was sending him to Lawrence.

Quantrill protested; he would rather die than be sent there. He asked for a weapon to defend himself against Snyder. Snyder drew his pistol, menacing Quantrill with it until the constable shoved him away. Quantrill took refuge behind the counter. One of Snyder's men hoisted himself up on the counter and fumbled with his rifle, pretending something was wrong with it. When the constable was looking elsewhere, the man placed the barrel against Quantrill's chest and pulled the trigger. The gun misfired.

Sixteen armed men from Paola, alerted by Bennings's son, arrived in Stanton prepared to do battle to save Quantrill, one of their own. They took on the town "with that brazen assurance, loud profanity, and vulgar swagger then common to the border-ruffians." They looked so fierce and were so belligerent, they cowed even the tough Eli Snyder and his Jayhawkers. They also outnumbered them.

The justice of the peace handed Quantrill over to the Border
Ruffians, along with his arrest warrant. They promised to escort
him to Paola and keep him in the jail there, knowing he would
not stay incarcerated long. The judge had no other option, not
when the Border Ruffians warned that if he failed to release
Quantrill to them, they would "strew the road, between here &
Paola with dead men." That was a fine incentive.

Quantrill was driven in an open buggy to Paola, where he was
treated as the guest of honor at a banquet at Colonel Torrey's
hotel. Once again a celebrity, a hero, Quantrill was soon regal-
ing his audience with the story of how he had escaped the
clutches of that damned Jayhawker Eli Snyder. After dinner, he
was taken to jail, where one of the Border Ruffians confiscated
his pistol. After the jailer searched Quantrill, they returned his
gun, in case a lynch mob showed up. The jailer recalled: "I told
him in case the jail was attackted [sic], to remain, back in his cell,
& make every shot tell. I told him that as soon as I heard one shot
that I would be among them with some thirty or more armed
men and would commence firing on any mob, that would attempt to take him out of Jail."

Quantrill was kept in jail three days, while his supporters secured a writ of habeus corpus on the grounds that his arrest had
been malicious and illegal. Judge Thomas Roberts found no reason to detain Quantrill, and he ordered his immediate release.
A jubilant crowd accompanied Quantrill to Torrey's hotel, where
they lunched on sandwiches and cakes. Quantrill filled his pockets with food; Torrey and others advised him to get out of town
and not return to Kansas for a while. There was still the outstanding warrant for his arrest in Lawrence, and Eli Snyder was
no doubt obtaining another one from some other judge.
Quantrill agreed.

His friends led him outside, where Black Bess was saddled
and waiting. Just as he mounted, Eli Snyder and his cronies, with
the sheriff of a neighboring county, drew up, waving a new warrant for Quantrill's arrest. Quantrill thumbed his nose at them.
Then he bent over and patted his butt in a vulgar gesture of contempt. Trusting his supporters to block Snyder's gang from pur-

suit, Quantrill put his spurs to Black Bess, waved his pistol over his head, and raced off toward the Missouri border.

Nine days later, on April 12, 1861, at 4:30 A.M., the first shot was fired on Fort Sumter.

LIFE SEEMED EMPTY of promise for William Clarke
Quantrill after his escape from Eli Snyder. He rode back
over the border to Blue Springs, Missouri—where else was
there to go?—where once he had been lionized. How long,
though, could he keep feeding off the same old story about
avenging his fictitious dead brother and saving Morgan Walker's
life? Since then, he had done nothing except to escape after his
foolhardy return to Kansas, where he had taunted old enemies
and lost. He had deceived no one but himself, and he had been
forced to run.

He grew morose and despondent. His resentment at the way
life treated him, which was never far from the surface, swept up
like a sudden summer storm. He vowed to get even with everybody who had wronged him. But Kansas was closed to him. He
would not dare to go back unless it was at the head of an avenging army, a force large and merciless enough to fulfill his desire
to rob and loot, to inflict death and destruction. But Quantrill
had no army to lead and no prospect of forming one.

It was true there was a war on and real armies were gathering to do battle, but he was not cut out to be a common soldier. He knew he could not tolerate anyone ordering him about or the constant marching and drilling and regimentation. If he was going to fight in this war, it would have to be on his own terms—the terms by which he always fought his personal war—free to go his own way, to do as he damned pleased for whatever would bring in a dollar. And a bullet to anyone who tried to stop him.

He continued to visit with Morgan Walker and his neighbors, listening to their stories of the new nation, the Confederate States of America, but talk of politics and preserving the Southern way of life bored him. After an increasingly bleak month, he decided he'd had enough of Missourians and their talk of a noble cause. When one man announced he was taking his slaves to Texas for the summer, to keep Jayhawkers from stealing them, Quantrill decided to go along.

He did not like Texas any better than Missouri, and he moved on to the Cherokee Nation in Indian Territory. He had lived among Indians before, and he liked their free life and the fact that their law enforcement was a lot less strict than in the white man's world. He admired the Cherokee guerrilla tactics in repulsing raids from rival tribes. There is no evidence he joined their fights, but he observed their tactics and would use them in the future.

For a time, Quantrill lived with a wealthy Cherokee man named Joel Mayes, who would become head chief of the Cherokee Nation. Many Indians had fine homes with lavish furnishings, where they practiced genteel manners and sophisticated ways, attended by black slaves. Like the majority of well-to-do Cherokee, Mayes believed in the Southern way of life and the slave society it maintained, as strongly as any Virginian or South Carolinian.

Mayes was willing to fight for this lifestyle, even as a private soldier. He enlisted with the First Cherokee Regiment, which headed east to Arkansas to join forces with a Confederate army under the command of Brig. Gen. Ben McCulloch. Quantrill rode with Mayes, though he did not enlist in the army. He became a camp follower, a hanger-on, looking for a chance to make money.

On August 10, 1861, McCulloch's Confederates beat a Union force at Wilson's Creek in southern Missouri. During the fight, Quantrill and the Cherokees lingered on the fringes of the battleground to carry away anything of value, including more than a few scalps.

Quantrill soon left the Indians and attached himself to a Confederate army led by Brig. Gen. Sterling Price. He may have chosen to follow Price's army because it was moving north to the Missouri River, close to his old haunts along the Kansas-Missouri border—and closer to Nannie Wilson, his mistress at Blue Springs.

On September 2, 1861, Price's army collided with a Union force at Dry Wood Creek. It was not much of a battle, barely mentioned in history books, and it ended with a Confederate retreat in the face of an inferior number of Yankees. Quantrill was standing near a cannon when a Union shell scored a direct hit. Several Southerners were killed and maimed. Although unhurt, Quantrill decided he'd had his fill of soldiering.

He left Price's army in November, returned to Blue Springs and his mistress, and took up his self-proclaimed calling as a detective. Blue Springs remained peaceful, seven months after the onset of war, untouched by the fighting that had ripped the nation. Although Morgan Walker and his neighbors were Confederate in their sympathies and not interested in freeing their slaves, they felt no urgency about joining the fight to keep them. Few young men there were rushing to join the colors. It looked like the war might bypass Blue Springs altogether.

Shortly after Quantrill returned, a band of Kansas Jayhawkers started raiding farmhouses north of Blue Springs. Quantrill, ever on the lookout for trouble and the opportunities that came with it, scouted the area, playing detective, and reported the raids to Andrew Walker. Walker formed an eleven-man posse, Quantrill among them, to pursue the Kansas raiders. They traced the Jayhawkers to a farmhouse they had looted and set afire, where they found a woman who had been pistol-whipped. Striking a woman was unpardonable; there was no justification for such outrageous behavior. Walker and his men pursued the raiders with renewed fury.

They caught up with them half a mile away, as the outlaws were leaving another burning farmhouse. Walker, Quantrill, and the posse charged, yelling and firing wildly. Legend has it that Quantrill fired the shot that killed the man who had struck the woman, but whoever did it killed him instantly, and two other Jayhawkers were wounded so severely, they later died. The others got away.

The Kansans were apparently a quasi-military unit, a militia outfit operating under official orders of the Union army. Two of Walker's men, identified by the survivors, were arrested by civilian authorities and charged with murder. Quantrill, perhaps wanting all the glory, went to the justice of the peace who had issued the warrants and claimed responsibility for the killings, absolving the others in his group. After explaining why they had chased down the Kansans, Quantrill and the others were released. He returned to Blue Springs, to a new round of acclaim.

Quantrill had found a place for himself in the war, as an irregular, a partisan, a guerrilla. But he was still only a follower. Although Quantrill was credited with bravery and daring, Andrew Walker was the undisputed leader. A few weeks later, however, Morgan Walker insisted that his son return to farming. Later, Andrew Walker recalled the moment: "I had, in obedience to the advice of my father, returned to the farm, and given up bushwhacking. . . . Quantrill had by that time become the leading spirit among the guerrillas."

By Christmas 1861, Quantrill had assumed control of the Blue Springs outfit. Now, he had his own army. There were only ten men to start with, but they were tough and determined, prepared to follow William Clarke Quantrill wherever he would lead them. Only half would survive the war, but at the time, they formed the nucleus of a guerrilla band that would grow to thirty times their number and hack a bloody trail over two states.

Quantrill seemed the natural choice to take over after Andrew Walker left. He could ride faster and shoot straighter than most of the men. He was better educated, having not only attended school but taught, as well. He had proven himself a fearless fighter for the cause, having saved Morgan Walker from those damned abolitionist Yankee Jayhawkers. In addition, he alone could claim, however falsely, that he had military combat experience. He spoke freely of his service with two Confederate armies, Ben McCulloch's and Sterling Price's.

He could also attest to expertise in guerrilla warfare, from his days in Kansas fighting the antislavery forces; at least that was his version of events. And he had killed, a feat not many in his group could yet claim. He knew the enemy from having lived among them, and was, above all, so he said, an ardent believer in the Confederate cause. He was Southern-born himself, from Maryland, he boasted, conveniently forgetting his Ohio roots. And he invented yet another older brother, serving with none other than Robert E. Lee. All this, plus his shrewd, cunning, charismatic personality, made Quantrill the logical and popular choice to lead the neophyte guerrilla band.

The men who rode with Quantrill were a mixed lot of idealists, opportunists, and rogues. There were those who joined out of principle, believing they were defending their homes and families and their ideal way of life against the misguided Yankees. Some fought to avenge their treatment at the hands of Union troops, who had destroyed their farms and killed fathers and friends. Some were looking for the excitement of a good fight, restless young men come west to escape the routine life back home, ready to "fight or frolic, and [they] often acted as though they perceived little or no difference between the two." Fighting was a game to them, a deadly game only the wildest and best could play well enough to win, and the game itself became their reward.

There were also the opportunists, like Quantrill, who viewed the war as a chance to make a dollar and to live outside the law. In peacetime, they had been criminals, driven by their hatred of those they believed had wronged them. This group comprised "some of the most psychopathic killers in American history." Their goal was "nothing more than robbery, revenge, or nihilistic love of violence."

One of these outlaws was "Bloody Bill" Anderson. Then in his early twenties—a sadistic, brutal, taciturn fellow—Anderson was known to tie a knot in a silken cord every time he killed a man. His final tally would be fifty-four. A crony described him as "a maniac in battle with no regard for the lives of his men. He would often cry and froth at the mouth in battle simply because he could not kill a whole regiment of the enemy in a few minutes."

It was rumored that sometimes Quantrill would spare a life, but Anderson never would. He was fearless, reckless and daring to an astonishing degree. "If I cared for my life," he once said, "I'd have lost it long ago. Wanting to lose it, I can't throw it away."

Bill Anderson was born in Missouri and raised on a farm in Kansas. The Anderson family had an unsavory reputation. "To kill, steal and plunder wagon trains of the Santa Fe trail and rob the settlers seemed to be their business." Bloody Bill's father had been shot and killed in a confrontation with the local judge over a stolen horse. Bill himself was freed on bail and promptly fled to Missouri with the rest of the family.

Two months later, he returned to Kansas with his brother, Jim, and a third man, reputed to be Quantrill. The judge and his brother-in-law were shot down and left in the cellar of the judge's store. They were still alive when the store was set afire. The brother-in-law escaped but died later from his wounds; the judge burned to death in the cellar. The killers were never caught, but their identities were an ill-kept secret.

Anderson was the handsomest and best dressed of Quantrill's guerrillas. He had sharp, angular features, and his long dark hair fell to his shoulders in ringlets. Before he became a bushwhacker—another term for Confederate guerrilla, from "one accustomed to beat about or travel through bushes"—Anderson was known as easygoing, entertaining, and affable. But people also recalled the vicious look in his eyes, "a sort of a cross between an eagle and a snake." A preacher who met Anderson before the war recalled, "Over his features continually there played a look of infinite conceit and a sneering smile of ineffable contempt."

George Todd, with blond hair and intense ice blue eyes, was nearly as handsome as Anderson and equally callous, brutal, and cruel. He was an expert shot and fearless in battle. A Union officer remembered Todd as a "blood thirsty cuss." Four years younger than Quantrill, Todd had the loyalty of the younger guerrillas, who idolized him without question. His goal was to kill Yankees—the more the better—though he never kept score the way Bloody Bill Anderson did.

No one knows why Todd turned bushwhacker. Born in Canada, he arrived in Kansas City in 1859, at the age of eighteen, and found work as a stonemason and ditchdigger. Illiterate, hot-tempered, and always spoiling for a fight, Todd would soon become the only man on whom Quantrill could depend. Eventually, he would be the only one to challenge Quantrill's leadership.

Archie Clements was eighteen when he joined Quantrill's band, though his allegiance was to Bloody Bill. Short and slender, with blond hair and gray eyes, "Little Archie" was as vicious as anyone in the outfit. He often smiled, especially when he was killing someone, and was equally adept with knife and gun. "An unfeeling savage, this child soldier scalped and mutilated his victims when it pleased him." There was neither mercy nor remorse in Clements's soul.

Frank James began the war as a soldier in Ben McCulloch's Confederate army. He was captured at the battle of Wilson's Creek and granted a parole. Paroles were common early in the war, because neither side wanted to be burdened with large numbers of prisoners to house and feed. Under the terms of a parole, a soldier pledged not to fight again until the other side announced it had received an equal number of parolees. Many soldiers adhered to this restriction because they had given their word, and a man's word was his bond. Others agreed out of a sense of relief at having this honorable way out of their obligation to fight.

The tall, lanky Frank James came from Missouri. A rabid Southerner, he chafed at no longer being able to fight for his cause. When he returned home, to a part of Missouri under Union control, he brandished a revolver in town and boasted about how badly the Yankees had been routed at Wilson's Creek. For this unwise behavior, he was arrested; he was released from jail only because of his mother's influence with local politicians. He left town but could not rejoin the Confederate army, because neither side allowed parolees to reenlist until they were formally released from parole. James grabbed what he saw as his only alternative, service with Quantrill's guerrillas.

A couple of years later, Frank James's younger brother Jesse ran afoul of some men from an outfit of the Missouri state militia, who whipped him and left him bleeding in a field when he refused to reveal the whereabouts of his brother and Quantrill. When Jesse dragged himself back home, he discovered his stepfather, Dr. Reuben Samuel, hanging from a tree. His mother and sister, forced to watch, seemed paralyzed by the horror. Samuel had been strung up because he wouldn't divulge where Frank James had gone. Jesse cut the man down, but his breathing had been stopped for too long; he was left mentally incapacitated. James's mother and sister were arrested and taken to prison in St. Joseph, where the sister contracted malaria. By the time they were released, Jesse James was also riding with Quantrill. His best friend would be Little Archie Clements.

Thomas Coleman Younger, who called himself Cole, was born in Missouri in 1844. He was one of fourteen children of Col. Henry Younger—the title was an honorary one—a wealthy landowner with five farms throughout the state. He was also a county magistrate and holder of several lucrative U.S. mail contracts. One of the richest men in all of Missouri, he kept slaves and held deep Southern sympathies, although he opposed secession.

As a boy, Cole Younger enjoyed a life of ease and luxury. Tall, broad-shouldered, and handsome, he was also high-spirited, impulsive, and quick-witted. Women found him charming, and he seemed to be admired by everyone. Like most boys reared in the West, he learned to hunt and became a crack shot with pistol and shotgun. His childhood games reflected the growing tensions between North and South. In these games of war, young Cole and his neighbors formed into squads of soldiers and did battle, using sticks for guns. The South always won, of course, and the conflicts were fierce. Occasionally, the children playing abolitionists were on the losing side of fistfights.

The confrontations became more vicious as the border wars flared and a man was pushed to declare his loyalty. People demanded to know who was sound on the goose and who was not. Colonel Younger, who maintained his opposition to secession, found himself increasingly distrusted by both sides. His course was to pray for peace and to argue for conciliation, but that was not enough, particularly when bands of Union militia were organizing.

In the fall of 1860, a gang of Kansas Jayhawkers, led by Charles Jennison, raided the Younger homestead, threatened the family, and stole forty horses and several wagons worth more than four thousand dollars. Seeing their property destroyed, Colonel Younger and Cole knew they could no longer resist secession.

At a neighborhood dance, held the night after Fort Sumter was fired on, a twenty-eight-year-old Union army captain, Irwin Walley, a blustering, drunken womanizer, asked one of Cole's sisters to dance, something no proper Southern woman would ever do with a Northerner.

"I don't care to dance with you, Captain Walley," she said in a voice loud enough to carry across the dance floor.

She had intended to humiliate the officer publicly, and she succeeded. Irate, Walley decided to take his revenge on Cole. The two men exchanged harsh words. Cole hit Walley in the face and knocked him down. Walley reached for his gun, but his friends, sizing up the situation, restrained him.

Cole told his father what had happened.

"That man's determined to ruin you for some reason or other," Colonel Younger said.

"I'll not run, Father," Cole said.

"No, son, and I'm not telling you to. But you ought to go to the farm in Jackson County for a while or to school in Kansas City."

Cole departed the next morning. A few hours later, Captain Walley called at the Younger home with six men in tow. Colonel Younger told them he did not know where Cole was.

"He's a spy against the Union," Walley shouted. "He'll hang for it."

"That's a lie and you know it. Cole's gone and you'll not find him."

"We'll see about it," Walley replied.

Walley never did catch Cole Younger, who was soon riding with Quantrill, but the family paid a terrible price. A year later, Captain Walley waylaid Colonel Younger, shot him to death, and robbed the corpse of $500; he missed $2,200 the colonel was carrying in a money belt. The following year, a band of Union soldiers invaded the Younger farm, searching for Cole. Infuriated that he was not there, they forced Mrs. Younger to set fire to the house. The woman had to walk eight miles through snow to find refuge with a neighbor.

The soldiers paid another visit to Mrs. Younger, looking for the money they had learned had been concealed on the colonel's body. When she said she did not have it, they threatened to kill her maid if she did not tell them where it was. When both Mrs. Younger and the maid denied any knowledge of the money, the men grabbed the maid, strung her up from a tree limb, and rode off. Cole's mother cut her down, their secret intact. The money had been sewn into the maid's skirt. Several of Cole's sisters were arrested, and two female cousins died as prisoners in a Union army jail when it mysteriously collapsed. Thus, the war against the North was intensely personal for Cole Younger.

Younger was among the first to join Quantrill's band, and later he would be among the first to leave. But while he rode with Quantrill, he was one of the most valued men in the outfit. Courageous and daring, a crack shot and cunning tactician, his plans more than once saved the group from disaster. Despite his desire for revenge, he was never bloodthirsty. He refused to kill except in battle or in self-defense. He never shot a man for the thrill. He occasionally saved the lives of innocent civilians, despite Quantrill's orders to kill everyone in their path. By the war's end, a lot of people owed their lives to Cole Younger. He behaved nobly when he was with Quantrill, fighting for a cause in which he believed, able to temper his anger with mercy. There were few like him.

John McCorkle began the war as a soldier in Sterling Price's army, but he lost heart when Price retreated after the battle of Dry Wood Creek. McCorkle gave up soldiering and returned to his Missouri home, determined to live in peace. He even took the oath of allegiance to the federal government. Despite this proclamation, his Yankee neighbors continued to suspect him of proslavery activities. He was harassed by the local militia and was once set upon and robbed by Union troops. McCorkle's moment of decision came in the summer of 1862, when he was ordered to join the militia, as a way of showing his support for the Union. He fled the family farm and joined Quantrill's raiders.

Frank Smith was fifteen when the war began. Although Southern in his sympathies, he was in no hurry to enlist in the Confederate army. He stayed on the family farm near Blue Springs, Missouri, not far from Morgan and Andrew Walker. By 1863, the situation in that part of Missouri was so dangerous, because of raiding bands of Jayhawkers and Border Ruffians, that it was no longer possible to plant crops.

Smith moved to Kansas, where he hoped to get a job. He was given an ultimatum: Join the local pro-Union marauders and vigilantes to prove he was sound on the goose, or be killed. He fled Kansas as fast as he could and joined up with Quantrill's raiders.

Then there was fourteen-year-old Riley Crawford, who lived with his family on their farm near Blue Springs. In 1862, Kansas Jayhawkers kidnapped and killed his father. Mrs. Crawford took Riley to Quantrill and asked him to make a soldier out of the boy, so he could kill Yankees and avenge his father's murder. "Little Riley Crawford was to kill every Union soldier who fell into his hands until he was shot dead at the age of sixteen."

John Thrailkill was another Missourian who rode for revenge. Before the war, he had been an artist, engaged to marry one of the prettiest women around. When Union militia broke into her house and murdered her invalid father, she went insane and died not long after. Thrailkill vowed to kill the twenty militiamen responsible. After he joined Quantrill, he got eighteen before the war was out.

Quantrill's raiders had several advantages over the Union army and militia groups they fought. The guerrillas were tough, hardy farm boys used to riding and shooting. Among them there were no city boys who had to be taught to sit a mount and hit a target nine times out of ten when firing from a charging horse. These were rough-and-ready men who knew how to fight.

They were younger than many of the Union troops, and single, and so they were free of that reluctance to take chances that comes with age, and a dependent wife and children. Years after the war, Frank James put it well:

> If you ever want to pick a company to do desperate work or to lead a forlorn hope, select young men from 17 to 21 years old. They will go anywhere in the world you will lead them. When men grow older they grow more cautious but at that age they are regular daredevils. Take our company and there has never been a more reckless lot of men. Only one or two were over 25. Most of them were under 21. Scarcely a dozen boasted a moustache. Wasn't it Bacon who said when a man had a wife and children he had given hostages to fortune? . . . The truth was we were nothing but great big boys.

Those "great big boys" had weapons that were far superior to those of the Union forces. While some carried carbines and Sharps rifles and a few had shotguns, their basic weapon was arguably the best revolver in the world—the six-shot Colt .44. It was commonly called "the Navy revolver" because of the depiction of a naval battle engraved on the cylinder. Most of Quantrill's men carried two Colts stuck in their belt and two more in saddle holsters; some carried as many as eight. They could keep up sustained fire without having to stop to reload; when one gun was empty, they pulled out another.

The guerrillas fabricated their own powder charges rather than using standard amounts the way Union soldiers did. They discovered, through trial and error, that they could shoot more accurately with a smaller charge because the revolvers did not kick or recoil and ruin their aim. The ball went just as far and was just as deadly as with a larger charge. Not only did this refinement improve their accuracy; it also used less powder, a commodity not so easily obtainable. Unlike regular troops, Quantrill's raiders had no quartermaster corps to keep them supplied with weapons and ammunition.

Quantrill's men were among the best shots of any outfit, North or South. They could fire revolvers simultaneously from each hand. Their aim was never by sighting along the pistol barrel, but by intuition and judgment. The pistol was brought to the target and fired instantly and with ease, but the ball rarely missed.

The Union forces were no match for them. They carried single-shot carbines that had to be reloaded every time they fired. They also carried sabers, which were useless against an opponent who could return fire a couple of dozen times in rapid succession. By the time a Yankee unsheathed his saber and raised it overhead to strike, the guerrillas would have riddled his body with bullets. No guerrilla was ever killed by a saber.

Union cavalry officers complained to the War Department about their inferior weapons and they begged for revolvers. They did not get them until later in the war, and they made little difference in fighting the guerrillas. "The Federals' pistols were of poor quality, and according to the bushwhackers the Yankees couldn't hit anything with them anyway."

Quantrill's outfit also had the best horses. The western Missouri counties were noted for their fine horses—perhaps the best in all the West, it was said—and the guerrillas got the pick of that lot in terms of speed and endurance. The Union forces in Missouri, by contrast, rode some of the worst nags in the Union army. The better horses went to major theaters of war. Missouri, a backwater, got what was left over. Worse for the Federals, many units in Missouri and Kansas were infantry, which were useless in a contest involving lightning cavalry raids. Thus, the guerrillas enjoyed the advantage of mobility denied to their enemies.

The raiders boasted superior men and tactics. Most of the Union troops in the Kansas-Missouri area were second-rate regiments and citizen militia units. The best outfits were with the larger armies fighting on other fronts. The border region got what was left—poorly trained troops, officers deficient in leadership skills, poor morale and unit cohesion, and men who were terrified at the thought of confronting Quantrill's guerrillas.

Quantrill's men did not adhere to traditional ways of fighting; they did not follow the tactics taught at West Point and described in Union army field manuals. They preferred to wait in ambush, strung out along a road, hidden among trees and undergrowth, to pounce on some unsuspecting Yankee patrol.

When the soldiers drew close, the bushwhackers would suddenly come charging out of the brush on horseback, screaming the terrifying rebel yell and blazing away with their pistols. In a matter of seconds the whole affair would be over. The guerrillas would strip their victims' bodies, round up their horses, and disappear once more into the forests and thickets.

Another favorite tactic was to dress in uniforms of Union blue, amble up to a Yankee outfit and offer friendly greetings, and open fire at point-blank range. Few Northern troops survived these surprise attacks. Union commanders caught on to the trick and insisted on the use of passwords and signs and countersigns. But their officers grew lazy and rarely changed the passwords. It was easy for the guerrillas to give the proper password, ride among a Union patrol, and shoot down the lot in seconds.

The guerrillas were helped by the terrain of western Missouri, the area that came to be called "Quantrill Country." Much of the land was open prairie, ideal for their swift cavalry raids. Yet the same land offered good hiding places, large stands of woods that provided cover. Because most of Quantrill's men had been raised in the area, they knew every hill, forest, thicket, and trail. The Union troops did not know the terrain and did not trouble to scout it. They traveled mostly on the main roads, while the bush-whackers used paths that easily concealed their movements.

The land also offered a haven to which Quantrill's men could retreat, on those rare occasions they were pressed too hard by a pursuing force or simply needed to rest. A wild area seven miles wide and thirty miles deep known as the Sni-A-Bar—a place of deep gorges, thick woods, overgrown bush, and narrow, winding trails—it could be defended by a few well-armed men. Only the largest Union forces ventured into that forbidding place. They did not linger.

The guerrillas could count on the assistance of the local population. They had no trouble finding horses, clothing, food, information about enemy troop movements, a barn to take shelter, medical care for wounds. Many of the residents helped willingly—they had relatives and friends riding with Quantrill—and most others were grateful for what the raiders were doing to the Yankees. Even children did their part, collecting small pieces of lead for making bullets.

Those who opposed the war or who were secret Union sympathizers had no choice about aiding the guerrillas. Anyone who did not provide food or shelter or whatever else was necessary risked being beaten or killed. As a result, Union troops could not expect help from the residents, which made their job much more difficult.

The Union army tried to punish the locals for helping Quantrill. They levied fines and jail terms, burned their homes and crops, and even put some to death. But these repressive measures only made the locals hate the Yankees more.

Helping Quantrill's men became an accepted part of daily life, as routine as milking the cows or planting the crops. One local resident remembered this story about his grandfather:

[H]e would wake up in the night and see somebody in front of the fireplace taking off his boots. Then, walking in his sock feet, the person would go into a room that was seldom used and go to bed. Sometimes the outside door would be silently opened and clothes put inside the house. This was a sign they needed to be mended; and this my grandmother would do, and in a few days someone would call for them. Sometimes, when my grandfather went to the stable in the morning, he would find one of his horses gone and a strange horse in its stall, usually lame, or one that had lost a shoe. As soon as the lameness was gone, my grandfather would replace the shoe. In a few days he would go again to the stable and there would be his own horse, and the other would be gone. This is the way our people helped each other.

The populace of Quantrill Country became Quantrill's quartermaster corps and commissary, supplying his needs and keeping him and his men better fed, equipped, and clothed than most regular Confederate army units.

Quantrill's guerrillas adopted a unique style of dress, a kind of uniform that became recognizable and feared all over the border country. The major distinguishing feature was the guerrilla shirt, a blouse worn over a regular shirt. Seen in every color from scarlet to butternut, the guerrilla shirt was cut low in front, like a vest with sleeves, the point ending just above the belt in a rosette or ruffle. The shirts had four enormous pockets, two on each side—handy for holding ammunition—which were trimmed with swatches of brightly colored cloth and decorated with beads and needlework. Most of the shirts had been sewn by mothers or sweethearts from whatever material was available.

The men wore large round-rimmed hats tilted at rakish angles, the crown sporting a feather or a shiny metal star. Baggy trousers were tucked into the tops of their high boots, and wide leather belts held their Colt .44 Navy revolvers.

The story was told by some of the raiders about a black flag under which they rode, although others, including Frank James and Cole Younger, claimed never to have seen it. "I never saw it," Cole Younger told a reporter years later, "but [I] heard it was destroyed." The legend may have arisen from the tale of a young Missouri woman, Annie Fickle, who in 1861 spread the word that she wanted to meet Quantrill. They finally got together near a church in Sni-A-Bar Township. She lavished praise on Quantrill

and his men, proclaiming, "And ever let your battle cry be—
Quantrill and Southern supremacy!"

Then she raised the eight-foot pole she had carried with her
and unfurled a three-by-five-foot black banner of quilted alpaca
with the name QUANTRILL stitched in bloodred thread across the
center. The truth of this incident has not been verified, and
there is no evidence that the banner, if it existed, was carried into
battle. However, one of the guerrillas, Kit Dalton, lent credence
to the tale when he wrote a book about his experiences, entitled
Under the Black Flag.

Another unverified tale that became part of the myth of
Quantrill's raiders involves the Black Oath, which the men were
allegedly required to swear before joining the band. Supposedly,
each man was told the following:

> You have voluntarily signified a desire to cast your fortunes
> with us. By so doing, remember that our purpose is to tear
> down, lay waste, despoil and kill our enemies. Mercy belongs
> to sycophants and emasculated soldiers. It is no part of a
> fighter's outfit. To us it is but a vision repugnant to our obli-
> gation and our practices. We recognize but one power to sep-
> arate us in the hour of peril, and to succor one another at all
> hazards we have pledged ourselves more sacredly, and are
> bound by ties much stronger than honor can impose. With this
> understanding of what will be required of you, are you willing
> to proceed?

If the candidate said yes, the Black Oath was read to him slowly
so he could repeat each phrase aloud.

> In the name of God and Devil, one to punish, the other to re-
> ward, and by the powers of light and darkness, good and evil,
> here under the black arch of heaven's avenging symbol, I
> pledge and consecrate my heart, my brain, my body, and my
> limbs, and I swear by all the powers of hell and heaven to de-
> vote my life to obedience to my superiors; that no danger or
> peril shall deter me from executing their orders; that I will

exert every possible means in my power for the extermination of Federals, Jayhawkers and their abettors; that in fighting those whose serpent trail has winnowed the fair fields and possessions of our allies and sympathizers, I will show no mercy, but strike with an avenging arm, so long as breath remains.

New recruits pledged they would never betray a comrade, even under the most diabolical of tortures and the most horrible of deaths, and would never forsake a comrade by allowing him to fall into the hands of his enemies. Should they violate any article of the oath, they would

pray an avenging God and an unmerciful devil to tear out my heart and roast it over flames of sulphur; that my head may be split open and my brains scattered over the earth; that my body be ripped up and my bowels torn out and fed to carrion birds; that each of my limbs be broken with stones and then cut off by inches, that they may be fed to the foulest birds of the air; and lastly, may my soul be given into torment that it may be submerged in melted metal and be stiffened by the fumes of hell, and may this punishment be meted out to me through all eternity, in the name of God and the Devil. Amen.

Kit Dalton wrote that the oath was used only in the group's early days and was discontinued when the outfit grew larger. Cole Younger, writing thirty years later, discredited the idea of the oath. "The 'Black Oath' is a myth originating in the brain of some irresponsible, badly informed and reckless chronicler. It was all new to me, and had no existence in fact." However, this disclaimer was written in 1881, when Younger was in prison, serving the fifth year of a life sentence. He was applying for a pardon, and it is conceivable he was trying to downplay his violent past.

The lore, legend, myth, and reality of Quantrill and his guerrillas began shortly after he took over the leadership of the group, at the time they killed their first man, a Confederate deserter from Sterling Price's army. The victim, George Searcy, had committed several robberies in the Blue Springs area and, most un-wisely, had taken a shot at Quantrill. The guerrillas tracked him down, hanged him in the woods along the Little Blue River, and returned the horses and mules he had stolen to their owners, even though some of the owners were Union sympathizers.

A few days later, Quantrill's band had their first encounter with Yankee troops. It occurred near the Little Blue River when they ambushed an unwary Union patrol on the road to Inde-pendence. Caught by surprise, several of the soldiers were wounded; the rest surrendered. Quantrill confiscated their weapons and ammunition, then paroled the men, acting just as the regular army would have done.

The war in Missouri took an ugly turn against civilians on December 22, 1861, when the Union commander of the De-partment of the Missouri, Maj. Gen. Henry W. Halleck, issued General Orders Number 32. Rebels in the northern part of the state, far from Quantrill Country, had been burning bridges, de-stroying railroad tracks and telegraph wires, and creating a nui-sance for the Union forces. Halleck was irate, and he insisted that partisan acts by civilians be punished.

General Orders Number 32 stated the following concerning persons who destroyed federal property:

> [They] are guilty of the highest crime known to the code of war and the punishment is death. Any one caught in the act will be immediately shot, and any one accused of this crime will be arrested and placed in close confinement until his case can be examined by a military commission, and, if found guilty, he also will suffer death.

When General Halleck issued these orders, he had not heard of Quantrill. That name had yet to appear in any Union army dis-patch. But the year 1862 would open a new chapter in the bloody story of the war in the border counties and bring considerable attention to William Clarke Quantrill.

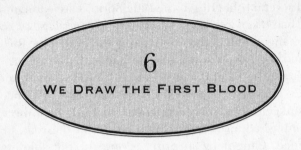

6

WE DRAW THE FIRST BLOOD

Seventh Missouri Infantry
Independence, Mo., February 3, 1862
Brig. Gen. John Pope,
General: I have just returned from an expedition which I was com-
pelled to undertake in search of the notorious Quantrill and his
gang of robbers in the vicinity of Blue Springs. Without mounted men
at my disposal, despite numerous applications to various points, I
have seen this infamous scoundrel rob mails, steal the coaches and
horses, and commit other similar outrages upon society even within
sight of this city. Mounted on the best horses of the country, he has
defied pursuit. . . . I mounted a company of my command and went
to Blue Springs. The first night there myself, with 5 men, were am-
bushed by him and fired upon. We killed 2 of his men (of which he
had 18 or 20) and wounded a third. The next day we killed 4 more
of the worst of the gang, and before we left succeeded in dispersing
them. . . .

*   Quantrill will not leave this section unless he is chastised and dri-*
ven from it. I hear of him to-night 15 miles from here, with new re-

*cruits, committing outrages on Union men, a large body of whom have
come in to-night, driven out by him. . . .*

> W. S. *Oliver*
> *Capt., Commanding*

Quantrill's war against the Union was well under way, some
two months after taking charge of Andrew Walker's group in
Blue Springs, and his name had been formally entered in official Union army files. He led his men, still no more than two
dozen or so, against Jayhawkers and soldiers alike in a series of
lightning raids and ambushes that made him a hero and a symbol of Southern resistance.

Already he was a hunted man. Union patrols were searching
for him. Bands of Jayhawkers scoured the woods. In January, a
farmer from Blue Springs, with more courage than common
sense, had set a trap to catch Quantrill. One Riley Alley announced he was going to hold a dance at his farmhouse. He
spread the word that all young people were welcome to come,
and he particularly wanted Bill Quantrill to be there.

Quantrill heard about it—nothing around Blue Springs escaped his attention—but suspected it was a trap. He cautioned
his men not to go. When the dancing and drinking were at their
peak, Union soldiers from Independence, alerted by Alley that
Quantrill and his men would be there, burst into the parlor with
guns drawn. They separated the men from the women and kept
them all under guard until the following night, waiting for
Quantrill to show up. When he did not, the soldiers proceeded
to get drunk on peach brandy.

They released the women and loaded the men into wagons
and took them to Independence. They dragged Riley Alley along
as a prisoner so no one would suspect his involvement with the
Yankees. They let him go before they reached Independence.

Quantrill and George Todd were waiting for Alley, but he
eluded them and kept on going, all the way to Kansas City. He
was smart enough not to return to Blue Springs. After a short stay,
the other prisoners were set free.

Ed Koger, one of Quantrill's men, whose brother John also rode with the group, wrote a song about Alley's ball, which he sang while strumming his banjo.

> *Old Rile Alley gave a ball,*
> *The Feds came down and took us all*
> *Over the ice and over the snow—*
> *Sing-Song Kitty, won't you kiss-me-o!*
>
> *Old Rile Alley gave a ball,*
> *Planned to catch Quantrill and bushwhack all,*
> *But Quant was smart and didn't go—*
> *Sing-Song Kitty, won't you kiss-me-o!*

Perhaps in retaliation for the arrests at Riley Alley's farm, or because he relished the idea of celebrating George Washington's birthday by ransacking a town controlled by Yankees, Quantrill, assuming that no soldiers would be around to bother him, took fifteen men on a raid to Independence on February twenty-second.

A regiment of Ohio cavalry had passed through town only minutes before, and the rear element was exiting by a southwesterly road when Quantrill and his men roared in from the northeast. The rear riders dashed to catch up with the regimental commander, who ordered his cavalry to wheel around and charge.

Visibility was poor due to fog, but for Quantrill there was no mistaking the sound of thundering hooves approaching. And it was easy to tell that there were many more Yankees than bushwhackers, perhaps more than one hundred to their fifteen.

Instead of retreating in the face of a superior force, Quantrill led his men down the street toward the Union cavalry. Troops and raiders fired at one another at point-blank range. Two of Quantrill's band went down, dead in the dirt street. Bill Gregg fired three times at a cavalryman, his pistol beside the man's ear, and three times the gun misfired. The Yankee drew his saber and chased Gregg down the street, slashing as he ran. He "proceeded to belabor me with his sabre," Gregg recalled; "the only harm he did was to blacken my arm from the elbow to the wrist," beating it with the flat of the blade.

Quantrill's band turned and ran, with the Northerners close behind. Once clear of the town, they scattered—every man for himself—and the Union soldiers could not maintain pursuit for long because of their mediocre horses. Still, they chased the bushwhackers into the woods.

A stray shot felled Quantrill's horse and nicked Quantrill in the leg. He appeared a few days later at the funeral of one of his dead buddies, walking with a cane. For the Washington's Birthday raid, the tally was two killed, one wounded, and the outfit forced to flee, while not one Union man was hit. It was not a promising beginning for the guerrillas.

It was the next foray that set the pattern for the successful raids that would make Quantrill a legend. On March seventh, he took more than thirty men across the state line to Aubry, Kansas, arriving at dawn. Jayhawkers were known to live there, and Quantrill wanted to pay them back in kind for incursions they had made into Missouri.

He issued orders to sack the town. The men rode into Aubry firing their pistols wildly, "screaming and swearing like devils." They plundered homes and shops, robbed every man of his cash and valuables, and set at least one building ablaze. From a second-floor window of a tavern, two overnight lodgers watched a group of Quantrill's men chase five residents across a field. They shot and killed each one, although the men were unarmed.

The lodgers, Abraham Ellis and 2d Lt. Reuben A. Randlett of the Fifth Kansas Regiment, dressed quickly. Peering through the frost-covered window, they saw a bushwhacker on horseback glance up and spot them. It was Quantrill. He whipped out his pistol and fired, striking Ellis in the forehead. Later, Quantrill described it as a "damn good shot." Ellis slumped to the floor, his face covered with blood.

A man rushed into the room and urged Lieutenant Randlett to join the other lodgers in fighting it out with the guerrillas. At first, Randlett was willing, but when he learned there were only three guns in the tavern, he knew resistance would be futile. Better to take their chances on surrendering, because it was inconceivable that the rebels would kill unarmed prisoners.

Randlett walked downstairs and surrendered his revolver to one of the guerrillas, explaining that as a soldier he had a right to be treated as a prisoner of war. The man laughed at him and turned him over to two others, who made it clear they had no use for the civilities of Yankee rules of war. They shouted curses at him and grabbed his arms. One pushed the muzzle of his gun into Randlett's ear; the other shoved his pistol in the lieutenant's mouth.

As Randlett felt and tasted the gun barrels, Bill Gregg yelled for them to stop. Quantrill wanted the officer alive, he said. He led Randlett into a room where Quantrill was waiting. Quantrill asked if Randlett had a horse. The lieutenant told Quantrill it was in the stable. Quantrill ordered one of his men to saddle the horse and bring it around to the front door.

A bloody, dizzy Abraham Ellis staggered into the room, looking as if he had risen from the dead. They gaped at him in shock. Quantrill's bullet had torn through the top of one window sash and the bottom of the other, which slowed it down considerably, before it hit Ellis. "I was struck in the center of the forehead," Ellis wrote seventeen years later, "where the brains of most men are supposed to be located." He became known as "Bullet-Hole" Ellis, because of the deep dent in his forehead, and may have been the only man to be shot by William Clarke Quantrill who lived to joke about it.

While Randlett was downstairs attempting to surrender, Ellis had regained consciousness, to find two men standing over him with revolvers pointed at his head.

"If you have any money, God damn you, give it to me in a minute or I'll blow you to *Hell*," one of the bushwhackers said.

"And as I had no hankering after [that] place," Ellis recalled, "I passed over the checks—(or in other words) I handed him $250.00. . . . They then ordered me down stairs & said that I was not dead by a damned sight."

Quantrill stared, openmouthed, when Ellis staggered into the room.

"Why, Ellis," he exclaimed, "is that you?"

Abe Ellis allowed as how indeed it was, and he felt over-whelming relief to be face-to-face with the young man he had examined for a teaching certificate back in 1859 in Stanton. Ellis had been superintendent of schools when Quantrill taught there.

"Ellis, I am damned sorry I shot you," Quantrill said. "You are one of the Kansas men I do *not* want to shoot!"

For a few minutes, they reminisced about old times, and Ellis was struck by how Quantrill had changed in three years. He seemed much tougher, and so were his men. Ellis described them as "the most desperate Demons that ever disgraced the name of man."

Quantrill said again he was sorry for what had happened and assured him that nothing of his would be stolen, but Ellis was too groggy to mention his $250. Quantrill had Ellis's horse and buggy brought around before he left, with Randlett in tow. Ellis fainted before they were out of sight. He remembered that he "lay on the frozen ground about four hours senseless and motionless and to all appearances dead, and all who saw me pronounced me dead."

Quantrill kept Lieutenant Randlett hostage for eleven days, intending to exchange him for Matt Brady, one of his men held prisoner at Fort Leavenworth. He wrote several letters to the commanding officer but received no reply. Quantrill was an outlaw; no one at Leavenworth was disposed to negotiate with the likes of him.

Frustrated at the official silence, Quantrill ordered Randlett to write, asking for the exchange of prisoners. They heard nothing. Randlett's value as a hostage was fast diminishing; if the Union would not give up Quantrill's man, then he had no value at all. Yet the bushwhackers treated him well, and even took him on a pursuit of Kansas raiders who were burning houses in a neighboring county. They allowed him to watch the fight, under guard.

Quantrill's outfit captured two men claiming to be Union army deserters; they said they were looking to join a rebel outfit. They seemed to know about Randlett and urged Quantrill to hang the Yankee from the nearest tree. Quantrill brought Randlett to talk with the men; the lieutenant wore the coat of one of his guards rather than his uniform, so the deserters would assume he was one of Quantrill's men. The deserters repeated to Randlett and Quantrill that the no-good Yankee Randlett should be strung up right away.

In private, Quantrill asked Randlett what he thought of the two men. Randlett knew if he said he thought they were legitimate deserters who wanted to fight for the South, he might be signing his own death warrant. He told Quantrill he believed they were spies or thieves. A few minutes later, he heard gunshots; he never saw the men again.

Apparently, Quantrill trusted Randlett, because he proposed paroling him for a period of ten days, during which time Randlett agreed to go to Fort Leavenworth to try to effect his exchange for Quantrill's man. Quantrill escorted the lieutenant to Independence, which was empty of Union troops, and left him in a hotel in the main square.

Randlett found himself in trouble right away. A rowdy bunch of local men, drinking in the hotel bar, recognized Quantrill when he brought Randlett in. They began debating Randlett's sympathies and quickly concluded Randlett had to be in league with the rebels and thus deserved to die. Randlett overheard their threats; they seemed increasingly determined to kill him. An elderly man in the bar also overheard the wild talk. He gestured for Randlett to follow and took him to the stable, urging him to hide beneath a pile of hay. The man, openly pro-Union, was nevertheless a friend of Quantrill's. The next morning, he sent Randlett on his way across the border to Kansas and safety.

Randlett went to Union army authorities in Kansas City and Fort Leavenworth but found that no one would deal with Quantrill. There would be no prisoner exchange. A Union army colonel ordered Randlett to lead a company of cavalry to Quantrill's camp so they could kill him. Randlett refused; he had given his word to Quantrill and was honor-bound to keep it. When the colonel persisted, Randlett stormed out of the room in such a fury that he knocked another officer off the sidewalk.

At Fort Leavenworth, Gen. Sam Sturgis took the same position. He would have absolutely no dealings with a bushwhacker like Quantrill. However, he said that Randlett was free to do as he pleased. The general advised him not to return to Independence, warning that Quantrill might kill him. Randlett was aware of that risk, but he was too much a gentleman to go back on his word and violate the terms of the parole Quantrill had granted him.

When Randlett returned to Independence, he found the town full of Union soldiers, nearly a thousand troops decamped there. Through a contact, he sent a message to Quantrill, saying he had been unable to bring about the exchange. With that, Randlett believed he had fulfilled his part of the bargain. He returned to Kansas and never saw Quantrill again. Randlett survived the war, one of a tiny band of Union officers captured by Quantrill who lived to tell the tale.

On March eighteenth, Quantrill and forty men rowed across the Missouri River in small boats, with their horses swimming alongside. Their objective was to attack an eight-man Union detachment in Liberty, Kansas. On the outskirts of town, they met a soldier from that detachment; he refused to divulge the whereabouts of the others. Quantrill promptly shot him down. The other soldiers may have been few, but they were a determined lot and had the good fortune to take refuge in a stout brick building.

A vicious gunfight raged for three hours before the Union commander was wounded and the detachment surrendered. Quantrill paroled them all, then rode off, leaving the town untouched. No buildings were put to the torch; no one was robbed. The people of Liberty were supporters of the South, despite their unfortunate location in Kansas.

The following day, Quantrill read in a St. Louis newspaper

about a new order from General Halleck officially condemning guerrillas as outlaws and calling for their extermination. From that date, March nineteenth, all such bandits would be executed upon capture, like common horse thieves or murderers. No prisoners would be taken; it was to be a war without mercy. The Union was hoisting the black flag.

Quantrill was infuriated, and in his mind, he savagely altered his approach to the war. Cole Younger described the change.

> Where at first there was only killing in ordinary battle, there became to be no quarter shown. The wounded of the enemy next felt the might of this individual vengeance, acting through a community of bitter memories, and from every stricken field there began, by and by, to come up the substance of this awful bulletin: Dead, such and such a number— wounded, none.

Quantrill assembled his sixty men and explained the Yankees' new policy. If they continued to ride with him, they faced immediate execution if captured, death by shooting or hanging. There would be no confinement as prisoners of war, no parole, no trial, and no appeal. They would forfeit all rights as citizens and would be hunted and killed like animals. With his flair for the dramatic, Quantrill drew a line in the dirt and urged his horse across it.

"Now, boys," he said, "I accept the challenge. All of you who wish to remain and fight with me ride over on this side of the line. All of you who wish to leave the outfit go ahead and nothing will be held against you. Every man now will make his own choice."

About forty of the raiders crossed over to Quantrill's side of the line. The others were new to the outfit, having joined the day before. They viewed General Halleck's order as a grim welcome. As Bill Gregg put it, "They were disgusted at the idea of being outlawed and the hoisting of the black flag by the enemy." They decided to return home, but before long they would be back with Quantrill, persecuted by their neighbors and by federal troops on the suspicion that they were guerrillas.

Quantrill intended to strike hard and fast in retaliation for Halleck's policy. The next morning, he led the largest force he had ever assembled, nearly one hundred men, to Independence. He believed the town held only seventy-five troops, a force he knew he could beat, but as he approached, he learned the garrison had been reinforced. It was now three hundred strong, too many for his band to take on. He would have to exact his vengeance elsewhere.

Two days later, on March twenty-second, Quantrill and his men rode to the outskirts of Kansas City, hunting Yankee soldiers to kill. They found only one, at the bridge over the Big Blue River, a sergeant who was immediately disarmed. Quantrill pulled out his revolver and, without a word, shot the man dead. He raised the smoking gun above his head and faced his men.

"Boys," he yelled, "Halleck issued the order, but we draw the first blood!"

They spied the bridge's toll keeper and dragged him out of his hut. The man's young son, playing nearby, watched silently, looking from the dead trooper in the road to the rough mob with drawn guns shouting at his father. The raiders accused the toll keeper of being a spy. Quantrill ordered a hasty mock trial, pronounced sentence, and had the man killed. Before they rode away, they set fire to the bridge.

For Quantrill, this new kind of war was a reversion to his earlier life, little different from torturing animals as a child or thieving and killing as Charley Hart in Lawrence. General Halleck's order had given him an excuse. He no longer felt hindered by any rules of war. All restraints were off.

Quantrill and his men set out to the southeast of Kansas City. After about eighteen miles, they stopped for food at the home of a sympathizer. They rode on to the farmhouse of another supporter, David Tate and his family, some three miles from the Missouri line. Quantrill and about two dozen of his men put up at Tate's home, while the rest took shelter at neighboring farms. Quantrill posted two guards one hundred yards from the house and turned in for the night, sharing the only spare bed with Cole Younger. The other men slept on the floor.

Units of the Federals' Second and Fourth Kansas Cavalry were scouring the countryside on the trail of the murderers of the two men at the Big Blue River bridge. Two companies of the Second Cavalry, under the command of Maj. James M. Pomeroy, rode for the Tate house with orders to arrest Tate and bring him in for questioning. Tate was known to be a supporter of Quantrill.

Quantrill's guards were caught by surprise, apparently asleep at their post. They escaped into the woods but had no time to sound the alarm. Pomeroy led his cavalry up to the farmhouse, climbed the steps onto the porch, and pounded on the front door. Quantrill and his men were awake by then, having heard the troopers approach. He told the others to remain quiet while he made his way to the door. He fired a single shot right through it.

The bullet missed its target. Major Pomeroy leapt off the porch, unhurt, and shouted for his men to open fire. A hail of bullets thudded into the thick log walls of the house, doing no damage to the guerrillas but terrifying the Tate women and children. When Pomeroy heard their shrieks, he ordered his soldiers to cease firing. He shouted for whoever was inside to send out the women and children. Quantrill complied.

While the Tate family filed outside, Quantrill's band stacked furniture and mattresses against the doors and windows. They knew they could not surrender, not in the face of Halleck's order. They would be gunned down without question, no prison or parole. Pomeroy ordered his men to resume firing, and the two sides traded volleys in the darkness.

One of the bushwhackers, Perry Hoy, told Quantrill he was afraid of being burned to death in the house. He would rather surrender and take his chances on being shot. Quantrill shouted the news to Major Pomeroy that one of his men wanted to give himself up. Both sides stopped firing while Hoy and a companion climbed out a window. As the two approached Pomeroy, determined to surrender, they tried to persuade the major they were farmers, not guerrillas. They revealed that Quantrill and twenty-six others were barricaded inside the Tate house. Pomeroy ordered them taken prisoner, and Hoy later faced a firing squad.

Major Pomeroy then ordered Quantrill to surrender. If he refused, the troopers would burn the house. Quantrill had anticipated this plan and had searched for a way out. Along a lower wall at the rear of the house, he had found a section covered with thin weatherboard instead of logs. That was where they could make their break when the fire got too close.

Pomeroy waved some of his men closer to the house. They stacked kindling against the side of the house and struck matches to set it ablaze, but in the intense shooting from inside the house, the major and a private were wounded. The men withdrew. Pomeroy turned over command to Capt. Amaziah Moore, who tried twice more to get a fire going.

Flames lit up the night and swiftly enveloped the front of the house. As they spread toward the rear, Quantrill knew it was time to get out.

"Steady, boys," he said. "Follow me."

He picked up a piece of furniture and smashed it through the weatherboard. The guerrillas burst out of the blazing house, each man firing two Navy Colts at the startled Union troops. The Yankees got off only a few wild shots before the bushwhackers disappeared into the woods behind the house.

One Union soldier was killed, two of Quantrill's men were found dead in the house, and Cole Younger's dignity had been impaired. In the excitement, he had forgotten to put on his boots. To reach the safety of the trees, the men ran through a patch of prickly gooseberry bushes. John McCorkle said, "Cole Younger suffered more from the gooseberry bushes than any of us, having run out of the house without his boots, and we teased him a good deal about the Federals running him out of his boots." For a long time after, Younger was taking quick, dainty steps.

When the bushwhackers had time to take stock of events at the Tate house and to appreciate what a tight spot they had been in, they realized the debt they owed to William Clarke Quantrill. He had remained calm and had acted with courage and ingenuity.

If anyone had doubted him before, they did not after that fra-
cas. A historian commented: "The Tate house fight, which became one of the most famous episodes in bushwhacker annals,
increased Quantrill's prestige among the West Missouri guerrillas and strengthened his leadership."

Nevertheless, the fight was a major defeat. The horses had
been lost, and the men were scattered in small groups throughout the area, pursued by Union troops. The Yankees set fire to
many houses and barns, places that had once provided shelter
for the guerrillas.

Quantrill walked all night and finally found a friendly farmer
who took him in, but he was so bone-weary, he could hardly
stand. His clothes had been torn to shreds. As soon as he had
rested, he sent out word to his men—using willing farmers and
their families as couriers—to obtain fresh horses and meet him
at Sam Clark's farm near Pink Hill, nineteen miles southeast of
Independence.

A week later, on March thirtieth, Quantrill, George Todd, and
some thirty other men met at the Clark place. They were enjoying a relaxed Sunday morning, unaware that Capt. Albert P.
Peabody and his First Missouri Cavalry were close by. Peabody
sent thirty-five men off in one direction and kept thirty with him
to search the countryside for signs of the guerrillas.

Peabody spotted a log house and some outbuildings on high
ground overlooking a road. He could see several men in the front
yard. He dismounted his troops and led them toward the house,
prepared to attack. Bill Gregg recalled that morning:

> [I was] acting barber, cutting a comrade's hair in the front
> yard. John Koger had ridden out to the house of an acquain-
> tance, returned and dismounted in front of the house, where
> he was hitching his horse. Suddenly Koger made a move that
> showed he had sighted the enemy. Immediately after Koger
> had shown this sign . . . the enemy fired upon him, one of their
> bullets struck a rail in [the] fence, glanced [off] striking Koger

on the "buttock," burning severely but did not break the skin.
I imagine I can see Koger holding the burnt spot now.

The guerrillas ran to the house for cover. Quickly, they knocked holes in the chinking between the logs to make ports through which they could return fire. Quantrill positioned himself downstairs with eight men. George Todd was on the second floor with eight more, and Bill Gregg had another eight in the slave cabins. The rest vanished on foot as soon as the firing started. All the horses were in the barn, about two hundred feet away. Once again, they were trapped. Peabody sent for his other detachment and soon outnumbered the guerrillas more than two to one.

The fight raged for over an hour, with neither side inflicting casualties. A half hour later, Peabody assembled a force and led his troops in a charge, which Quantrill's men easily repulsed. Time was on the Yankees' side, however. It was early in the day, and Quantrill knew the Union soldiers could keep them pinned down until they ran out of ammunition. And if Peabody got reinforcements, he would surely try another charge or burn the guerrillas out.

Quantrill realized they had to escape, and he was determined to do so on horseback. Not only did they need to get out of the house without being hit by gunfire but they also had to cross the two-hundred-foot field to the barn and ride out without being picked off by the troops who were safely under cover.

He ordered Todd's group to maintain a withering fire from upstairs while he and his men dashed to the barn for the horses. But just as Quantrill ran out of the house, Captain Peabody began another charge. Todd yelled a warning; he could not hold off the assault by himself. Quantrill returned to the house along with Gregg and the others. Years later, Gregg blamed Todd for the outcome, commenting that "before we had accomplished anything, Todd became alarmed and yelled for us to come to his aid, for which, there was no plausible excuse. . . . I contended then, and have always contended, that if Todd had done his whole duty, we would have saved our horses."

Quantrill was resigned to abandoning the horses. He ordered six of his men to create a diversion. They would burst through the front door and pretend to head for the barn. As soon as the Union troops shot off a volley, they would run back inside.

The Yankee soldiers fired their single-shot carbines all at once. Before they had time to reload, Quantrill and his men rushed outside toward the trees. They all made it unscathed and scattered in the woods. They had lost their horses and Quantrill had left behind his prized spyglass. The Federals had three men wounded.

The bushwhackers crossed woods and gullies until they reached a ford on Sni Creek. There they regrouped and took up defensive positions behind rocks and trees. From this situation, they were able to ambush fifty-one troopers who were on their way to join Peabody. Quantrill waited until the troopers stopped in the middle of the creek to water their horses. The guerrillas took aim and cut down several Yankees before the rest reached cover and returned the fire. The soldiers charged, but Quantrill beat them back until Peabody's force rallied to join them. Peabody now had more than one hundred men in his command.

Quantrill knew it was suicidal to remain there any longer. He ordered his men to scatter, find fresh horses, and rendezvous at a house ten miles south of Independence. When they reassembled, riding fine horses provided by Southern sympathizers, Quantrill's plan was to attack a Union garrison. He sent out a patrol to scout the area, but they reported the garrison to be much larger than he had thought. They also brought the news that Captain Peabody's outfit was dangerously close. Quantrill told his men to saddle up, and he led them to an abandoned farmhouse, the Jordan Lowe place, sixteen miles southeast of Kansas City. It was April 15, 1862.

Determined never again to be caught by surprise and trapped inside a house, Quantrill and the bushwhackers made camp in the woods. Early in the evening, they were awakened by a heavy rainstorm. They were so soaked and miserable that they rushed inside the farmhouse for shelter. Quantrill left the horses hitched to a fence behind the house. He did not post sentinels, believing that the awful weather would keep the Yankees from patrolling.

Quantrill was wrong. The Seventh Missouri Cavalry, under the command of Lieutenant Colonel Brown, had been on his trail for five days. A scout reported at midnight that he had found Quantrill at the Jordan Lowe place, and that the guerrillas had turned in for the night. Colonel Brown sent Lt. G. W. Nash with thirty troopers of the First Missouri Cavalry to attack them.

Lieutenant Nash reached the Lowe house at dawn. He posted his men in a ring around the house and quietly led the bushwhackers' horses away. He shouted a demand for surrender, waking the guerrillas. Quantrill refused. The troopers opened fire from all sides. Bill Gregg described the men as "addled and confused" when the firing started. Quantrill rallied them and assured them they could shoot their way out.

With two guns blazing, Quantrill led his men outside and headed for the woods. Two raiders were shot down as they ran, but the rest made it to safety. Cole Younger glanced back and saw three men, including George Todd, firing from the upstairs loft. They had been asleep and had missed Quantrill's order to get out. Younger raced for the house, braving the deadly fire, and brought Todd out unharmed. The other two men, Andrew Blunt and Joe Gilchrist, were captured.

According to Bill Gregg's recollection, the two prisoners were "set upon a stump for a target. Gilchrist was killed, Blunt's arm broken, [Lieutenant] Nash coming up at this juncture, stopped the shooting and saved Blunt."

Blunt was taken to a hospital in Independence. With the help of a local doctor, a Southern sympathizer who had been forced to work for the Union, Blunt escaped and later rejoined Quantrill. The Federals suffered no casualties at the Lowe house.

In the years following the war, whenever Quantrill's men got together to rehash old times, they never talked about events at the Lowe house. One historian wrote:

Little wonder. For the third time in less than a month they had been surprised, lost their horses, and almost been wiped out. Only Quantrill's quick thinking had saved them from the firing squad or the hangman's noose—that and the incredible ineptitude of the Federal troops, who had thrice trapped them and thrice allowed them to escape with only minor losses. But the bushwhackers profited from these near-disasters. Never again did Quantrill fail to post adequate sentries around his camp, never again did a Union force catch Quantrill's band completely unawares—that is, not until a certain rainy spring morning in Kentucky, several years hence.

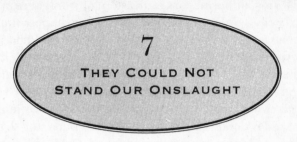

7

THEY COULD NOT
STAND OUR ONSLAUGHT

April 21, 1862
It is represented on reliable authority at these headquarters that bands
of jayhawkers, guerrillas, marauders, murderers, and every species of
outlaw are infesting to an alarming extent all the southeastern por-
tion of Jackson County, and that persons of influence and wealth in
these vicinities are knowingly harboring and thus encouraging (if not
more culpably connected with) these bands of desperadoes. . . . Mur-
ders and robberies have been committed; Union men threatened and
driven from their homes; the U.S. mails have been stopped; farmers
have been prohibited planting by the proclamation of a well-known and
desperate leader of these outlaws by the name of Quantrill, and the
whole country designated reduced to a state of anarchy. This state of
things must be terminated and the guilty punished. All those found
in arms and opposition to the laws and legitimate authorities, who are
known familiarly as guerrillas, jayhawkers, murderers, marauders,
and horse-thieves, will be shot down by the military upon the spot when
found perpetrating their foul acts.

> *James Totten*
> *Brigadier General*
> *Central District, Commanding*

The Union authorities in southeastern Missouri were trying to restore law and order to a lawless place and to impose their rule so that the people who wanted to live in peace could do so.

On April nineteenth, Col. Egbert Brown, commander of the local militia, had called a public meeting at Independence, at which he vilified the acts of guerrilla bands on both sides. He told the large civilian crowd that he had arrested Charles Jennison, the Kansas Jayhawker leader, in an effort to put a stop to depredations from Jennison's pro-Union band. Colonel Brown also castigated Quantrill as the most infamous anti-Union guerrilla leader. He called on all men of goodwill to put down their arms and let the Union militia maintain order. Quantrill's answer was to issue a proclamation warning Union sympathizers in his corner of Missouri not to bother planting crops that spring, because they would not be around by autumn to harvest them.

During this period, Quantrill's guerrillas were operating not as a single unit but in small independent groups, striking anywhere that would disrupt life for the Federals. They targeted the U.S. mail service, robbing so many carriers that ever-larger units of Union cavalry had to be detached from other duties to escort the mail. Before long, all of Jackson County where Quantrill reigned was cut off from the rest of the state, with no mail coming in or going out. Kansas City received no mail from St. Louis for three weeks that spring, until cavalry patrols rode escort for the mail wagons.

Dividing the cavalry into smaller units to protect the mail routes only made them more vulnerable and offered the guerrillas easier targets. Whereas before, bandits would ambush a stagecoach or a mail wagon and its driver, now they hit the wagon as well as its cavalry escort, ambushing them from rocks and trees or down ravines and passes. It was the rare night Union patrols returned to headquarters at Independence without wounded or dead troopers slung over their saddles. Protecting the mail was dangerous duty that weakened morale and increased the determination of Union commanders to stop Quantrill.

Quantrill did no raiding himself in late April and May. He had left Jackson County, though few people were aware of it. So freewheeling were the operations of his men in the weeks following the Lowe house fiasco that most guerrillas did not know he was gone.

Quantrill and George Todd were 180 miles away in Hannibal, Missouri, to buy the pistol caps needed to fire the cartridges in the Colt Navy revolvers. Jackson County ladies ordinarily supplied all the caps, lead, and powder the guerrillas needed, purchasing them in Kansas City, but the supply of caps had run low, and Quantrill decided to look for them himself.

They rode to Hannibal on old, exhausted horses, which they promptly sold for enough money to buy fifty thousand pistol caps. Quantrill and Todd purchased the caps over four days so as not to arouse the suspicion of Union authorities. They began the journey home by train to St. Joseph, Missouri, where they rented a carriage and driver. After they crossed the Missouri River from Kansas City during the night, they were stopped by a Union guard.

If they were caught with fifty thousand caps in their possession, they would be arrested for questioning, but gunning down the guard would attract the attention of other troops, and Quantrill and Todd would be lucky to escape on foot. And if they ran, they would have to abandon the caps.

While the Yankee sentinel questioned the driver, Quantrill and Todd slipped out the door on the far side of the closed carriage and made their way along the riverbank, searching for a place to cross. They walked throughout the night and into the next day, careful to avoid Union patrols, but did not find a point where they could cross the broad river.

They spotted two fishermen in a small boat and hailed them, hoping for a ride across. To their surprise, the men who greeted them were guerrillas, Bill Bledsoe and Andrew Blunt, the latter having escaped from the Union hospital at Independence after his capture at the Lowe house.

By the end of May, Quantrill reassembled his men and prepared to resume large-scale raids. All the men—experienced guerrillas and new recruits alike—arrived well provisioned and riding fresh horses. For two months, the guerrillas roamed freely, striking at easy targets. They ambushed Yankee cavalry patrols, robbed the U.S. mails, and attacked a ferry on the Little Blue River.

On June twenty-seventh, they forced their way aboard a Missouri River steamboat, the *Little Blue,* when it docked at a landing. Among the passengers were forty sick and wounded Union soldiers. The bushwhackers menaced them and shoved them around before carrying off their loot, an enormous quantity of Union military supplies.

A Seventh Cavalry unit from Lexington, Missouri, Maj. Eliphalet Bredlett commanding, was sent in pursuit of Quantrill's men. The cavalry scoured the countryside in two counties and rounded up 107 men—farmers, mostly—whom they imprisoned in Lexington's jailhouse. Major Bredlett found much of the equipment stolen from the *Little Blue* hidden in cellars, haystacks, and outhouses, but he never caught sight of Quantrill and his band. Quantrill had led them twelve miles south, out of the cavalry's line of march.

To the Federals, the guerrillas had become too daring, elusive, and embarrassing. Something had to be done. A punitive expedition was organized by the Union army to hunt them down and kill them. But first, the Yankees had to find them. On July eighth, they did.

Quantrill took his men eighty miles south of his usual Jackson County haunts at the request of Col. Upton Hayes of the regular Confederate army. Hayes was in Jackson County to recruit men for a new cavalry regiment, but he could not travel freely through the countryside while the Yankees were riding out after Quantrill. Hayes asked Quantrill to shift his operations south to draw away the Union forces. Quantrill agreed. Hayes rode with them until he was certain the Federals knew where the bushwhackers had gone; then he returned to Jackson County to carry on his recruiting mission. He asked Quantrill for an escort, and Quantrill detailed George Todd and thirty men to accompany Hayes, leaving Quantrill with a group of sixty-five.

A few days later, Maj. James Gower of the First Iowa Cavalry heard that Quantrill was camped on Sugar Creek, near Wades-burg, Missouri. Gower sent ninety men with orders to make a sur-prise attack at dawn to catch the guerrillas unprepared. The troopers found the camp, but one eager Union lieutenant led his men forward without waiting for the main body of troops. Quantrill's men easily repulsed the attack. The Yankees made sev-eral charges, and Quantrill beat them back every time. As the Yankees suffered more casualties, their enthusiasm dwindled. Convinced they faced a superior force, they retreated.

Major Gower was furious. He dispatched couriers to neigh-boring Union outposts, directing them to send every available man to meet him at a farmhouse near the guerrilla camp. He in-tended to lead the attack himself. The next morning at eleven o'clock, Gower arrived at the rendezvous point with seventy-five soldiers. Other soldiers joined him, and soon he had a force of 265 troopers, to oppose Quantrill's 65.

Gower led them cautiously along Sugar Creek toward Quantrill's camp. It was empty; the guerrillas had vanished. He divided his command into four columns and ordered them off separately to continue the search. That afternoon, the sixty-three-man column commanded by Capt. Martin Kehoe of the First Mis-souri Cavalry picked up Quantrill's trail and began shadowing the guerrillas. He sent a messenger to Major Gower, telling him where the bushwhackers were heading.

By dusk, Gower's men had covered fifty miles under the blaz-ing July sun. Men and horses needed a rest. Gower was confident he would strike the guerrillas early in the morning. Captain Kehoe was also confident and eager. He craved the glory and the honor of being the man who killed the notorious Quantrill. In violation of orders and all rules of common sense, Kehoe roused his sixty-three men early and led them out, not waiting for the rest of the troopers in Gower's command.

Quantrill and his men had made camp in a clearing near a farmhouse and passed a miserable night in the rain. When they awoke, the sky was clear. Bill Gregg recalled, "The morning was bright and lovely, the many wild birds were carrolling in the woods. Our boys were jubilant. Hicks George and Bob Houk was sent on our back trail as pickets. Blankets, overcoats, etc., hanged upon the [corral] fence to dry."

Shots rang out when Kehoe's men were fired on by the pickets. The bushwhackers grabbed blankets and gear and saddled their horses, ready to ride out as fast as they could. As Kehoe's men got closer, however, Quantrill saw that the Yankee force was approximately the same size as his, and he decided to stay and fight it out.

Quantrill ordered the horses moved to a ravine for safety and placed his men in position. Because the Federals had to file down a narrow lane to reach the camp in the clearing, Quantrill deployed men behind the corral fence facing the lane. Others waited in the woods alongside the lane.

The Union troops—six men with a sergeant in the lead—drew sabers, cheered, and charged down the lane. Quantrill watched from the corral fence, resting his hand on the gate. He told his men to hold their fire, even as the Yankees advanced shooting. Finally, after what Bill Gregg said "seemed to me an hour," Quantrill shouted the order to fire. The Union troops were no more than sixty feet away. "Seven Federals fell in a heap, the horses coming straight toward the gate. I yelled to Quantrill to open the gate, which he did, the horses coming into the lot," Gregg remembered.

Nine more Yankees were wounded, including the eager Captain Kehoe, who took a round in the shoulder. Kehoe ordered his men to fall back, a maneuver for which they needed no encouragement. As the Yankees withdrew, Quantrill's men ran out into the lane and looted the bodies of the fallen troopers. They found six Colt carbines, seven Colt Navy revolvers, and seven canteens of whiskey.

Kehoe regrouped his men one hundred yards away and began peppering the guerrillas with long-range fire from their carbines. One guerrilla was killed and two others wounded. The Yankees were too far away for accurate return fire—the Navy Colts and shotguns lacked the range—so Quantrill ordered a charge, killing two Yankees, although failing to dislodge the rest from their position.

Quantrill drew back to the farmhouse to tend to his casualties. He wanted to get the wounded out as fast as possible and to give a decent burial to the dead. The guerrillas hitched a yoke of cattle to the farmer's wagon and placed two feather beds in it to cushion the ride for the wounded.

Meanwhile, the rest of Major Gower's troops had arrived, and he formed them up to attack. Gower ordered them forward through the pasture in which Quantrill had placed Dave Pool and one other man to serve as lookouts. The two men were so intent on watching the Yankees that they did not notice a jackass that was apparently upset by their presence. Just as Gower's men started toward the pasture, the ass headed for Quantrill's men. The animal, Bill Gregg recalled, "made a dash for them at a dead run, with his tail hoisted straight in the air, his immense ears laid back, braying at every jump. Pool said afterwards that he was in double fear, and did not know by which he would be run down, the Federals, or the Jack."

They escaped from both and rejoined Quantrill, who was just realizing how large the enemy force was. He had violated a cardinal rule of guerrilla warfare—never to do battle with a force larger than your own—but it was too late now. The Yankees were almost on them, so close that Quantrill's men had to abandon their dead and wounded in the rush to fall back.

Quantrill led them a half mile back into a ravine with banks five to seven feet high. The Yankees attacked almost immediately, precipitating what Bill Gregg described as "the greatest, most unequal battle scene that I ever witnessed." He admitted that the federal troops were "well trained, brave soldiers."

Capt. William Martin of the Seventh Missouri Cavalry dismounted his men and led them forward, telling them not to fire until they reached the gorge's rim. They stood on the edge and fired into the ravine, then leapt down and fought hand to hand with the guerrillas, using Bowie knives and rifle stocks and pistol butts, until Quantrill's men were forced to run from the ravine and retreat to a thicket. Gower had positioned men near the woods, and the guerrillas ran headlong into them. The troops drove them back to the ravine, where Captain Martin's men were waiting. After another fierce hand-to-hand struggle, with no quarter given, Quantrill led his men to another part of the thicket.

Most of them had long since abandoned their horses, with their saddlebags full of ammunition, and many men were running out of bullets. Dave Pool had been in charge of the extra supply, but he had lost it in his haste to get away from the charging jackass. Captain Martin's men made one assault after another, but the guerrillas beat them back. Still they came. Quantrill was hit in the thigh; other men were shot and fell all around him. The bushwhackers were forced to fight with stones and with crude clubs fashioned from stout tree limbs torn off with their bare hands. Quantrill knew they could not hold out long throwing rocks at the enemy. They had to get out of there.

Quantrill told Bill Gregg to take the twenty-one men who still had horses and to fight their way through the enemy on one side of their position. Quantrill led the dismounted men against the enemy line on the opposite side. Once they cut their way through the Yankees, they scattered in the woods, breaking up into small parties and disappearing into the countryside.

It was a costly battle on both sides. Union forces reported eleven dead and twenty-one wounded. Quantrill admitted to five dead and from ten to twelve wounded, but Major Gower's report of the battle estimated eighteen bushwhackers killed and as many as thirty wounded. Bill Gregg wrote that the wounded men the guerrillas left behind were well treated by Major Gower, "the only time our wounded were treated with anything like courtesy by the Federal government."

Quantrill and his men took a monthlong rest to regroup and obtain fresh horses and supplies. Quantrill sought refuge in a farmhouse to nurse his injured thigh and to plan his revenge against the Federals for the disgraceful defeat they had inflicted on him.

Farther north, near Blue Springs, George Todd had been escorting Colonel Hayes around the county while he recruited men and boys, some as young as fourteen, for the Confederate cause. The colonel had formed a new regiment of three hundred men. Lt. Col. James T. Buel, the Union commander at Independence, acting on an informant's tip that Quantrill's men often forded the Little Blue River at a particular crossing point, sent a detachment there to wait. One day in late July, Todd, John Little, and Ed Koger, made for that spot.

Halfway across the river, they stopped to water their horses, perfect stationary targets for the Federals hidden along the riverbank. The Union detachment opened fire, killing Little and Koger. Todd fled into the woods. The Yankees apparently figured that two out of three was a good enough day's work, so they did not pursue Todd.

In his haste to put distance between himself and the troops at the river, Todd rode straight between two boulders. The gap was so narrow that his horse became wedged. Fearing the Yankees were chasing him, Todd abandoned the unfortunate animal. It was later found stuck there, dead from starvation.

Embittered by the loss of his friends Little and Koger, Todd vowed to kill as many Yankees as he could. His daring and ruthlessness grew, and he became more contemptuous of danger.

Col. John Hughes and Col. Gideon Thompson were recruiting men in the northern part of the Missouri. Colonel Hughes, with a force of seventy-five men, made camp at the farm of Charles Cowherd near Lee's Summit, a few miles outside Independence. Hughes raised the Confederate Stars and Bars on a pole so tall that the flag was visible from the courthouse roof in Independence.

Colonel Hughes believed his chances of enlisting new soldiers for the Confederacy would be improved if he could capture Independence, a major Yankee outpost. A victory of that magnitude would stir considerable patriotism among Missouri's Southern sympathizers. Also, if he could drive the three-hundred-man Union garrison out of Independence, then it would be easier for him and his men to leave the state safely and return to Confederate territory once he finished his recruiting drive up north. The

Independence garrison was the only force large enough to cut off Hughes's escape route south.

Colonel Hughes knew he couldn't capture Independence with his seventy-five-man outfit, so he sent couriers to request assistance from Colonel Hayes and from Quantrill. Both readily agreed. Hayes arrived at the camp near Lee's Summit on August tenth with his force of three hundred recruits. They were raw and untrained, but they were country boys spoiling for a fight, and Hayes figured they would do just fine. Quantrill reached camp the same day with twenty-five men, raising Hughes's force to about four hundred.

The Confederates were unaware that a Mrs. Wilson, a Union supporter, had seen Hayes and his men marching past her farm. She guessed where they were going and what they planned to do. She saddled her horse and rode into Independence to warn the Union commander, Lt. Col. James T. Buel.

Colonel Buel was an arrogant sort who did not take kindly to people interfering with his job and telling him what to do—particularly civilians; more particularly, women. He was rude to Mrs. Wilson and discounted her information. Although one of Buel's officers vouched for her reliability and honesty, Buel dismissed her story. He said he knew what he was doing and wished people like Mrs. Wilson would stop spreading tales about rebels wanting to attack Independence.

Buel knew Confederate soldiers were camped at Lee's Summit, but he did not believe they were a threat to the Union garrison. The local civilians were not so sure. A few had climbed to the roof of the courthouse to see the big rebel flag. Not about to take chances, many townspeople fled for Kansas City.

Buel believed his force of three hundred was sufficient to repulse even the idea of an attack. Thus confident and secure, Buel had organized the dispersal of his troops, leaving them in an indefensible position. The bulk of the men were quartered in an open tent camp a half mile west of the courthouse square. Buel's comfortable headquarters were in a sturdy bank building on the square, but the headquarters guard company was housed across the street. A block north, a provost marshal detachment was ensconced in the city jail. Buel as commanding officer was isolated from most of his troops and would not be able to communicate with them should headquarters be cut off. But Buel was sure there was no chance of that happening.

He made no attempt to keep the garrison troops on alert, nor did he dispatch patrols to scout the area between Independence and the rebel camp. So certain was Buel there would be no attack that he did not even post extra guards as lookouts on the outskirts of town. Even the greenest lieutenant would not have been so inept.

Colonel Hughes knew nothing of the garrison's lack of preparedness. Before planning his assault, he needed detailed information on Union troop strength and disposition that only a personal reconnaissance could supply. Someone would have to go to Independence, posing as a spy. He assigned the task to Quantrill, who chose Morgan Mattox for the job. Mattox went into town, disguised as a farmer, and wandered about freely, selling onions and pies to the soldiers.

Cole Younger later claimed that he, too, went into Independence to spy on the Union troops. As he told the story, he dressed as an old woman, complete with wig and bonnet. He said he rode sidesaddle and carried a basket of fruits and vegetables. For some reason, perhaps having to do with his size (nearly six feet tall, 170 pounds), a mounted soldier became suspicious and called after him.

"Wait a minute, Granny. I want to talk to you."

Younger rode on, pretending not to hear. The soldier shouted again, and a detachment of six others hurried to follow the old woman. Younger whipped his horse a bit faster.

"Damn you," the trooper yelled. "I'll teach you something! Stop!"

Cole Younger spurred his horse, but the soldier grabbed the reins. Younger yanked out his pistol, shot the man dead, and galloped down the street, the Yankees in pursuit. He eluded them, then returned to the rebel camp to brief Colonel Hughes on the town's defenses. Cole loved to retell the story, particularly to impressionable young boys, one of whom wrote it down for posterity.

Whether from Mattox or Younger, Colonel Hughes got the information he needed to plan the raid on Independence. Quantrill and his twenty-five men would spearhead the attack, cut Buel off from the rest of his troops, and kill him.

"You will be well supported," Colonel Hughes assured Quantrill. "I shall be right behind you when you enter the public square."

Hughes, with his larger force, would take on the main Union force at their tent camp a half mile away.

At 4:30 on the morning of August eleventh, just before daybreak, Quantrill led his men into Independence, followed by Hughes and his troops. Quantrill's group took the small band of guards by surprise. They raced into the courthouse square with guns blazing and easily shot the guards down. The sudden flurry of shots, some of which shattered Colonel Buel's bedroom window, awakened him. Across the street, the sentinel outside the building housing the headquarters guard detachment yelled a futile challenge to the guerrillas, demanding that they halt. When the guerrillas showed no sign of stopping, he fired his rifle to alert the sleeping guards inside.

Half-awake and only partially dressed, the guards grabbed their weapons and started firing from the second-floor windows. One of Quantrill's men shouted, "For God's sake don't fire. It's your own men."

The guard commander, Capt. William Rodewald, believed the ruse and led his men outside to see what was going on. The first person he encountered, he knew to be a rebel, and he immediately ordered his men to resume firing. Buel leaned out the window and shouted for the men to cease firing and take cover in the bank building. Quantrill's outfit quickly surrounded the building and poured volley after volley of rifle fire through the windows. Buel and his guard detachment were trapped. There was no way he could communicate with his main force.

Quantrill ordered George Todd to take a squad up the street

to deal with the provost marshal's detail at the jail. When the Union troops saw the bushwhackers coming, they fired one volley and ran away as fast as they could. Later that day, some of the provost marshal's men arrived in Kansas City, some ten miles away. Todd used a sledgehammer to smash the locks off the cells, freeing the prisoners. Anyone jailed by the Yankees could not be all that bad. But there was one exception. When Todd saw him, "an expression of fiendish glee" came over his face.

The man was Jim Knowles, the town marshal, who had been jailed for killing a rowdy old drunk. Todd had learned that Jim Knowles was the person who had informed Colonel Buel about the river crossing, leading to the ambush of Todd and the murder of his friends John Little and Ed Koger. Todd confronted Knowles, pulled out both pistols, and fired until the guns were empty. Then Todd's men found the lieutenant who had led the ambush. They shot him dead in his hotel room, mutilated the body, and kicked it down a flight of stairs.

Quantrill was waiting at the courthouse square, annoyed and increasingly impatient. Buel and the headquarters guard in the bank building, returning fire, had held him off for ninety minutes. It was time to put an end to it. He ordered his men to set fire to the adjoining building.

"Surrender or roast!" he warned Buel.

Colonel Buel did not waste any time. He yelled back that he would surrender only if he would be treated as a prisoner of war and not turned over to Quantrill's men to be executed. Colonel Thompson gave his word to Buel that he and his men would be well treated and paroled. Accepting that assurance, Buel hoisted the white flag.

A half a mile out of town, Colonel Hughes was fighting the main body of Yankees. The battle there had started out well enough. The Confederates' attack had routed the Federals from their tents and sent them running, undressed and half-awake, some all the way to Kansas City. One courageous Union officer, Capt. Jacob Axline, who had reported for duty there only the day before, rallied seventy-five men and put them in a strong position behind a stone wall. Colonel Hughes's troops, once they had overrun the camp, busied themselves plundering the tents instead of paying attention to the battle, a consequence of their being new recruits. They were adequate fighters, but they had not yet learned to obey orders and maintain discipline.

Hughes finally got them organized and led them against the men behind the stone wall, but he took a fatal bullet in the forehead. Colonel Thompson then assumed command and charged again, but he was wounded in the leg in the attempt. Colonel Hayes took over next and kept up a steady rate of fire against the Yankees, but prudently he did not order another charge. Even so, he was shot in the foot.

Axline had set up an impregnable position. One colonel had been killed and two wounded trying to take it. He could probably have held out until nightfall and saved the day, and the town, for the Union, but Buel's surrender applied to his troops also. At first, Axline refused to surrender, but he was finally persuaded to do so by some of his junior officers, who were not made of such stern stuff as he was.

Buel and the surviving Union troops were paroled, and they left Independence a few days later to be mustered out of the army. Charges of conspiracy and cowardice were later brought against Buel and one of Axline's officers, but the proceedings were not yet complete when they left the service, and so they escaped official retribution. The Union losses had been high, twenty dead and seventy-four wounded. Twenty-three Confederates were killed and an undetermined number wounded. According to Bill Gregg's recollections, only one bushwhacker was lost in the battle.

The defeat was a stunning blow to the Union presence in Missouri, and it spread shock and fear throughout the entire border region. For the first time, a guerrilla force had captured a major Union outpost. If such a large town as Independence with its garrison of three hundred soldiers was not safe from the rebels, then no place was. A lot of Union supporters in smaller towns, and alone on their farms, looked out over the prairie with a new sense of vulnerability whenever they saw a dust cloud in the distance. The victory at Independence was a morale booster for the South, and William Clarke Quantrill had played a major part in it.

Quantrill and his men left the Confederate troops and rode back to the Morgan Walker farm at Blue Springs. They stayed there only one day before moving on to the Ingraham farm about six miles west of the town of Lone Jack. There, on August fifteenth, he and his men were officially mustered into the Confederate army as a Confederate partisan ranger company. Col. Gideon Thompson, recovering from his wound taken at Independence, did the honors, commissioning Quantrill as a captain. One historian noted: "From the fifteenth day of August, 1862, the Confederate government was responsible for all the acts of Quantrill and his men. From that day they were regular Confederate soldiers, properly enrolled, with officers regularly commissioned."

The government may have been responsible for the guerrillas in a legal sense, but it would find that it had absolutely no control over Quantrill or any of his men. He was no more prone to take orders now than when he was an outlaw before the war.

After the formal mustering-in ceremony, the men elected the rest of their officers themselves, in accordance with the custom of the day. George Todd was elected second lieutenant, Bill Gregg, third lieutenant, and, to be second in command to Quantrill, William Hallar was elected as first lieutenant. Why Hallar was chosen for such an important post has remained a mystery. He was rarely mentioned by any of Quantrill's men who wrote about their experiences, and even today, nothing is known about him except that he was among the first seven followers of Quantrill. Todd resented Hallar's election, believing that the post should have gone to him. Relations between the two men turned openly hostile, and when Hallar left the outfit a month or so later, Todd became first lieutenant.

The formal designation of officers, except for Quantrill's position, meant nothing in terms of their daily operations. The band never became a disciplined military organization, and most of the men would probably have left it the moment it had. Many of them were old friends from childhood who tended to form their own cliques and units based on those friendships, and all were of a highly independent nature, men who, like Quantrill, resented being told what to do.

Also, the band did not always operate as a cohesive large unit. It formed and reformed, grouped and regrouped, often attacking in small parties, then scattering and coming together again with men from other groups. The real leaders of these parties emerged because of their particular style, bearing, personality, courage, knowledge of the specific terrain, or how long those around them at that particular moment had known them. Quantrill's band was fluid and continually changing, and sometimes not even he was in total command of all the men all the time.

The day after the commissioning ceremony, Capt. William Clarke Quantrill took sixty of his men back to Independence. No Union troops had yet dared to return, and so the bushwhackers were able to complete their plunder of Union supplies. Among other needed items, they loaded several wagons full of barrels of gunpowder, enough to keep them shooting for quite some time. He left ninety men back at the Ingraham farm, with orders to Hallar not to leave there for any reason before he returned.

Later that same day, a major battle erupted a few miles away at Lone Jack. Colonel Hayes and Colonel Thompson, with their 375 men, had been reinforced by 1,000 more troops under the leadership of two other colonels. This large force attacked a column of eight hundred Federals, commanded by a Missourian, Maj. Emory Foster, who had been out looking for rebel units.

It was a vicious, bloody battle, which Foster, even though outnumbered, seemed to be winning. His men beat back repeated rebel charges, and they made some assaults themselves. The rebels needed more men, so Colonel Hayes, who was in overall command, sent a courier to the guerrilla camp asking them to come to his aid as quickly as possible. Hallar refused—his orders from Quantrill were to stay put—but later in the day, Hayes sent a second, more urgent request for help. Hallar refused again, but then, under pressure from Gregg, he finally agreed to go.

Most of the bushwhackers got to Lone Jack too late to join in the fight, which the Confederates had won, but a few of them did, most notably Cole Younger. When he reached the battlefield, the rebs were running out of ammunition, and he took it upon himself to single-handedly replenish their supply. He raced back and forth twice on horseback between the front line and a springhouse a mile away where the reserve ammunition had been stored.

Each time, he filled a large basket with as much as it would hold, crooked it over his arm, and sped back to the battle. There he blatantly rode up and down the line, the only man on horseback, tossing out ammunition while just about every Yankee soldier tried to pick him off. Both times, he got through completely unscathed. After his second trip, Colonel Hayes ordered him not to try it again, telling him that if he did not get down out of his saddle and obey the order, he would shoot Younger's horse. Younger dismounted, and as he did, the Yankees across the way let out a rousing cheer in admiration of his bravery. Cole was offended; he thought the Federals believed him to have been hit and that was why they cheered.

"Halloo and be damned," he shouted at them, "you ain't killed nobody!"

Major Foster, the Union commander, was wounded during the fight, then captured when his side lost. As he lay on a cot in a makeshift hospital, a bushwhacker strolled by, then stopped when he saw the uniform of a Union officer. He cursed Foster, then pulled out his pistol and said he was going to shoot him dead then and there. Cole happened by at that moment and told the man to put away his gun and leave Foster in peace. That only made the bushwhacker angrier, and more determined than ever to shoot Foster. Cole grabbed him, pushed him out the door, and said that if he ever came back, he would kill him.

Major Foster, obviously believing he could trust Cole, told him he had seven hundred dollars on his person.

"I want you to promise me that you will take it to my mother in Warrensburg," he said.

Cole said he would, put the money in his pocket, and later made good on his promise.

There is no indication that Quantrill got angry at Hallar for disobeying his orders. In fact, at least one writer has suggested that Quantrill went to Independence that day specifically to avoid getting involved in the battle. He had known before he left the camp that the Union force was not far away and that a large body of Confederate reinforcements was also nearby. He had to have known, or at least suspected, that a fight was possible. Yet he deliberately rode away to pick up supplies at Independence.

Why? Perhaps he was upset at the presence of so many high-ranking officers—four colonels—in his realm, and he only a captain. Or perhaps the reason was

[that he] decided to let these "big guns" fight their own battle. He resented their invasion of his territory. They brought soldierly rules and permitted no murder of prisoners. He made war in no such feminine fashion. If mawkish sentiment was to prevail upon the gory field he would be absent and employ himself in lugging off the loot of a former action.

Whatever the reason for missing the battle of Lone Jack, Quantrill soon got the chance to fight the war in his own way again—bloody and awful and vengeful.

Quantrill established a new camp four miles northeast of Lee's Summit, where he stayed for ten days, during which time Colonel Hayes left Missouri to take his troops back to Arkansas. Now Quantrill had his territory all to himself. He was once more king of his realm. Quantrill asked Hayes to give him one of the prisoners taken at the battle of Lone Jack. He wanted a hostage to trade for Perry Hoy, the man held captive at Fort Leavenworth, whose release he had been trying to arrange. The federal authorities at Fort Leavenworth had not been willing to deal with Quantrill, but maybe they would now that he was a captain—an officer in the Confederate army. He was determined to get Hoy back.

The man Colonel Hayes turned over to him was Lt. Levi Copeland, whom the bushwhackers hated for his role in harassing and killing a number of Southern sympathizers. If it were not for his possible value in getting their comrade back, they would have cut him down on the spot. One evening, a few days after Hayes left, the farmer with that most appropriate name of Charles Cowherd stopped by the camp and gave Quantrill a copy of a recent issue of the *Missouri Republican*.

Quantrill sat down at a small table to catch up on the news. Bill Gregg hovered nearby, waiting for his turn at the paper. Gregg recalled: "[S]uddenly I saw a change in Quantrill's countenance and, the paper fell from his hand, without saying a word, he drew a blank book from his pocket, penned a note on a leaf, folded and handed it to me, saying 'give this to [Andrew] Blunt.' "

Quantrill told Gregg what he had read in the newspaper: the news that Perry Hoy had been executed by a firing squad at Fort Leavenworth. Gregg opened the note and read it. "Take Lieut. Copeland out and shoot him," it said.

The note also said to take two other Union prisoners from a nearby camp and shoot them, too. Gregg delivered the note to Blunt; then later he retrieved the fallen newspaper and read the story that had upset Quantrill so much. While he was reading, he heard several shots ring out from the forest. Not long after, Andy Blunt appeared and reported that the order had been carried out. Quantrill immediately ordered all the men to saddle up and get ready to ride. Gregg asked him where they were going.

"We are going to go to Kansas and kill ten more men for poor Perry!"

They spent that night and most of the next day camped near the Kansas line before heading across the border to Olathe the next evening, September sixth. Quantrill had 140 men with him. According to Bill Gregg's brief account of the journey, nothing much happened along the way except that they killed ten men before even reaching Olathe. But the deaths of ten Yankees, both soldiers and civilians, were not so remarkable anymore, and certainly not in the heated aftermath of Perry Hoy's death. Quantrill had already paid the Federals back many times over for that, with thirteen lives exchanged for one.

On the outskirts of Olathe, Quantrill detailed Gregg to take sixty men and surround the town to prevent anyone from escaping. Then he calmly led the other eighty into town. He stopped at the courthouse square, opposite 125 militiamen lined up in orderly fashion on the sidewalk, looking for all the world as if they were ready to do battle. Clearly, Quantrill had been expected, and this was the welcoming party.

Quantrill, however, had no intention of fighting a force so much larger than his own in an open square that provided no place to take up defensive positions. Instead, he planned to call their bluff and capture the lot of them without firing a shot. The bushwhackers behaved as peacefully as if they were local farmers come to town for supplies. Following Quantrill's orders, they hitched their horses close together to the fence around the courthouse, then stood in a line facing the militiamen on the other side of the square. As soon as they had formed into that closely packed line, they drew their revolvers, each man holding two, and told the Yankees to surrender. All but one of them did. One man refused to give up his gun and was instantly shot down. "We had killed fourteen men for Hoy," Gregg said, adding up the score in that deadly contest.

The rest of the militiamen were disarmed and placed under guard while the bushwhackers had their way with the town. They stole horses, clothes, money, jewelry, watches, weapons, ammunition, and all the wagons they needed to carry their booty. They smashed the presses of the local newspaper, invaded homes, stores, and hotel rooms, terrorizing the residents the whole night long.

Strolling through the town, watching his men at work, Quantrill spied a man by the name of Robinson, whom he knew to be a judge. He called him over and the two men sat together on a bench and talked about old times for over an hour. At one point, the judge called him Bill, the name he had used before the war.

"He very politely requested me to address him as 'Captain Quantrill,' and took from his pocket and showed me what he claimed was a commission from the Confederate Government," Robinson recalled nearly twenty years later. Clearly, the commission meant a great deal to Quantrill.

The next morning, with stolen wagons full to bursting with stolen goods, Quantrill's men left Olathe, leading the long column of 124 militiamen out onto the open prairie. All of them had been stripped to their underwear, their clothes and boots stowed in the wagons. They stopped two miles out of town, where there was no one around to see or hear them—or help them. They were terrified as they stood there, helpless and almost naked, facing the most dangerous and feared bushwhackers in the region. But there was to be no massacre that morning. Instead, Quantrill paroled them and set them free, "with the admonition to return home and be good boys."

The Federals wanted revenge for the sacking of Olathe and the embarrassment of having 124 of their militiamen taken without a shot being fired in their defense. Col. John Burris of the Fourth Kansas Cavalry was to be the instrument of vengeance this time. Burris caught up with Quantrill's men near Columbus, Missouri, and chased them through four counties for ten days without killing or capturing a single man. They did, however, recover most of the plundered goods taken from Olathe. The pursuit was too close for the guerrillas to keep the lumbering wagons. The Yankees also burned down some farmhouses belonging to Southern sympathizers, and they liberated sixty slaves from their owners.

Quantrill's men finally came to rest on October fifth, at the town of Sibley, near Independence. It appeared that they had lost their pursuers, but the next day, their pickets were driven in by what, at first, looked like a large force of Union cavalry. They turned out to be a militia patrol instead, fair game for attack, for they were usually not as steadfast as regular troops. Quantrill led his men after them, chasing them in a running gunfight to a bridge over the Sni River where the militia finally stopped and tried to stand their ground. The bushwhackers just kept coming, stampeding across the bridge and killing some of the Yankees and scattering the rest. "As usual," Bill Gregg said in his matter-of-fact style, "they could not stand our onslaught."

It was a nice little victory, but the guerrillas had no time to savor it. Colonel Burris had caught up with them again, ruining their breakfast the next morning when he attacked their camp and sent them running. These were not untrained, skittish militia troops, and they kept after the guerrillas all day, hounding them until four o'clock, when they got close enough to kill a couple of them in a sharp fight. This time, it was Quantrill's men who scattered and ran.

They regrouped five days later and set up a new camp in a river bottom one mile from Sibley, but the Yankees were not about to let them rest. They were still determined to pay Quantrill back for Olathe. Their pursuer was Capt. Daniel David of the Fifth Missouri Cavalry; he was leading a force of 150 troopers. Even though Quantrill's force numbered only one hundred that day, he decided to take on David's men and proceeded some distance away, where he set up an ambush.

While the men waited for the Yankees to do their part by showing up at the trap, Quantrill was approached by Col. Dick Chiles, who had just fallen in with the guerrillas a few hours earlier. Chiles led a group of twenty-five men who may have been a part of Colonel Hayes's outfit and somehow got left behind. At any rate, whatever they were doing there, Colonel Chiles was determined to make his presence count. He was a firebrand, hungry for action, and he asked Quantrill to let him hit the Federals first.

"No," Quantrill said, "I do not know you. I do not know if you would carry out my instructions. Here are my Lieuts. Gregg and Todd. I know that either of them will do just as I tell them."

Gregg and Todd spoke up quickly, perhaps less enthusiastic at the idea of spearheading the ambush. Both men urged Quantrill to let the colonel have the honor. Quantrill agreed.

"You must obey these orders," he told Chiles. "When you meet the enemy, you must not stop, but go right into them. I will be there to support you. Now go."

Chiles led his men off with great dash and eagerness, but when he met the enemy, he immediately disobeyed Quantrill's orders by stopping and dismounting his men. He thus lost the element of surprise and gave the Yankees time to take possession of a log house and assume a position behind a rail fence. Chiles led his men forward on foot and was shot through the lung, which left his troops less than eager to continue. Quantrill watched and decided that it would be futile to attack such a strongly defended position.

He left the mortally wounded Colonel Chiles at a farmhouse and retreated into the woods. Captain David was persistent, and he followed the bushwhackers, pressing them hard, allowing them no time to rest. The chase continued throughout the night and far into the next day, until Quantrill ordered his men to break up into small bands and scatter once again.

Things were getting too hot in Missouri, so he decided to cross over into Kansas again and raid another town. The target was Shawneetown, where they hoped to get more clothes. They were a pretty ragged-looking bunch after being on the run for so long, and having lost all they had stolen in Olathe. They left on October seventeenth, but before they reached Shawneetown, they happened upon a Yankee wagon train on the Santa Fe Trail. It was guarded by a detachment of about thirty soldiers, who had unwisely taken a break and posted no guards. Most of the troops were asleep when the bushwhackers struck, and in no more than a few minutes, fifteen of them lay dead as the rest ran for their lives.

The guerrillas were in a fine state of excitement by then and ready to shoot down anything that moved. They roared down on the tiny hamlet of Shawneetown and killed seven civilians, looted every home and business, and put the entire town to the torch. When they rode away, there was nothing left but burned timbers, weeping women, and an agonizing sorrow.

Word of the attack spread almost as fast as fire in a field of dry grass. Quantrill had struck again. For the second time, he had savaged a town in Kansas. "Settlers living in the Kansas border counties were gripped by panic. Hundreds of them fled to the interior or left the state altogether. The few who remained cried out desperately for protection against Quantrill's raiders," according to one account.

By early November, winter—the only real protection from Quantrill the settlers of Kansas knew—was setting in. When the trees lost their leaves, the woods and forests no longer offered refuge, sanctuary, a place to hide from pursuing federal cavalry. Then it was time for the guerrillas' annual trek south to Arkansas for the safety provided by the Confederate troops stationed there.

On November third, Quantrill started south with 150 men, as well as a number of farmers and their families who no longer felt safe from Yankee reprisals with Quantrill gone. Cole Younger and a handful of others elected to stay behind for the winter. At the same time that the long column of bushwhackers began their journey, thirteen empty Union wagons with an escort of twenty-one troopers started to the northeast on a route that would take them directly across Quantrill's path.

Not long after the wagons left, Col. Edwin Catherwood of the Sixth Missouri Cavalry, the man who had dispatched the train, received a report from a scout of the guerrillas' movement south. Catherwood grew worried about the safety of the twenty-one escorts. He immediately ordered a force of 150 men to catch up to the wagons, but they were too late.

Quantrill spotted the wagon train at sundown and ordered Bill Gregg and forty men to go after it. In a matter of minutes, four soldiers and six teamsters were dead, the wagons were on fire, the survivors running over the prairie, and a federal lieutenant and several privates were prisoners. It happened so fast that it hardly slowed down the trek south at all. Two miles from the line of burning wagons, the men stopped to eat before pushing on. That was where they were found by Colonel Catherwood and his 150 troops, who were mad as hell after seeing the bullet-riddled bodies of their comrades.

They drove in Quantrill's pickets and sent all of them running and scattering once again into small groups that disappeared in the night. They recaptured the prisoners and claimed to have killed six bushwhackers and wounded twenty-one, though Bill Gregg's report of the fight, in which he emerged as a hero, indicated no casualties on their side. Over the course of the next day, Quantrill collected his men and made his way through two more counties, leaving Colonel Catherwood far behind.

On November fifth, they came across some three hundred rebel cavalry commanded by Col. Warner Lewis. The colonel told Quantrill that they were only a few miles from Lamar, and he persuaded Quantrill to join forces in a combined attack on the small Union garrison headquartered there. They agreed to strike at 10:00 P.M., with Quantrill's men riding into town from the north while Lewis's troops came in from the south. Quantrill's men did their part, charging into the courthouse square, yelling and blazing away with their Navy Colts, but Lewis and his men never showed up, then or later.

Worse, the Yankee garrison had learned of the attack and Union troops were waiting for the raiders behind the thick walls of the brick courthouse. The guerrillas fought on for an hour and a half, losing as many as six dead and more wounded without being able to dislodge the federal troops. Disgusted and angry, Quantrill called off the attack, and on his way out of town, he set fires, which burned down a third of the houses. Perhaps he had forgotten—or maybe he was too angry to care—that Lamar was not in Kansas but in Missouri. It was a Southern town and it suffered far more from Quantrill than it ever did from its Yankee occupiers.

The guerrillas continued south, passing through the Osage Nation and into Arkansas, where their arrival caused considerable excitement among the Confederate troops. Everybody wanted to see the legendary Quantrill. Gen. Thomas Hindman, the Confederate commander in Arkansas, lauded Quantrill as an "extremely zealous and useful" leader to the South.

The year 1862 had been good for William Clarke Quantrill. He had every reason to feel pleased with what he had accomplished and to believe that 1863 would hold greater promise. By God, people had heard of him now. They would not soon forget his name. Quantrill had come a long way from the Charley Hart who had hung around the ferry landing in Lawrence.

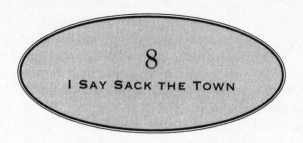

8

I Say Sack the Town

IN ARKANSAS THAT December of 1862, Capt. William Clarke Quantrill became fired with dreams of greater glory. The praise lavished on him by General Hindman and other Confederate officers inflated his already exaggerated sense of self-importance to the Southern war effort. His ambition for fame—his outright hunger for it—intensified, and he began to see himself as a figure of national, not just regional, prominence. If so many people in Arkansas and the border region viewed him as a hero, savior, and leader, then others throughout the South must also know of his exploits and idolize him, he assumed.

And if he was that well known and praised, Quantrill reasoned, if he was single-handedly saving Missouri from Yankee domination, imagine what he could do on a larger scale. Surely he deserved his own regiment and a commission as a colonel. He had earned it and fought for it; it was his due. And after that, why not a general's star? A division? Who could say how far someone with his talents might rise in wartime? The prospects were intoxicating. His mind placed no limits on how far he could go.

But first he had to obtain a commission, and there was no better place for that than Richmond, where he would likely be hailed as the hero he was. Old Jeff Davis would probably want to meet him. There would be fancy dinners and elegant balls and interviews with newspaper reporters. He expected that he would be asked to give the leaders of the government the benefit of his hard-earned knowledge of the only way to beat the Yankees, by waging total, brutal war.

Quantrill left Arkansas in the middle of December, accompanied by Andrew Blunt and Charles Higbee. He did not see President Jefferson Davis, but he was able to present his case to James A. Seddon, the Confederacy's patrician Virginia-born secretary of war. The scholarly Seddon was "gaunt and emaciated with long straggling hair." He was said to look like a dead man; "his eyes are sunken and his features have the hue of a man who has been in his grave a full month."

The only surviving description of Quantrill's meeting with Seddon was provided by Maj. John Edwards, a journalist with Gen. Jo Shelby's cavalry in Arkansas, who claimed to have known many of Quantrill's raiders. After the war, Edwards wrote two books about Shelby and one about the guerrillas. The latter book, *Noted Guerrillas,* published in 1877, included stories about Quantrill, based on information Edwards said was told to him by members of Quantrill's band, particularly Frank and Jesse James. The book has been described by one historian as "extravagantly romantic in temperament, bitterly pro-Southern in outlook, and completely devoid of a sense of historical objectivity and integrity." Edwards wrote that what occurred in the meeting between Quantrill and Seddon was told to him by Louis Wigfall of Texas, the only other person present.

According to Edwards's account, Quantrill asked Secretary of War Seddon for a colonel's commission under the Partisan Ranger Act. He claimed he could raise enough men to equip a regiment in a month, and he vowed a war without mercy. In flowery prose, typical of all the characters in Edwards's books, Quantrill allegedly described to Seddon how he would lead the South to victory.

"I would cover the armies of the Confederacy all over with

blood. I would invade. I would reward audacity. I would exterminate. I would break up foreign enlistments [in the Union army] by indiscriminate massacre. I would win the independence of my people or I would find them graves."

"And our prisoners, what of them?" Seddon asked.

"Nothing of them; there would be no prisoners. Do they take any prisoners from me? Surrounded, I do not surrender; surprised, I do not give way to panic; outnumbered, I rely upon common sense and stubborn fighting; proscribed, I answer proclamation with proclamation; outlawed, I feel through it my power; hunted, I hunt my hunters in turn; hated and made blacker than a dozen devils, I add to my hoofs the swiftness of the horse, and to my horns the terrors of a savage following. Kansas should be laid waste at once. Meet the torch with the torch, pillage with pillage, slaughter with slaughter, subjugation with extermination. You have my ideas of war, Mr. Secretary."

Whatever Quantrill actually said to the secretary of war, Seddon was apparently not impressed; he did not give Quantrill a commission as a colonel. That decision did not stop Quantrill from assuming the rank. He simply lied about it, as he had lied about so much in his life, and claimed to his men that the commission had been granted in person by none other than the Honorable James A. Seddon. Quantrill had a photograph taken in a colonel's uniform, and he signed dispatches and orders with this rank.

But the truth of Seddon's action weighed heavily on him. Once again, those in authority had dealt him a crushing blow. Worse, he had been ignored by the official and social elite of Richmond. There had been no dinners in his honor, no grand balls, no recognition for the sacrifices he had made for his country. It was as though he did not exist; he was a nobody, a nonentity, skulking in the shadows of the glitter and honors that enveloped so many others in the capital of the Confederacy. Richmond was full of heroes, but he was not one of them.

Heading back to Arkansas under his assumed title of Colonel Quantrill, he was disconsolate and discouraged about his future. He grew even more dispirited when he reached Arkansas and saw

how small his band had become in his absence, how unkempt
and ragged they looked compared with the regular troops he had
seen in Richmond. His men had fought alongside General Hindman's troops in several battles in Arkansas and southern Missouri, where they had suffered a major defeat and had retreated
south of the Arkansas River.

Some of the bushwhackers disliked being soldiers in the regular army. There was too much regimentation and little opportunity for plunder or independent action. George Todd was one
who hated taking orders, and he and a number of others had deserted Hindman's army two hours before a battle, returning to
Missouri for the remainder of the winter. Bill Gregg had also left.
He had been sent north by Hindman with several other guerrillas on a recruiting expedition. Other members of Quantrill's
band were on scouting missions for the army. With those ab-
sences, there were no more than two dozen of Quantrill's men
in camp when he returned to Hindman's headquarters in January of 1863. It was a sorry-looking command he returned to, un-
worthy of a colonel.

Quantrill complained about his disappointment to Maj. Gen.
Sterling Price. Called "Old Pap" by his men, Price was a sympathetic listener who knew what it was like to be rejected by the
politicians in Richmond—Jefferson Davis could not stand him—
and he tried to talk Quantrill out of his despondency. He assured
Quantrill there would be many chances for him to achieve distinction.

Price urged Quantrill to give up his old ways—bushwhacking,
robbing, looting, burning homes, and stealing from civilians—
if he wanted recognition from the Confederate government. He
suggested Quantrill form his men into a regular military unit, at-
tach itself to one of the Confederate armies in the area, and obey
orders, fighting against the Union army in the conventional way.

Quantrill considered Price's advice and talked with some of
his men about it, although it is doubtful he would have been able
to operate for long within the military's narrow confines. Nor
were his men in favor of such a plan. Talking about joining the
army "was the worst possible course he could have taken with his

men, especially with his officers. They in a manner deserted him." Thus, Quantrill lost their allegiance and loyalty. His power over them waned. While they recognized him as being in over-all command, they began taking more initiative, operating in-dependently in small bands.

When Quantrill returned to Missouri in May of 1863, it was to a different kind of warfare, one in which he no longer played the central role. While his officers and men were planning and exe-cuting one daring raid after another, he was not leading them or even riding with them. He remained aloof, like some super-numerary general at headquarters who is kept informed but who issues no orders and is not consulted for advice and certainly not for permission. Bill Gregg described the new situation.

On Quantrill's return to the state, military operations began in earnest, however, on a different line from the previous year, during the year 1862 the men were kept close together and all under the watchful eye of Quantrill. Not so in 1863. There was Todd, Pool, Blunt, Younger and others, each had companies, often widely separated, and only called together on special oc-casions.

These separate bands were on the move almost daily, striking at Union outposts, patrols, wagon trains, and towns in widely scat-tered raids. There were so many bands attacking so often that the Union forces could not possibly catch up with all of them. The raids were effective, but Quantrill was involved with only two of them.

The boldest raid, the kind of strike only Quantrill could have planned just the year before, was led by Dick Yeager, who took his group of two dozen men 130 miles into Kansas undetected and undeterred by Yankee troops. Riding first to the town of Council Grove, he terrified the residents by forming up outside the town limits and waiting, leaving them to wonder when the guerrillas intended to strike.

To the astonishment of the townspeople, only one man rode into the main square. It was Yeager, in desperate need of a dentist. The local dentist agreed to treat Yeager, but only if he agreed to spare the town. The painful tooth was pulled and the raiders rode off to sack Diamond Springs. They returned to Missouri, leaving a trail of death and devastation behind them—ruined towns, stagecoaches, and farmhouses, civilians and soldiers shot down, and Union troops riding in circles trying to find them.

Kansans were irate. If one small band could venture so deep into the state and escape unscathed, what prevented a larger force from crossing the border and inflicting greater damage?

Criticism mounted against the Union commander in Kansas, Brig. Gen. James Blunt. A Kansas-born physician and abolitionist, Blunt had received his commission as a general through the influence of Senator Jim Lane. Blunt was a stubby, overweight man with deep-set dark eyes, a bristling black mustache, and a pointy goatee. Licentious and coarse, Blunt drank heavily and traveled with a coterie of "female servants" to tend to his needs. He threw gala banquets, rollicking late-night parties, and grand parades in his honor. He was reputed to be as thoroughly dissolute as the Bible-quoting Jim Lane.

Blunt was not much of a soldier, and he seemed helpless in preventing guerrilla incursions into Kansas. All he appeared capable of doing was ordering his troopers out whenever there was a raid, but they rarely had any success. "This method of protecting burned towns, dead bodies and destroyed private property, don't suit us," wrote a newspaper editor in Lawrence. "Give us a *live* man to take charge of Kansas."

Blunt's response was not to undertake a vigorous campaign against the guerrillas or attempt to seal the border but, rather, to string up one of Quantrill's bushwhackers. The unlucky man was twenty-three-year-old Jim Vaughn, who had made the mistake of getting a haircut. He and a friend walked into a barbershop in Wyandotte, Kansas, took off their gunbelts, got comfortable in the barber's chairs, and were immediately arrested by Union soldiers.

Vaughn was hanged on May twenty-ninth before a large crowd at Fort Leavenworth. He told the excited spectators that he hoped he would go to a better world. He asked that his friends be told how he died and that he be given a proper Christian burial. Then he delivered a threat: "We can be killed but we cannot be conquered. Taking my life today will cost you one hundred lives, and this debt my friends will pay in a very short time."

Union authorities in Missouri were also trying to crack down on the bushwhackers. The new commander at Independence, Col. William Penick of the Fifth Missouri State Militia Cavalry, believed the only way to deal with guerrillas was to kill them, along with their civilian supporters. Penick was doing a good job of it, shooting and hanging three farmers in Quantrill's Blue Springs neighborhood and terrorizing many more. The situation got so bad there that virtually all the old men and boys went into hiding, left the state, or joined the bushwhackers.

The guerrillas retaliated for every incident, usually more effectively than the Yankees, striking down Union troops and Union sympathizers throughout the border region. In early June, Quantrill went back into action. With George Todd and a couple of other men, he attacked one of Colonel Penick's patrols. The first volley killed five soldiers. Four more were cut down as they fled in panic. Quantrill ordered the bodies loaded into a wagon and persuaded a farmer to deliver it to Penick, along with the message that any Yankee soldier who ventured out of Independence would end up the same way.

On June sixth, Quantrill struck at Shawneetown again, killing four civilians and torching nine homes. On June sixteenth, George Todd attacked a column of troopers 150 strong outside of Kansas City. The Yankees were tired; they had been out all day under a scorching sun hunting for bushwhackers. Believing nobody would dare attack so large a force so near Kansas City, they felt secure enough to strap their carbines to their saddles. When the brief fight was over and twenty Union soldiers lay dead, a bushwhacker wrote a note and stuffed it in the mouth of one of the bodies: "Remember the dying words of Jim Vaughn."

Quantrill did no more fighting over the next two months. He had become increasingly depressed, perhaps because Todd and his other officers were raiding so successfully without him. He left his Blue Springs camp and spent most of his time holed up in an abandoned log house in another county with a fifteen-year-old girl named Kate Clarke.

Many stories have been told about Kate Clarke, suggesting she was kidnapped by Quantrill and forced to become his mistress until she reconciled herself to her fate and even became infatuated with him. It was not until 1992 that the facts emerged. Her real name was Kate King, and she had been raised near Blue Springs. She was thirteen when she first met Quantrill in 1861. They began seeing each other secretly, taking long horseback rides over the countryside. Her father was furious and ordered her to end the relationship. His attitude served to intensify her determination to see Quantrill, and she would often sneak out of the house at night to meet him.

Charles Taylor, one of Quantrill's men, reported that Quantrill once borrowed his gray mare and rode with Kate six miles from camp to the home of a preacher, who then married them. She had adopted the habit of wearing men's clothing to ride with Quantrill on raids, just to be near him.

> Most of her time with Quantrill was spent in a tent near his men during the summers and in places farther south during the cold Missouri winters. Hardly anyone knew she was not a member of the band. She assumed the name of Kate Clarke as a safeguard in case she was ever captured by Federal authorities. By using Quantrill's mother's maiden name (his own middle name as well) it would have saved her embarrassment had she been questioned.

Quantrill might have abandoned the war and stayed happily with Kate Clarke in his log cabin if a new Yankee general had not been appointed and a building in Kansas City had not collapsed.

Brig. Gen. Thomas Ewing, Jr., came from a socially and politically prominent Ohio family. His father, a longtime U.S. senator, served as secretary of the treasury and as the first secretary of the interior. In addition to rearing his own seven sons, the elder Ewing took responsibility for a skinny red-haired youngster, the son of a close friend who had died. Tom junior and the orphan boy, whom everyone called "Cump," grew closer than many brothers and spent their school years together until Cump, then known as William Tecumseh Sherman, went to the military academy at West Point, New York.

Tom junior studied law, married, and moved to Fort Leavenworth in 1856, where he established a law and real estate business. Cump Sherman, having left the army to seek better opportunities, joined the business, which was called Sherman & Ewing. Like his father, Tom became active in politics and received an appointment as chief justice of the Kansas Supreme Court.

When the war came, Cump was suddenly a major general and Tom's brother Hugh was also rising fast in rank. Feeling left out, Tom called on his political mentor, Senator Jim Lane, to inquire about getting a commission. And so Colonel Ewing, with no military experience or training, found himself in command of the Eleventh Kansas Cavalry.

He turned out to be a good soldier, performing with distinction in his first battle against rebel troops. By the spring of 1863, not quite seven months after he first put on a uniform, he was promoted to brigadier general and given the toughest job of his life: to put down the guerrillas in Kansas. Before he was through, the thirty-three-year-old Ewing would be called "the monster of monsters."

On June sixteenth, a new command structure was established in Kansas, with the ineffectual Blunt shifted to western Kansas and put in charge of the District of the Frontier. Ewing replaced him in eastern Kansas as commander of the District of the Border. Ewing immediately ordered attacks on the bushwhackers, surprising them in ambushes, then chasing them down until his inferior Union horses could run no more. He infiltrated various guerrilla bands by using spies, who reported on the outlaws' movements and plans.

Residents of the border region soon noticed the change. There were fewer guerrilla raids, and when Union patrols returned from a mission, more often than not it was with dead bushwhackers strapped over their saddles. Kansans finally had a "live" man in charge. Ewing kept up the pressure, both in the field with his aggressive tactics and in speeches with fiery and inspiring rhetoric that he delivered around the state.

A week after taking command, Ewing addressed an enthusiastic crowd in Olathe, offering the kind of talk people wanted to hear from their general.

> I hope soon to have troops enough on the Missouri side not only to prevent raids into Kansas, but also to drive out or exterminate every band of guerrillas now haunting that region. I will keep a thousand men in the saddle daily in pursuit of them and will redden with their blood every road and bridle path of the border.

It began to look as though the long years of fear and misery would be coming to an end, and many local farmers expressed the belief they might live long enough to harvest that year's crop, and perhaps even long enough to see the end of this godawful war. Not only was Ewing chasing the raiders over the border into Missouri, where they belonged, but he was also working to seal off the border to keep them there. No one had ever been able to do that.

The most dangerous stretch of the border was the ninety miles from Kansas City south to the banks of the Osage River. That was bushwhacker country, the wild, forbidding terrain that fostered, fed, and sheltered Quantrill's men. If Ewing could close that gap, he would eliminate the guerrilla menace to Kansas. He set about the task with calculation and deliberation. He established a series of small outposts along the border—spaced thirteen miles apart—and stationed more than one hundred troopers at each. The soldiers were equipped with the best weapons and horses available.

Throughout the day and night, patrols were regularly dispatched from each post in both directions along the border, and the troopers would not head back until they had made contact with their comrades from the neighboring stations. If any outpost was attacked—an unlikely possibility, because bushwhackers had learned not to assault fortified positions—men from the next posts could reach them quickly. Ewing also supplied the local militia units with better weapons and sent troops to defend the towns located within easy striking distance of the border.

However, Ewing was not satisfied, despite the praise newspaper editors and civic leaders were lavishing on him. There was another step he wanted to take. It was not enough to keep the bushwhackers on their side of the border; he wanted to drive them from their territory altogether. He knew he did not have sufficient troops to chase them out of their easily defended home ground, but if he could arrange it so no one there gave them food or shelter, or dressed their wounds, or provided them with lead and powder, then they would have no choice but to leave. And to Ewing's methodical mind, the only way to accomplish that goal was to sweep the area clean of the guerrillas' families and friends, of everyone who supported and aided them.

Of the farm families in the border region, Ewing estimated:

> About two-thirds . . . are of kin to the guerrillas, and are actively and heartily engaged in feeding, clothing, and sustaining them. The presence of these families is the cause of the presence there of the guerrillas. I can see no prospect of an early and complete end to the war on the border, without a great increase of troops, so long as those families remain there. While they stay there, these men will also stay. . . . I think that the families of several hundred of the worst of these men should be sent, with their clothes and bedding, to some rebel district south.

In early August, Ewing went downriver to St. Louis to obtain approval for his plan from his superior, Maj. Gen. John Schofield, commander of the Department of the Missouri. Schofield, a

West Point graduate who before the war had been a professor of physics at Washington University in St. Louis, considered Ewing's forced removal plan for almost two weeks before giving his consent. However, he cautioned Ewing that the number of people removed should be kept to a minimum. Only the worst of the lot should be sent away. He also warned Ewing to be alert for retaliation from Quantrill's men.

Ewing immediately issued General Orders Number 10. His directions to his officers were:

[A]rrest, and send to the district provost-marshal for punishment, all men (and all women not heads of families) who willingly aid and encourage guerrillas, with a written statement of the names and residences of such persons and of the proof against them. They will discriminate as carefully as possible between those who are compelled, by threats or fears, to aid the rebels and those who aid them from disloyal motives. The wives and children of known guerrillas, and also women who are heads of families and are willfully engaged in aiding guerrillas, will be notified by such officers to remove out of this district and out of the State of Missouri forthwith. They will be permitted to take, unmolested, their stock, provisions, and household goods. If they fail to remove promptly, they will be sent by such officers, under escort, to Kansas City for shipment south, with their clothes and such necessary household furniture and provision as may be worth removing.

Everything was in readiness to carry out the forced removal, but before Ewing's troops could start rounding up the suspect families, a calamity struck that was to change the lives of hundreds of people, make Ewing the target of blame and recrimination, and bring William Clarke Quantrill back into the war in a way that exceeded his wildest dreams.

Before Ewing had sought permission to evacuate families from the border region, he had arrested seventeen young women thought to have aided the guerrillas. They regularly rode into Kansas City to spy for the bushwhackers, conveying to them the latest information on Union troop movements and dispositions. The women purchased pistol caps, powder, and lead and delivered these supplies to Quantrill's men, and they provided food and hiding places when needed. These friends and relatives of the guerrillas included John McCorkle's sister and sister-in-law, two cousins of Cole Younger, and three sisters of Bill Anderson.

Two of the Anderson women, Josephine and Mary, had been arrested at a farmhouse where Bloody Bill stayed between raids. They were taken away by a squad of fourteen Union soldiers, who left their ten-year-old sister, Jennie, behind. The women screamed so loudly as they were led off that Anderson and his men, who happened to be nearby, heard them and raced to the rescue. They found the Federals riding along a narrow road bordered on both sides by a rail fence. The guerrillas drew their guns and faced the Yankees, demanding the release of the women. Two soldiers walking alongside the sisters' horses immediately mounted, grabbing the women from behind.

It was a standoff. Anderson and his men could not open fire without risking injury to the women. And the Yankees threatened to kill the women if any soldiers or horses were shot. Anderson backed off and his sisters were led away. Not long after, young Jennie, lonely living by herself, went to Kansas City to be with Josephine and Mary.

The women prisoners were housed in a three-story brick building on Grand Avenue, to be detained until they could be banished from Missouri and sent south to Confederate territory. The ramshackle building was owned by the noted Missouri artist George Caleb Bingham, who had once used it as a studio. Poorly constructed to begin with, the structure had been allowed to deteriorate. Bingham, however, was in Europe and unaware of the building's condition.

The foundation was weak and timbers had been laid in place to shore up the floor beams. Large chunks of plaster had fallen from the walls and ceilings, and occasionally the building shook as if in the grip of an earthquake. Hogs rooted in the dirt below the floorboards, further weakening the foundation. Prostitutes had taken up residence on the top floor. The second floor was reserved for the women prisoners.

A Union army doctor, ordered to check on the health of the prisoners, was alarmed by the dilapidated condition of the quarters. He urged Ewing to move the prisoners someplace safer. Ewing sent a sergeant to conduct an inspection, but the man reported that everything looked fine to him.

However, on August fourteenth, in the early afternoon, a disaster occurred.

[One of the guards] heard a creaking sound; glancing up he saw the walls slowly separating from the ceiling. Swiftly the man dove to safety, shouting for everyone to jump. But there was no time. Within seconds the walls fell inward; moments later only dust and debris remained. A huge crowd gathered. Muffled cries and moans drifted up from the wreckage as rescue efforts began. Pulled from the rubble, bloody and broken, survivors became hysterical, screaming that the Federals were murderers, that the building had been a death trap.

Josephine Anderson, Bloody Bill's sister, was dead, along with one of Cole Younger's cousins and three other women. Mary Anderson was left crippled, and most of the rest of the prisoners suffered terrible injuries. As the dead and injured were taken away, the bystanders grew restless. Troopers with fixed bayonets were called in to disperse them, but the cries of "Murder" could not be so easily dismissed. They intensified as the crowd became more unruly, and the rumor circulated that Union authorities had deliberately undermined the prison's foundation so it would collapse and kill them all.

The idea was ridiculous; no one deliberately killed women in the Civil War, not even Quantrill, and the Federals would have known such an act would create a firestorm of hatred and vengeance that could engulf all of them. They had nothing to gain and everything to lose by the women's deaths. But Cole Younger believed this had been an intentional act, as did Bloody

Bill and many people on the Southern side. And they echoed the same cry: "Vengeance is in my heart, death in my hand; blood and revenge are hammering in my head."

The collapse of the building and the consequent injuries and deaths were just what Quantrill needed to revive his flagging leadership of the guerrillas and to give vent to his hatred of the Kansas town that had humiliated him by daring to place him under arrest before the war. "He raged against Kansas day and night. He thought of nothing but the humiliation and destruction of her people. Quantrill . . . longed to get even." He wanted to burn Lawrence to the ground for what it had done to him.

There were other reasons, not the least of which was the passion that had driven him since his days as Charley Hart down by the ferry landing in Lawrence: loot. Lawrence was a rich town. Money was there for the taking, and lots of it, as well as fine horses and clothing and anything else a man might want.

In addition, such a daring attack would rally his men around him again, Quantrill believed. Although some of his leaders had abandoned him, his men still worshipped him—he was sure of that. And they would be seething to avenge themselves against the Yankees for what had been done to their women. There was nothing like an outside threat to erase internal squabbles and unite like-minded men. They would ride with him again, and the Greggs and the Todds, and those others who had broken away, would have no choice but to ride with them. He would show his men what a real leader was like by taking them on the biggest raid ever, one that would go down in the history books.

In the process, he would show the Honorable James A. Seddon, and everyone else in Richmond who had treated him like a nobody, who had ignored him, what a daring military commander he was. No one, not even the foppish Jeb Stuart, whom everyone in Richmond fawned over so much, had dared to attack a Union city, a center of abolitionism, and destroy it. Quantrill believed that by the time he was finished, they would beg him to accept a colonel's commission.

* * *

Two days after the collapse of the prison building, Quantrill gathered the leaders of his various guerrilla bands and told them of his plan.

"Let's go to Lawrence," he said. "Lawrence is the great hotbed of abolitionism in Kansas, and all the plunder (or the bulk of it) stolen from Missouri, will be found stored away in Lawrence, and we can get more revenge, and more money there than anywhere else in the state."

Not everyone was in favor of the raid at first, despite their anger and their hunger for revenge against the Yankees. Some argued with Quantrill that going to Lawrence was too hazardous. It was forty miles from the border, and there were those new outposts Ewing had put up every thirteen miles. How were they to get past those undetected? The Yankees would know they had crossed over and would send every soldier in Kansas after them. They could be ambushed long before they reached Lawrence. And even if they got there, it was a big city, with almost three thousand residents, a home guard, federal troops, and strong brick buildings. Every man in Lawrence would have a gun. And even if they managed to sack the town, how would they ever make it all the way back to Missouri? No, it was just too risky.

"I know," Quantrill said. "I consider it almost a forlorn hope, for, if we go, I don't know if anyone of us will get back to tell the story." Then he added, "But if you never risk, you will never gain."

They argued for all of twenty-four hours, with Quantrill at his most persuasive. In a sense, he was fighting for his life as he responded to their arguments. If he could not get them to follow him to Lawrence, while their fury was at such a high pitch, then he would never again persuade them to follow him anywhere.

He told them he had recently sent two men to survey the situation in Lawrence (revealing that he had been planning such an attack before the prison building's collapse). These men had told him they thought it would not be too difficult to slip across the border between Ewing's outposts. Once across, the country between the border and Lawrence was sparsely populated, which meant there were few people who might spot them. If they rode hard, Quantrill assured them, they would catch the residents of Lawrence, and the garrison, by surprise.

Quantrill made two additional points. He talked about the obvious success of Yeager and his band in riding 130 miles inside Kansas and returning unscathed. If he could do it, so could they. Second, because Lawrence was so large and so far from the border, and since it had never been attacked, the Yankees would never imagine that anyone would attack it. As a result, a surprise attack would be that much easier.

"The march to Lawrence is a long one," Quantrill agreed, in the florid prose of Maj. John Edwards's description of the scene.

In every little town there are soldiers; we leave soldiers behind us; we march through soldiers; we attack the town garrisoned by soldiers; we retreat through soldiers; and when we would rest and refit after the exhaustive expedition, we have to do the best we can in the midst of a multitude of soldiers.

Then he put the question to his leaders, one by one, until each had had his say.

"Anderson, what about you?"
"Lawrence and be damned. Kill all the males."
"Todd?"
"I'm with Bill Anderson. Lawrence it is."
"Gregg?"
"It is the home of that damned Lane, and that's enough for me. Make it Lawrence or death."
"Shepherd?"
"Lawrence should be wiped out. I'm ready now."
"Jarrette?"
"Burn it to the ground as Lane did Osceola."
"Maddox?"
"I'm in for burning Lawrence and killing all the men in the damned town."

"Yeager?"

"Lawrence or hell. Let's be quick."

"Blunt?"

"Lawrence it is."

"And you Cole Younger? How do you feel about it?"

"I say sack the town."

"It's Lawrence," Quantrill said when the roll call was ended. "Kill every man and burn every house. Saddle up!"

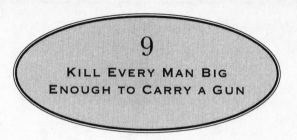

9

KILL EVERY MAN BIG
ENOUGH TO CARRY A GUN

IN THE SUMMER of 1863, Lawrence, Kansas, was a boom-town, made prosperous and sprawling by the Civil War. Money poured in from government contracts for hauling and storing military supplies, as well as for the purchase of produce, horses, and cattle. Immigrants passing through town spent their hard-earned dollars on goods and supplies. They knew there was no place farther west where they would have such an abundant choice of food, clothing, guns, and everything else they would need for new lives in the wilderness.

Travelers and locals alike shopped or looked covetously at the dazzling array of goods filling the shelves of the two-story Ridenour & Baker's, thought to be the largest grocery store in all of Kansas. There was little they did not carry, from the basics such as sugar and salt to luxuries including canned oysters and figs. R&Bs, as the locals referred to it, was located on Massachusetts Street, and it was surrounded for three blocks by other fine shops. If folks could not find what they were looking for, it was said, then it was probably something they didn't really need.

Lawrence's downtown buildings and the houses on the ad-

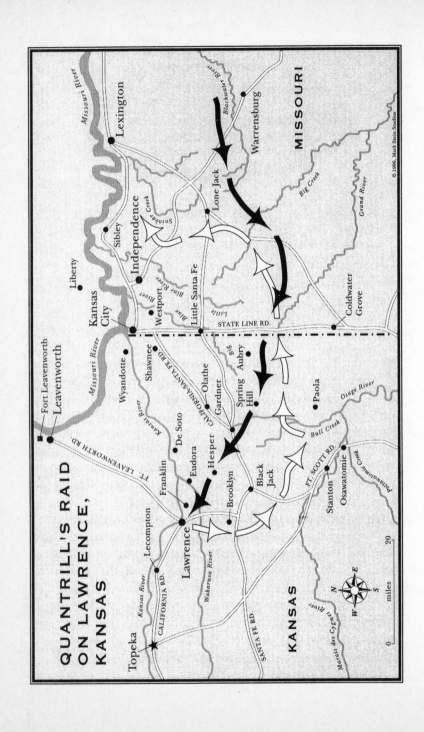

joining streets were substantial, fine-looking properties. There was nothing shoddy or makeshift about them. Few towns along the western border could compare. Elsewhere, construction of new homes was stagnant—few people had money because of the war—but Lawrence was having a building boom. The sound of hammering filled the air. It was not unusual for families to double up in one house while waiting for the carpenters to complete theirs.

Like all cities on the prairie, Lawrence was laid out in a grid, with streets running in orderly fashion east and west, north and south, intersecting one another at precise right angles. From the heights of Mount Oread on the western edge of town, Lawrence appeared to be a city in miniature, neat, attractive, prosperous, as formidable and sturdy as the hill itself.

At the base of Mount Oread's northern slope stood the area where the rich and powerful lived. The mayor's home was there, and the mansion of Senator James H. Lane, the man who was first on Quantrill's long death list. To the east of those fine homes, separated by a tree-lined ravine, was the older part of town, comprising the business district and other handsome homes. Massachusetts Street ran north and south, ending close to the bank of the wide Kansas River at the northern end and running through South Park at the other.

Two blocks south of the river loomed the four-story, one-hundred-foot-wide Eldridge House, formerly the Free State Hotel, the largest building in town. It had been rebuilt—and now was even grander than before—since the attack in 1856 when the Missourians under David Atchison had shelled it, set off explosives in the doorway, and finally gutted it by fire. Behind its graceful street-level archways sat an impressive row of shops and offices. There was no finer hotel west of the Mississippi. None other than that peripatetic newspaper editor from New York City, Mr. Horace Greeley of the *Herald Tribune*, had pronounced it "magnificent."

A block west of Massachusetts Street, not far from South Park, twenty black soldiers of the Second Kansas Colored Regiment were encamped, Capt. (and the Reverend) Samuel S. Snyder, commanding. The men were new recruits who had barely received enough military training to know how to march, but they were more than welcome in abolitionist Lawrence as a symbol of what the war was all about.

Two blocks away on the east side of Massachusetts Street, in a separate but equal facility, twenty-two white recruits of the Fourteenth Regiment of Kansas Volunteers were bivouacked in a vacant lot. These were local boys, too young for active duty but eager to learn how to play soldier. One resident recalled: "They had been dressed up in blue clothes and furnished with tents and hard tack. . . . They had no discipline, and to all appearances nobody competent to teach or enforce its rules." They had no guns or ammunition, not so much as a shotgun or old musket with which to drill. But what need would they have for guns? Lawrence was as safe from the rebels as the peak of Mount Oread was from summer floods. If the boys had guns, they might hurt themselves.

Lawrence had sent many of its sons off to war, to join the Union side, of course, but otherwise its citizens had not been touched by the fighting. They felt safe and secure in the conviction that their sheer size protected them from rebel attack. Certainly no bushwhackers would dare to take on a city of three thousand souls. People knew that a force large enough to risk attacking Lawrence would be spotted immediately by General Ewing's border outposts and be hunted down long before it could threaten the town.

Oh, there had been the occasional scare, the odd rumor that Quantrill's men were approaching, but it had never turned out to be true. An incident at the end of July had upset people no end and caused such trouble, disruption, and embarrassment that it would be a long time before people believed another story like that one. Most people blamed the mayor, George Washington Collamore, and young Lt. T. J. Hadley, in command of twenty troops on the far side of the Kansas River, for overreacting and riling folks up for no reason.

Hadley and his men had been camped across the river from Lawrence since June, sent there by General Ewing in response to an urgent request from the mayor for troops to defend his town. There had been nothing to defend against until the end of July, when Lieutenant Hadley received a letter from his brother, who was on Ewing's staff, saying that the Union army had a spy in Quantrill's camp on the Sni River. The spy had reported that "Quantrill is coming at the light of the moon," planning to attack Lawrence sometime within the next several nights when the moon was full.

Hadley showed the letter to Mayor Collamore, who decided to call out the militia, thinking it foolish and irresponsible to ignore a warning from an official source. However unlikely such a raid might seem, the mayor believed it was his duty to put the town on alert. At midnight on July thirty-first, he ordered the armory bell rung to sound the alarm. The local militiamen dragged themselves out of bed, sure that their nervous mayor was once more seeing danger where none existed. They had lost sleep before and fallen behind in their chores while playing soldier. This was probably more of the same, they reasoned.

Tired and sullen, the men took up their positions around town. The cannon was loaded and pointed down Massachusetts Street. Scouts were sent into the countryside and pickets ordered to patrol the roads leading into town from the lonely posts ten miles out. Several hundred increasingly angry men waited throughout the night and into the next day. For some reason Mayor Collamore never made clear, he told no one of Hadley's letter announcing Quantrill's forthcoming attack. Neither did Lieutenant Hadley. The men had nothing but rumor and gossip to feed on.

The following day, one hundred additional militia came in from outlying areas, along with some soldiers and a cannon. More patrols were dispatched, and people settled down to wait through another bright moonlit night. Mayor Collamore and Lieutenant Hadley maintained their inexplicable secrecy, a lapse in judgment that caused morale to plummet. Stories abounded that Quantrill was heading for Lawrence, but neither leader would confirm or deny them.

The townspeople waited through another night, and when the scouts returned at dawn, they reported no signs of the rebels. More soldiers showed up the following day, en route to duty elsewhere, and they stopped to wait with everyone else through a third sleepless night when no enemy appeared.

On the next day, Mayor Collamore canceled the alert. The period of the full moon was coming to a close. The story of a pending attack had obviously been a mistake or a hoax, leaving hundreds of people mad as hell at the mayor and Hadley for disrupting their lives. Most of the troops left town, the cannon was wheeled back into its ceremonial place in front of the courthouse, and the militia disbanded. Men went back to their farms to thresh wheat, cut hay, and tell tales about their fool of a mayor.

At one time, Mayor Collamore had let the men of Lawrence's militia keep their government-supplied weapons at home, but too many guns had been damaged through neglect or abuse. Now he required all guns to be turned in after every alert or drill. The men neatly stacked their weapons in the Massachusetts Street armory, where they would be safe until needed again.

Lieutenant Hadley moved back across the river with a reduced force of fifteen men; five had been sent to Fort Leavenworth. Hadley's camp had a fine view of the city, but there was no bridge. If they needed to get to town, they had to rely on a slow ferry manned by civilians. "They could not have been posted anywhere in the same proximity to the town, where they would have been safer themselves from harm, or more utterly harmless to the guerrillas."

There no longer seemed to be anything to fear, however. General Ewing had made Kansas safe again—everybody said so. In addition, there were the triumphs of early July, the staggering Union victories at Gettysburg and Vicksburg. The rebels were finished. It was only a matter of time, and not much time at that. It was just as the Reverend George Paddock had said in his sermon at the Methodist church: "the beginning of the end unmistakably appears. Hope begins to smile again over the land."

* * *

In the early morning hours of August eighteenth, William Clarke Quantrill led 150 men out of their camp near Blue Springs. They rode in a southeasterly direction to Captain Perdee's farm near Lee's Summit, where they joined Andy Blunt and Bill Anderson with their 140 men.

George Todd led his band on a detour, riding up to the house of a man named Wallace. Todd called Wallace outside and accused him of giving information to the Yankees; Wallace denied it. Todd was in no mood for denials. As far as he was concerned, Wallace was guilty. Todd pulled out his Navy Colt revolver and pointed it at Wallace. The man cringed, begging for mercy. Todd did not fire. He leaned down from his saddle and struck Wallace across the face with the gun barrel.

"If I ever hear of you talking any more," Todd warned, "we'll come back and kill you!"

Todd dismounted, walked around Wallace's crumpled body, and went inside the house. He looked around, calmly sat down at the organ, and played a tune for a few minutes. Then he and his men rode away, to rendezvous with Quantrill at the Perdee farm.

Quantrill's men had covered ten miles and had seen no federal soldiers, nor had they been spotted by any. They headed west, camping at noon at the Potter farm not far from the town of Lone Jack. Quantrill assembled the men, to tell the rank and file, for the first time, their destination. "You, one and all, will understand that the undertaking we are about to commence is one of extreme hazard. It might be that the entire command will be overwhelmed, the ranks decimated as they never have before. So, I say to one and all, if any refuse to go along, they will not be censured."

Quantrill paused and looked expectantly at the mass of men. About a dozen quietly got up, walked to their horses, and rode away. Quantrill nodded his acceptance and went on with his speech, repeating what he had told his lieutenants the night before.

The Kansan has been murdering and robbing our people for two years and more. They have burned our houses by districts, hauled our household goods to Kansas, stolen our livestock. I say that forbearance has ceased to be a virtue.

Lawrence is the great hotbed of abolitionism in Kansas. All the plunder stolen in Missouri will be found at Lawrence. We can get more revenge and get more money there than anywhere else in Kansas.

Shortly after sundown, he led the men off again to ride through the night. He posted a cordon of vedettes, or outriders, in every direction, to watch for signs of the enemy. Their pace was a slow march, because Quantrill ordered the vedettes to report in person every hour. Much time was lost as the outriders trotted back and forth between the main column and their posts. At seven the next morning, they set up camp and slept until three in the afternoon.

They stopped periodically during the night to allow time for men and horses to eat; it was more important that the horses be well fed. South of the Blue River, Quantrill's vedettes spotted a long column of riders heading south. This was no time or place for a gunfight, not so close to the border, near General Ewing's outposts, from which more Yankees would come running at the sound of gunfire. But luck was running well with Quantrill; the troops were quickly identified as Confederate soldiers—Col. John Holt leading 104 recruits south for training. Quantrill saw this as an opportunity to swell his ranks, and he asked Holt to bring his men along, to christen them in combat. Holt readily agreed.

The next morning, the men set up camp along the headwaters of the Grand River, only four miles from the border. Fifty more guerrillas from neighboring counties rode in to join the raid on Lawrence. Quantrill's army now numbered 448 men, the largest force he had commanded, perhaps the largest independent guerrilla force ever assembled during the Civil War. Now he had to lead them across a well-defended border deep into enemy territory, and bring them safely out again, from a state that held some four thousand Union troops, nearly ten times their number.

Quantrill's army left for the border at 3:30 P.M., crossing into Kansas about three hours later at a point one and a half miles below the town of Aubry, the site of one of Ewing's new outposts. Two companies of Union cavalry, numbering approximately fifty men each, were stationed there under the command of Capt. Joshua A. Pike. Pike, who was from Lawrence, may have been one of the least competent and certainly among the least aggressive officers in the Union army. It was Quantrill's continuing good fortune that Pike was in command at Aubry. If he had not been, Lawrence would probably have been spared.

Around seven that evening, a farmer living seven miles from Aubry rode into town to spread the word that a large body of men claiming to be Union troops had passed his farm earlier in the day. He suspected they might not be federal soldiers, because when some of the riders saw him counting the number of men on horseback, they had grabbed him and held him captive behind the farmhouse, out of sight of the passing parade. The farmer reported to Captain Pike that he believed the force numbered between seven and eight hundred well-armed men and that they appeared to be heading into Kansas. It had to be Quantrill. Only the guerrilla leader could assemble so large a force.

Pike sent two couriers north and south to spread the word of the sighting to the outposts along the border. Unbelievably, stupidly, Pike did not send couriers westward, into the area of Kansas where the bushwhackers were obviously heading. A messenger could have reached Lawrence no later than one o'clock in the morning, giving the residents a few hours to prepare to defend themselves. Nor did Pike make any attempt to follow them. Instead, he brought his troops out on the prairie, where they watched the guerrillas pass. Pike gave no orders to fire on or to pursue the bushwhackers.

Bill Gregg described Pike's troops riding out from Aubry. He exaggerated their number, doubling the force to two hundred.

"In the bright sun-light of the evening, these troops rode out on the prairie formed, and looked at us pass. Not a man of ours broke ranks. Not a shot [was] fired."

Fifty-four years later, in 1917, Captain Pike wrote his own account of events that night in an effort to clear his name. Referring to himself in the third person, Pike noted: "He was so severely criticized that he for many years refused to make any statement whatever concerning the Quantrill raid, believing that it would be impossible for him to be accorded justice, or even a fair hearing."

Pike went on to explain that he had not had enough troops to go chasing after Quantrill and his alleged eight hundred guerrillas. Of the one hundred cavalry in Pike's command, he had, according to his story, only twenty-one fit and available for duty. He said five men were on sick call and the rest were away on scouting and other missions. After talking over the sighting of Quantrill's force with one of his officers, Pike claimed, he concluded it would be suicidal to attack so large an army with only twenty-one men. He chose to await reinforcements from the nearest outpost before pursuing the enemy.

General Ewing, writing his official report a week after the incident occurred, chastised Pike for not sending word of the enemy force west to the towns in Kansas and for not pursuing the raiders with his entire command, which Ewing believed was at or near its full complement. "By Captain Pike's error of judgment in failing to follow promptly and closely, the surest means of arresting the terrible blow was thrown away, for Quantrill would never have gone as far as Lawrence, or attacked it, with 100 men close on his rear."

Capt. Joshua Pike had much to answer for that night, but no charges were ever filed against him. And recriminations would have been of no value to the piles of corpses soon littering Lawrence's streets.

Quantrill's force paused at 7:30 that night to graze their horses—and, as it turned out, to kill a man. They stopped two miles south of Squiresville, about ten miles inside Kansas, making good time. They could afford the time to deal with one Colonel Sims, a pro-Union man who used to live in Missouri and was now on Quantrill's death list. Sims knew he was wanted, and for two years he had rarely spent a night at home. In good weather, he slept in the cornfield; otherwise, he stayed with neighbors.

Quantrill sent a band of men after Sims. They were disappointed not to find him at home. They searched the house and demanded that Mrs. Sims cook supper for them. While they ate, they questioned her about her husband, but she stuck to her story that she had no idea of his whereabouts.

They also questioned Sims's young nephew, but he claimed he didn't know anything, either. The bushwhackers left the house, not "as empty handed as they came. A nice blanket lay handy and as they retired, it clung to their fingers like iron to a magnet."

At eight o'clock that night, a little after Quantrill's men rode up to the Sims place, the first of Captain Pike's two couriers reached his destination, one of Ewing's border outposts. The place was Little Sante Fe, twelve miles north of Aubry, under the command of Capt. Charles Coleman. He read Pike's message announcing that eight hundred raiders had crossed into Kansas and wrote out two dispatches of his own. He sent one rider to General Ewing's headquarters in Kansas City and another to Olathe, eighteen miles to the west, asking the federal commander there to relay the warning farther west. Coleman also issued orders for his entire force—some eighty men in condition to ride—to prepare to move out.

At about the same time, Pike's second courier reached Coldwater Grove, thirteen miles south of Aubry. Lt. Col. Charles Clark, commander of that outpost, immediately sent riders to his outlying patrols, ordering them to return. He summoned a courier to carry a reply to Pike, telling him to "watch the movement of the enemy and report." Then, having taken such prompt and decisive action, Colonel Clark elected to stay put and await word on further developments.

At nine o'clock that night, Captain Coleman led his eighty

men out of Little Sante Fe and headed south toward Aubry, reaching there an hour later. Wasting no time, he assumed command and led his and Pike's men west in pursuit of the raiders. In a report written nine days later, Coleman noted: "My force then consisted of about 180 men," giving lie to Pike's later claim that he had only 21 men fit and ready for duty that night.

They picked up Quantrill's trail five miles south of Aubry and began tracking the band. "The night was very dark," Pike recalled, "so much so that the scout had to strike matches to find the trail."

Quantrill had left Squiresville. The long, silent column of guerrillas headed southwest two miles to the hamlet of Spring Hill. A couple of Yankee soldiers were there, but Quantrill issued orders to leave them unmolested so as not to alert the residents. Apparently, the soldiers saw nothing unusual about the sight of 450 men riding slowly through town. Given the darkness, and with some bushwhackers wearing blue uniforms, the Federals took them to be Union cavalry.

Quantrill turned his column to the northwest after leaving Spring Hill and reached the town of Gardner at about eleven o'clock that night. A few curious bystanders watched them pass. A couple of Union soldiers asked the riders who they were and where they were headed. On their way to Lawrence, Quantrill's men replied, to have their horses shod. Again, no one became suspicious. No one imagined a rebel force could be that deep into Kansas without the whole countryside knowing about it.

Quantrill had told his men to stay together, not to separate, straggle, or break ranks, but when they reached Gardner, some chose to disobey his instructions. A few men at the rear of the column stopped at the house of a Mr. Rue to draw water from his well. To make conversation, or because he was suspicious, Rue asked what outfit they were with and where they were headed. Major Ransom's command, Rue was told, as Quantrill's men concocted a name on the spot—on their way to Lexington, Missouri, from Fort Scott, Kansas.

Rue was skeptical. If the outfit was headed for Missouri, it was going in the wrong direction. Then, when Quantrill's men asked for directions to Fort Leavenworth, Rue's doubts about them increased. But they were wearing Union blue and were part of an outfit so large, it could only be federal to be so far inside the Kansas border. Rue kept his questions to himself.

Another band of Quantrill's men, fifteen in all, returned to Gardner because they wanted a decent meal before they went into battle. After stopping at the hotel to order supper, they walked to the stable and took two good horses, leaving two tired ones in their place. They explained that they were Union soldiers and would be back the next day to swap horses.

Riding to catch up with the main body, a few stopped at the home of the pro-Union Dr. Shean. They pounded on his door, yelling that they needed to see him right away. Shean began to dress to answer the door, but his wife pleaded with him to slip out the back door and flee. She suspected the visitors were bushwhackers out to get him for his Union sympathies. The doctor agreed to go.

Mrs. Shean opened the window and called out that the doctor would come right down. Meanwhile, Shean slipped out the rear door and escaped into a field of tall weeds. Quantrill's men were furious when they found out he had gone. They did not harm Mrs. Shean, even though she had lied to them, but they were thorough in their search of the house and the field. Once or twice, they came within touching distance of Dr. Shean, but his luck held. Tiring of the pursuit, they rode off to catch up with the rest of Quantrill's outfit.

On the other side of Gardner, a lone Yankee soldier—a courier sent west from Olathe to warn the towns of Gardner and Lawrence that Quantrill was coming—reined in his horse when someone hailed him. A large number of mounted men had just passed through town, the stranger said. The soldier figured they had to be the bushwhackers he was supposed to warn people about. If they had already ridden through Gardner, then that town was safe. Lawrence was a different story. If the courier tried to reach Lawrence, Quantrill's men might spot him. Afraid to go on alone in the dark with the guerrilla army out there, the soldier turned around and headed back to Olathe. There would be no warning for Lawrence that night.

Sometime after midnight, Captain Coleman's messenger from Little Sante Fe reached Union headquarters in Kansas City. General Ewing was not there; he had gone to Leavenworth, nearly twenty miles away. It would take a fast rider two hours to cover that distance, and time was critical if anyone hoped to catch up with Quantrill's men. Ewing's chief of staff, Maj. Preston Plumb, considered using the telegraph link between Kansas City and Leavenworth. With that new invention of almost instant communication, the general could be notified in minutes. But the telegraph office closed down at eleven o'clock every night, and no one knew where to find the telegrapher. Plumb knew he could not wait for morning to take action. He sent couriers to outlying stations, ordering every fit man to saddle up and head south after the guerrillas. At one o'clock in the morning, he roused the headquarters company and led the fifty men out across the border toward Olathe, Kansas.

Captain Coleman, leading the reluctant Captain Pike and 180 men, picked up Quantrill's trail. Even in the darkness, it was hard to miss signs of the passage of 450 horses cutting a twenty-foot swath across the prairie. But the trail petered out after only three miles. Quantrill had ordered his men to scatter and then to reform a while later in order to confuse anyone who might be following them. Now it was painstaking work, even for the most experienced tracker. "Crouching low to the ground, often striking matches, straining their eyes for flattened grass, hoofprints, and fresh droppings, Coleman's force moved west through the black, still night."

Quantrill's tactic of splitting up his force proved effective. "In again finding [the trail]," Coleman wrote, "I lost near two hours." It was 3:00 A.M., and Coleman was a good six hours behind Quantrill. Coleman and his exhausted men urged their tired horses on, eventually picking up a trail the guerrillas no longer attempted to conceal. Along with routine signs of their passage, Quantrill's men were leaving a string of dead bodies.

Three miles outside Gardner, Quantrill turned the outfit north toward the tiny German settlement of Hesper. They were in danger of getting lost because they were in unfamiliar territory. Bill Gregg recalled: "We had now arrived at a point where none of our men knew the country, hence it became necessary to procure a guide." They tried to procure more than one.

The first house at which the raiders stopped belonged to a Mr. Myzee, formerly of Missouri. Fortunately for him, when the guerrillas roused him from a sound sleep, they discovered he was nearly blind. Thus, he was allowed to live, and also because no one recognized him as a Union man.

At the second house, the bushwhackers found two Union soldiers on leave. When the guerrillas learned their identity, they drew their guns. One of the Yankees, quicker than the other, ran into the bush, escaping with only a bullet through his wrist. The second Yankee raised his hands in surrender and was shot down where he stood. Quantrill's search for a guide was not going well.

German refugees from Missouri lived next door. The men were awakened and ordered to dress so they could lead the outfit to Lawrence. One man, realizing they would not survive the night if they allowed themselves to be taken by Quantrill's guerrillas, decided to act quickly. As he bent down to tie his shoes, he blew out the candle his wife was holding, plunging the cabin into darkness. He sprang for the open doorway and ran to safety through the cornfields. A volley of wild shots followed him.

The other man hid under a pile of rubbish, but the raiders found him and dragged him outside, two guerrillas twisting each of his arms. Powerfully built, the man shook off his captors and ran to the sanctuary of the cornfields.

The bushwhackers were now well beyond Hesper, moving in what they hoped was the right direction, still riding from farmhouse to farmhouse searching for a guide. The next house belonged to Joseph Stone, another displaced Missourian. He lived with his wife, a grown son, and a boy named Jacob Rote. They were awakened by pounding on the door and a shouted demand for a guide. The raiders said they were Union troops, but Mrs. Stone did not believe them. She went to the door and said her husband was too sick to travel but that the boy could guide them wherever they wanted to go.

The men agreed to accept young Jacob Rote and were about to ride off when George Todd spotted Stone and recognized him as the man who had once had him arrested in Kansas City. Todd was about to shoot him, but Quantrill warned that they were too close to Lawrence to risk arousing any neighboring farmer with the noise. If Todd was intent on killing Stone, he would have to do it quietly.

Todd remained intent, however, and he led Stone a quarter mile away from the house, but he could not find anything with which to kill the man. He sent someone back to the house for rope to make a noose, but the raider could not find any. Not wanting to return empty-handed, he brought back an antique musket, which Todd used to club Stone to death. His wife found the body in the morning.

Jacob Rote mounted up behind one of the bushwhackers, clinging to the man's waist. As they rode off, the man asked Jacob if he knew who they were. When Jacob said he did not, the raider told him they were Quantrill's men, on their way to destroy Lawrence. Jacob had heard of Quantrill—everybody had.

Describing their futile search for guides, Bill Gregg wrote, "Things went on this way until probably ten men had been killed." But young Rote was allowed to live. Forced to stay with the bushwhackers for five hours, until they were finished with their business in Lawrence, he witnessed much of the carnage. Gregg gave him a horse and a new suit, which he had stolen in town, and sent him on his way. Thus, Rote was a rare survivor of Quantrill's war.

At four o'clock in the morning, Quantrill led his men through Franklin, only five miles from Lawrence. The sky was clear and beginning to lighten and already it was hot. There was no breeze. It promised to be another day of brutal, scorching heat, close to one hundred degrees on the open, sun-drenched Kansas prairie.

The men were covered with dust, thirsty as a creek bed during a drought, hungry, and bone-weary. They had been riding for nearly thirty-six hours and were on their second night without sleep, save for some who strapped themselves to their saddles to doze while on the move. A few people, including a couple of Union soldiers, watched them ride through town in the dim predawn light, but no one seemed upset at the sight of 450 mounted men. Like everyone else, they assumed any force so large and so far from the state line had to be federal. Dr. R. L. Williams watched from his window. He counted as best he could and later estimated their number at 450. He heard someone, presumably Quantrill, call out a command: "Rush on, boys, it will be daylight before we are there! We ought to have been there an hour ago."

Bill Gregg recalled that at Franklin "the horses were hurried to a long trot, [then] the men were thrown into columns of fours and put to a gallop." They had to ride hard if they hoped to reach Lawrence while most people were still asleep—five miles to cover in less than an hour on tired horses.

Although Quantrill was getting closer by the minute, there was still an opportunity to save Lawrence. If only someone could get there ahead of the raiders in time to spread the alarm, in time for all able-bodied men to get their weapons out of the armory, in time to take up positions behind overturned wagons and inside doorways and windows. The army could not do it. Captain Coleman, leading his and Captain Pike's 180 men, was a good five hours behind.

There was still time for others, however, and several did try during those last moments before dawn. The wife of Capt. S. J. Jennings—the Union officer himself was off in Arkansas—lived not far from the farmhouse of Joseph Stone, where the Rote boy lived. The raiders had stopped at her house first, looking for a guide. Finding no man there, they had ridden on to Stone's place after drawing water from her well.

She was suspicious of them, and she walked half a mile north to the house of William Guest, whom she urged to ride to Lawrence to raise the alarm that hundreds of bushwhackers were coming. Guest did not believe her, and nothing she said changed his mind. Perhaps he was afraid or did not want to get involved. Mrs. Jennings was certain her visitors were bushwhackers headed for Lawrence, and there was not a thing she could do about it.

Henry Thompson, a black man who worked for Guest, volunteered to go to Lawrence if Guest would let him take one of his horses. When Guest refused even that, Thompson set out on foot. It was a futile gesture; he could never hope to walk there in time.

As he trudged along the road toward Eudora, he met Frederick Pilla, a justice of the peace who was returning home late on horseback from performing a wedding ceremony. Pilla believed Thompson's story, and he agreed to ride to Eudora to spread the news that Quantrill was on the loose. There he called for volunteers to ride to Lawrence.

Three men set out immediately. One of them, David Kraus, the town marshal, barely reached the edge of town when he was thrown from his horse. He survived but never recovered fully from his injuries. The other two men—Casper Marfelius and Jerry Reel—rode on side by side. Reel had the better horse, a black Kentucky mare, but it stumbled and fell on top of Reel. Marfelius, faced with the choice of trying to reach Lawrence ahead of Quantrill or stopping to help his friend, decided on the latter course. He turned for the nearest farmhouse to seek assistance, just about the time that Quantrill was riding into Lawrence. Reel died the next day.

The most valiant effort to warn the town, and certainly the longest, was made by Pelathe, a Shawnee Indian. Also known as the Eagle, Pelathe had ridden into Kansas City a little after midnight, accompanying Captain Coleman's courier. Pelathe went with the courier to General Ewing's headquarters and was there when Major Plumb, Ewing's chief of staff, learned about Quantrill crossing the border.

One of Ewing's best scouts, Theodore Bartles, was present, and when he heard the message, he was convinced Quantrill had only one destination: Lawrence. Enraged when he realized the army had not sent a warning to the town, he briefly considered going himself. But Lawrence was thirty miles from Kansas City.

Pelathe, an expert horseman and daring rider who knew the country well, said he wanted to try. Bartles said it was impossible but that if Pelathe was determined, he would give him his best horse. It was after one o'clock in the morning when Pelathe left, riding a Kentucky thoroughbred sorrel mare. He held the horse to a fast pace for two hours before she started breathing hard and he had to stop to rub her down.

The horse ran all out for hour upon hour, mile after mile throughout the night. Still an hour's ride from Lawrence, the magnificent animal faltered. "Her flanks heaved and her breathing was heavy. She was failing. She had done her best. Her wonderful powers of endurance were spent." Pelathe was determined to beat Quantrill to Lawrence, even if it meant sacrificing a noble horse. He knew it was a terrible thing to do, but so many lives—the entire population of Lawrence—were at stake.

He cut deep gashes into the horse's shoulders and rubbed gunpowder into the open wounds. The horse ran on in pain and terror, faster and faster, for one mile, then two, then three before pitching forward and expiring with a cry that sounded human. Pelathe leapt from the falling horse, running for all he was worth. Finally, near exhaustion, barely able to put one foot in front of the other, he saw in the faint light of early morning the village of the Delaware tribe. He knew he was not far from Lawrence.

Pelathe shouted a war cry as he neared the encampment. He quickly told the Delawares what was happening and took off on one of their ponies, riding hard for the ferry landing at Lawrence, the same place where Charley Hart used to hang out. He reached it at dawn, in time to hear the gunfire and the screams of terror. He was too late. Quantrill—alias Charley Hart—had gotten there first.

An hour's ride from Lawrence, Hoffman Collamore, the mayor's sixteen-year-old son, was spending the day hunting. He saw a large group of mounted men approaching. He assumed they were Union soldiers and paid them no heed—until they got close enough to ask where he was going, that is. Hunting, he said, and he kept on riding. Hoffman was not alarmed. Although it was too dark to see all the men clearly, he could tell they were strung out neatly in a column of fours, just like the cavalry.

Suddenly, the bushwhackers opened fire. The boy spurred his pony and headed into a field. The men kept firing until young Collamore and his pony fell to the ground. He lay still, in pain from a leg wound but barely daring to breathe, knowing he would be killed if they thought he was still alive. The raiders did not linger, and Collamore crawled to a farmhouse to get help. He was Lawrence's first casualty.

The Reverend Samuel S. Snyder awoke early, as usual, and went out in the yard to milk his cow. He had been busy recruiting black soldiers for his command, the Second Kansas Colored Regiment, twenty of whom were camped in Lawrence. Being an abolitionist was bad enough, as far as the bushwhackers were concerned, but putting niggers in uniform, giving them guns, and letting them think they were as good as anybody else was as low as a man could get. That was why Snyder was on Quantrill's list of men who deserved to die. And that was why Quantrill detached two men from the column; they shot Snyder dead in his yard.

Joe Savage had just gotten up and was rinsing his face in the water bucket behind his house. He did not answer the knock at the front door right away. The only thing that helped his sore eyes was to bathe them in water. By the time he finished and went to the door, he saw two horsemen riding out through his front gate to join a long column of riders. He remembered them well. "Low-crowned, broad-brimmed hats—all alike nearly—unshaven—stoop-shouldered—all without coats—nearly all wore red flannel shirts much begrimed with camp-grease and dirt." They had thrown away their coats. They knew they would find new ones in Lawrence.

Quantrill stopped on the outskirts of Lawrence as the city took on form and substance in the rising light. He sent Bill Gregg and five others ahead to see if the townspeople had been alerted and to find out if an armed defense force awaited them. He formed his army into forty-five-man units and assigned each a separate mission.

Although he appeared as tired as the rest of them, Quantrill was dressed much better. He wore a black slouch hat with a gold cord wrapped around it, gray pants and sharp-looking cavalry boots, and a brown guerrilla shirt. Four Navy Colts were stuffed into his broad belt. He wanted to make an impression on those who had known him as Charley Hart, those who had dismissed him as a ne'er-do-well and a common thief, those who had tried to have him arrested. He wanted them to remember him.

"Kill every man big enough to carry a gun," he shouted.

Some of the raiders were having second thoughts while they waited for Gregg and his party to return. The city spread out before them was huge and forbidding. What if the citizens of Lawrence were awake and alert, armed to the teeth and ready to spring a trap, an ambush in which Quantrill's men would be mercilessly gunned down as they rode along the main street? This was bigger than anything they had attempted before. Perhaps this was too great an undertaking. A few men began to voice their doubts about the whole enterprise, warning that they could be cut to pieces, that it was madness to go on.

Others suggested they turn around and head back, get out now while the getting was good. Quantrill heard the murmurs, saw the looks on their faces, read the uncertainty in the air. He knew he had to act at once. If he waited for Gregg to return, the contagion of doubt and fear might have spread too far.

"You can do as you please," Quantrill announced loudly. "I am going into Lawrence."

All chose to follow him. It was 5:15 on the morning of August 21, 1863.

10

A Tempest of Fire and Death

THE BOY SOLDIERS were the first to die—those white recruits camped on the east side of Massachusetts Street who were too young for active duty; who had no training and not a single weapon among them; who were still asleep in their tents at 5:15 in the morning; who never knew what hit them. In not much more time than it takes to tell it—Bill Gregg said it was over in three minutes—seventeen of the twenty-two boys were dead.

They had been awakened by the heart-stopping roar of 450 horses charging down the street, by the raucous shriek of the hair-raising rebel yell, by the sudden explosion, like bunches of firecrackers, of hundreds of pistol shots. The bushwhackers fired into the rows of white tents, shredding the canvas and staining it red, then rode the boys down, horses' hooves flashing and tearing at flesh and bone.

One of the raiders, Larkin Skaggs, preacher turned killer, hauled down the Union flag and tied it to the tail of his horse before galloping away, dragging the flag in the dirt. He and the others fired off potshots—like shooting at clay targets at a county fair—at the few boys who survived the initial onslaught. One was killed within fifteen feet of the nearest house, a sanctuary several tried to reach. Another made it almost to the porch before a bullet forced him to his knees. He raised his hands in supplication, as if reaching toward a merciful heaven.

"For God's sake don't murder me," he cried, but the only answer he received was a round that sent him sprawling in the dust.

"No quarter for you federal sons of bitches," was the reply.

Another boy approached a nearby house, clambered through the front door, and emerged from the back a few minutes later wearing civilian clothes. He walked past the bushwhacker who had chased him there, but the man paid him no heed. He was too intent on watching the front door, waiting for a lad dressed in a blue soldier suit to oblige him by coming out. The boy was one of the few from his outfit to escape.

The black recruits two blocks away, equally untrained and defenseless, were more fortunate. In the few minutes it took the guerrillas to massacre the white recruits, they were all able to flee, most by swimming across the river.

The raiders went about their assigned duties with the precision of a regular army outfit, according to Quantrill's plan. Some headed for the top of Mount Oread to act as lookouts, scanning the flat prairie for signs of federal troops. Others split off to the roads leading out of town in order to prevent anyone from escaping.

"On to the hotel! Be damned quick about it," Quantrill ordered.

The remaining men broke into three groups. The two smaller ones raced up Vermont Street and New Hampshire Street, parallel to Massachusetts, the main street. Their job was to see that no one escaped from the rear of the buildings along that prime stretch of business properties. Quantrill and Gregg led the rest, five and six abreast, up Massachusetts Street, a roaring, yelling, terrifying mob, firing revolvers at every window and doorway, at every person foolish enough to risk a glance outside. The raiders patrolling the parallel streets kept up a running fire into the rear of the buildings, trapping citizens in their shops or their second-floor living quarters.

The raiders pulled up in front of the imposing fortress of the Eldridge House. The rows of windows above them looked like opaque eyes in the still-dim light. The men stopped firing, although no one gave the order, and an unnatural silence fell over the street. Some of the men were apprehensive, knowing that the hotel was the only place in town constructed strongly enough to resist an attack. A score of armed men behind those stout brick walls could pick them off, holding them at bay until Yankee soldiers arrived. If there was to be an ambush, this was where it would be.

But there was no ambush, no trap, not even a thought of armed resistance among the disheveled, panic-stricken guests. They had no weapons. The fool mayor had issued an edict that no one within the city limits could be armed.

Capt. Alexander Banks, the Kansas provost marshal, lived in one of the hotel rooms. He convened a hasty meeting with several other occupants to plan what they should do.

Outside, the bushwhackers remained quiet as ghosts, their guns trained on the windows, expecting to see them flung open and gun barrels appear. The silence was shattered when the night clerk struck a gong, to awaken the guests and alert them to the danger.

The guerrillas edged away from the hotel, moving closer to the safety of the buildings on the opposite side of the street. No shots were fired; no one shouted; no one spoke.

Inside the hotel, Captain Banks and some of the other male residents concluded they had two choices: do nothing and let the rebels take over the hotel or try to negotiate a formal surrender in the hope of obtaining a guarantee of their safety. They agreed on the latter course.

Banks removed the sheet from his bed and waved it from the window. The raiders cheered; the hotel was theirs. Quantrill rode forward until he was beneath Banks's third-floor window.

"We'll surrender ourselves," Banks said, "if we are treated as prisoners of war."

"All right, agreed," Quantrill shouted back, and the deal was done.

Quantrill turned and nodded to his men. They knew the plan. Some would stay with Quantrill to deal with the hotel's occupants. The rest would form small groups to hunt down those on Quantrill's death list, to plunder and sack the town, and to murder anyone else they found—any man big enough to carry a gun.

"Kill!" Quantrill yelled. "Kill! And you will make no mistake. Lawrence is the hotbed and should be thoroughly cleansed, and the only way to cleanse it is to kill! Kill!"

While the rest rode off to carry out their missions, Quantrill and those who remained behind dismounted and strode into the lobby of the hotel like conquering heroes. Guards were set at the top of the stairs while the rest of the men pounced on those guests who had left their rooms and were milling about in the hallways. They were quickly and harshly relieved of their valuables—money, watches, jewelry—then ordered down the stairs.

Upstairs, fine ladies and gentlemen, scantily clad, had their rooms burst into by dirty, cursing men who with a splash of tobacco juice and wave of a gun ordered them out and down to the lobby. Trunks and carpet sacks were ripped open, and jewelry, currency, and ladies' apparel were crammed into pockets. The looting went from room to room as the stupefied boarders, bishops and priests included, fled down the staircase.

In the lobby, the night clerk was ordered to open the safe, from which rough, calloused hands scooped out money and more valuables. There was no ideology behind it, no charade of fighting for a noble cause. It was simple robbery, nothing more, nothing less. Charley Hart was back doing what he did best.

He watched it all from his perch on the second-floor landing. It was the supreme moment of his life. He was back in the town that had wronged him, the place he hated more than any other, and at that moment, he owned it and everyone in it. One word from him and any man would die before he could open his mouth to protest.

Some of those stumbling past Quantrill down the stairs recognized him from his prewar days. A few smiled tentatively, and others tried to flatter him in hopes of saving their lives. One man went so far as to congratulate him on his success in taking over the town so fast. Quantrill acknowledged the compliment with satisfaction and allowed that, yes, it was a great accomplishment.

Another man, Arthur Spicer, started reminiscing about the good old days before the war, and he mentioned Quantrill's outlaw name, Charley Hart. Quantrill fixed him with a deadly, furious stare and said it made no difference what he was called. Spicer backed away and wisely said no more, grateful to be alive, praying Quantrill would forget about him and what he had said.

When the looting and plundering was done, Quantrill placed a guard on the landing to prevent anyone from sneaking back upstairs. He left the hotel and commandeered a buggy drawn by two white horses. He drove around the town, admiring the handiwork of his men, the impressive number of bodies accumulating in the streets, and the houses and stores put to the torch.

The prisoners in the lobby of the Eldridge House milled about helplessly, with mounting concern for their safety. Sounds of gunshots and fearful screams and the smell of smoke from burning buildings filtered inside. A number of the raiders stormed into the hotel. They had looted the liquor store and were in a truculent and belligerent mood. They had already been on a killing spree and they were ready for more victims. They waved their guns at the hotel guests and began to threaten them. What was so special about them? the men demanded. Why should they be allowed to live while everybody else in town was being cut down?

The only thing that saved the hotel guests was the guard Quantrill had stationed at the head of the stairs. No one recalled his name, but he stood firm against the other bushwhackers, reminding them that Quantrill had decided the people in the hotel were prisoners of war and should be treated as such. One prisoner, the attorney R. S. Stevens, decided that something else had to be done. He would talk to Quantrill and persuade him to honor his agreement to protect the lives of those who had surrendered.

Stevens made his case to the guard, who was probably relieved at the prospect of having Quantrill back in control of the situation, thus taking it out of his hands. He convinced one of the more sober raiders to go find him. An angry Quantrill showed up at the hotel five minutes later, giving those present the impression that he had changed his mind about the prisoners—that he was sorry he had promised them protection and no longer felt bound by the agreement he had made with Captain Banks. "There was not much in his demeanor and tone when he came upon the landing and spoke, to encourage the prisoners."

"Who sent for me?" he demanded.

Stevens identified himself.

"What do you want, sir?" Quantrill asked, his voice haughty and cold.

Stevens was a persuasive man, suave and adroit, and he used his best courtroom manner on Quantrill. His words were not recorded, but whatever he said was effective. Quantrill assured Stevens he would not renege on his promise of protection, and he agreed to arrange for an escort to take them all to the City Hotel, which was run by his friend Nathan Stone.

Quantrill used to stay at the City Hotel when he was Charley Hart, and Stone had always treated him well. Now he was returning the favor. The City Hotel was the only building in town Quantrill had specifically ordered his men to leave alone. He told Stevens that he and the other Eldridge House prisoners would be safe with Nathan Stone.

"I once boarded there years ago," he said, "and the Stones were kind to me. Nothing will happen to their property so long as I am in Lawrence."

The guests at the Eldridge House survived the next four hours, but those who made their homes in Lawrence did not fare so well. "A tempest of fire and death swept through the adjacent streets," one man wrote. It was "Hell let loose," said another. Flames, screams, shots, shouts, and death by bullet and by fire engulfed Lawrence. Men died in their houses and shops, their gardens and fields, in the streets and alleys, and no amount of pleading, of cries for mercy from victims or their families, made any difference.

Possessions were rudely yanked from drawing rooms, rings from fingers, money from bureau drawers and purses. Pianos were chopped up like firewood, windows and mirrors smashed, furnishings torn and scarred and all set ablaze. The hopes and toil of a lifetime were gone in no more time than it took to strike a match. Smoke and flames rose from the ruined city, staining the clear blue morning sky and darkening the sun. Wails of despair could be heard over the crackling flames, along with the drunken oaths and cheers for Quantrill and Jeff Davis and the Confederacy.

Horses whinnied as they breathed the sulfurous smoke, adding to the cacophony of noise. Around the horses' tails the raiders tied small American flags looted from a bookstore. The raiders, drunk on more whiskey than many had seen in the two years of war, and on their orgy of killing and revenge, rode through the streets like demons, behaving beyond all reason, beyond all control. And the terrified people of Lawrence, driven to the edge of madness, felt thrust into Bedlam, the notorious lunatic asylum. But in Lawrence, the lunatics were in control.

John and Will Laurie, along with Will's wife, did not live in Lawrence, but they had come to town the day before from their farm twenty miles away to transact business. As soon as the gunfire started, they rushed from their boardinghouse and blundered from one street to another, seeking a way out, but the bushwhackers seemed to be everywhere.

John and Will were hit and fell to the ground, unable to get up. The men who shot them sat calmly in their saddles, reloading their revolvers and eyeing the men lying in the dirt. Will's wife, a baby in her arms, sank to her knees and begged the guerrillas to spare the brothers. John saw it was no use, yet he pleaded with the guerrillas to let Will live. Poor Will Laurie. He had survived at Shawneetown when Quantrill sacked it, and now the same men had found him again.

"We are not so particular about you," the raiders said to John, "but that fellow, we will put him through."

They put both men through, shooting them again and again until they lay quite still.

"We are fiends from Hell," they said to Will's wife, "get into the house, or by heavens, we will serve you the same."

The lodgers at the Johnson House, a hotel on Vermont Street, were treated the same way. It was a big stone house, one of the first places visited by the bushwhackers. The owner was known to be a rabid abolitionist. The raiders surrounded the house and shouted for the fourteen men inside to surrender. If they gave themselves up, they would be spared. Some figured the guerrillas were lying, believing they would not stand a chance if they came out. They jumped out the rear windows and were shot as soon as they landed.

Seven others, including Ralph Dix from next door, talked it over and decided to take their chances with the raiders. After all, they reasoned, they were civilians, not soldiers. They walked out the front door, hands held high. The raiders promptly relieved them of their money and valuables, led them out into the street, and shot them dead. Only James Finley made a run for it and dodged inside a building that was under construction.

Just as he dragged himself indoors, another man running for his life was shot down outside the house. When the two guerrillas chasing Finley asked the killers of the second man if they had seen anyone running that way, they said they had already killed him. Because of this confusion, Finley was spared any further pursuit. He lowered himself into a well inside the building, where he was found later that afternoon. He died six weeks later from his wounds.

One of the other seven men from the Johnson House, a Mr. Hampson, fell to the street, wounded but feigning death. He lay still, even when the heat from the burning Johnson House became intense. There were too many bushwhackers wandering about for him to dare move. He would be shot again before he took so much as a single step. Somehow his wife discovered he was still alive and she begged one of Quantrill's men to carry her husband's body away from the flames. Amazingly, he did, and even more amazingly, he did not discover that the corpse was still very much alive. Mrs. Hampson got him into a handcart and pushed him down the street in front of scores of killers. He lived.

Two doors away, Ralph Dix's wife, Getta, ran a boardinghouse for nine or ten men who worked in local stores. When the shooting began, her children screamed, and she implored her husband and her husband's brother to run for it while the guerrillas were busy with the Johnson House. They were paralyzed with fear, unable to move. All they could do was to tell one another that they would be all right if they did not offer any resistance. Besides, help would arrive any minute now. There were those soldiers across the river, and the militia was probably forming up by then. Best to wait.

Getta Dix agreed by then. She had seen men cut down as they jumped out of windows at the rear of the hotel. She barred the doors and said it was too late to try to get away; the bushwhackers were everywhere. All they could do was wait it out and hope nobody came to their house.

But now some of the men decided to move, and for some reason, they felt the safest place in town for them would be behind the stone walls of the Johnson House, which was already surrounded by raiders. Despite his wife's pleas to stay put, Dix and a couple of the others went up to the roof, crawled over the roofs of the adjoining buildings, and got inside the hotel just in time to surrender. Getta was frantic with worry. She left her children under the care of her maid in a coal shed behind her house, then ran for the hotel to try to save her husband.

She raced across the rear of the buildings and saw her brother-in-law tumble down the rear steps of the hotel as he tried to escape. She placed his head in her lap, but he was already dead. When she started to get up, his brain fell out of his shattered skull into her hands. When she reached the front of the hotel, dazed and bloody, she saw her husband and six other men being robbed by the raiders.

"Oh my God, Ralph. Why did you do it?" she sobbed. "I know they will kill you."

A man standing beside her husband handed a pistol he had kept, against the mayor's edict, to one of Quantrill's men. He was killed instantly. Getta Dix clung to her husband, who was begging her to save his life. Getta pleaded with the killers to let him go, and she was able to persuade two of them to promise not to harm him.

"No," the leader of the band said, "I won't let you take your husband away. I'm going to kill every damn one of them."

Getta watched her husband and the others shot in a dizzying swirl of smoke. She stood there as another group of raiders raced down an alley and trampled the dead under their horses' hooves.

Getta wandered along Massachusetts Street for some time— to a store where looting guerrillas chased her away, to a figure that was still breathing. But nothing, it seemed, could hold her attention. She continued to drift aimlessly until at last she found herself again in the alley. Noticing a straw hat laying nearby, Getta picked it up, quietly placed it over her husband's face, then calmly walked back to her burning home.

While most people were trying to figure out how to get out of town, several raced *into* Lawrence when the firing began. They did it because they thought they could help. They refused to stand by and do nothing while their neighbors were in trouble.

George Bell, the county clerk, saw the bushwhackers from his home on Mount Oread before they reached Lawrence. He watched them for some time, at first believing them to be Union troops—the only outfit of such a size that could possibly be on the loose that far inside Kansas. Then, when he saw five men ride ahead of the group into town and noticed that the long column flew no flag, he grew suspicious. He reached for his musket while his wife and family implored him to stay where he was. What could one man do against so many?

"If they take Lawrence," he replied, "they must do it over my dead body."

He ran down the hill, heading for the armory, determined to join the other citizens who must already be there, forming up to defend their town. By the time he reached Massachusetts Street, he realized the town was surrounded.

"Where shall we meet?" he asked others who were fleeing for their lives. It was too late to form up, they told him. It was every man for himself, they said as they ran on, and they urged him to get rid of his gun and get out of town. By then, shots were coming from all over and fires were burning everywhere around him. George Bell dropped his gun and started running. But it was too late to get back to his home. There were too many rebels in that direction. He was trapped.

He made his way into an unfinished house with another man. The two climbed up onto the roof joists, thinking they would be safe there. But they had been spotted by one of the guerrillas, who charged in after them and began firing. Bell glanced down and recognized the man. It was surely a miracle. He was an old friend who had often eaten dinner at Bell's house.

Bell identified himself and the bushwhacker agreed to spare their lives if they came down. They did—one can imagine with what relief—only to find themselves herded outside to face twenty others who were in no mood for clemency or mercy or gratitude for past favors.

"Shoot him, shoot him!" they shouted.

His onetime friend said nothing, and Bell, resigned to his fate, asked for a moment to say a prayer. When he finished, they shot him four times, along with his companion. The other man survived his wounds, but Bell died. Later, the group went to Bell's house and confronted his wife, who knew nothing of his fate.

"We have killed your husband," they told her, "and we have come to burn his house."

They set fire to it, but Mrs. Bell and her six children managed to save it after the raiders rode away.

Levi Gates lived a mile out of town, and he, too, grabbed his gun and headed for Lawrence when he heard the sound of shots. Like Bell, he thought he could help the residents fight off the attackers, but when he got there, he saw the situation was hopeless. He was a determined man, however, and believed himself to be a crack shot. He was not about to run away without doing what damage he could with his fine sporting rifle.

He squeezed off a round at long range and just missed a bushwhacker. He ran to the ravine to get a better shot but missed again. Before he could reload, raiders were all around him, and they did not miss. After he fell, they "pounded his head to a jelly and otherwise disfigured and mutilated his remains."

Sally Young, a seamstress at the Eldridge House, was out for her customary morning ride, accompanied by two suitors. They had seen the column of riders approach town but, like everyone else who saw them, thought nothing of it. They were not even unduly alarmed when they heard the sound of shots, thinking it to be no more than a ruckus among the soldiers. They began to suspect that it might be more serious when they rode by the home of the Reverend S. S. Snyder, the man who had been shot while milking his cow.

There they saw a number of women "weeping and wailing piteously," and they realized that grief in some form had been visited upon the household. But they still had no idea of what was going on until they got almost to town and saw the devastation taking place. Sally told her two young male friends to ride for their lives, to get as far away as quickly as they could. She guessed it was Quantrill attacking the town, and she vowed to go back to see what she could do.

"For God's sake do not go up there," said an elderly preacher she encountered.

"She replied that she would go if she was killed for it and went on."

When she reached town, the raiders stole her pony, but then they gave it back to her after a bit. She was pressed into service as a guide to show the rebels where certain men on their death list lived. She was not a very helpful guide—quite the contrary, in fact. She was determined to foil them at every turn. "Every other house it seemed was that of a brother, a cousin, or an uncle, and with tears rolling down her cheeks she begged the raiders to spare the home and occupants."

She did not seem to know where any of the condemned lived, and after awhile, the bushwhackers got disgusted and let her go. For some reason, she kept riding along after them, a point of confusion to some residents who saw her and figured she must be in league with the raiders.

Meanwhile, the killing continued as the circle of blood and flame spread out ever wider from the Eldridge House and the Johnson House. Three other families lived with Dr. Jerome Griswold at his large home: Harlow Baker, of Ridenour & Baker's grocery store; Simeon Thorp, a state senator; Josiah Trask, a newspaper editor; and their wives. Not long after the carnage in town began, five guerrillas rode up to their house with guns drawn. Josiah Trask was out on the balcony, wondering what all the noise was about, when he found himself facing men with revolvers, all pointed at him. The raiders shouted for the men in the house to come out and give themselves up immediately. Trask was told by the guerrillas:

> We have come to burn Lawrence, but we do not want to hurt anybody, and we do not want to get hurt. If the citizens will make us no trouble, we will do them no harm. We want you to go with us over to town where we can keep you under guard till we are through, then you can go. It will be better for everybody if you quietly go with us.

It sounded like a reasonable appeal. If they did not cause any trouble, they would be all right. Best not to get the raiders riled up. Best not to do anything to upset them. If they did, the bushwhackers would take it out on them, and maybe on the whole town.

"If it is going to help the town," Josiah Trask decided, "we had better go with them."

They were robbed as soon as they stepped out of the house and then lined up in a single file in the street. They were told they would be taken to the Eldridge House, where they would be held until the town was burned down. They started off with a raider riding by the side of each man and the fifth leading them. They had not gone more than twenty feet, with their wives watching tearfully from the house, when the guerrillas started cussing them out for dawdling.

They picked up their pace and were instantly shot down. Harlow Baker was hit in the neck and wrist and fell to the street, stunned and unable to move. Dr. Griswold was hit in several places, but he was a big, powerful man and he ran toward his fence, only to be shot fatally while he was climbing over it. Josiah Trask also fled, but he did not get far before being shot through the heart. Senator Thorp was wounded in the stomach, and he and Baker lay close to one another in the middle of the street where they fell. They were both still alive.

The wives of the four men ran to help their husbands, but the raiders kept them back. They left one man to guard the bodies, to keep the women away, while the others rampaged through the house, taking whatever they wanted. Then they robbed the women of their jewelry. Trask's wife begged them to let her keep her wedding ring.

"You have killed my husband," she pleaded, "let me keep his ring."

"No matter," one replied, cruelly twisting the ring off her finger.

Thorp and Baker lay in the broiling sun, whispering to each other, trying to keep up their spirits, whenever there were no raiders riding by. Thorp was in agony from his stomach wound. Baker was in better shape, but neither man dared move to try to get help. The men who had shot them had long since gone, but they had left one of their number not far away. Whenever the wives tried to reach their husbands, he charged toward them menacingly, frightening them back.

Presently, the other four men came back and looked at Thorp and Baker.

"Fred," one said to another, "one of them damned nigger-thieving abolitionists ain't dead yet. Go and kill him."

The one named Fred rode closer. Neither Thorp nor Baker knew which one of them was about to get shot again. Then Baker heard the horse stop beside him and knew he was the one. "It was but a breath, and the pistol cracked sharply. He felt a sudden sting in the right lung. Faintness followed, but he knew right where he was hit. The ball entered his back under the right shoulder and passed through his lungs." Baker heard Fred congratulate himself as he rode away.

The ordeal was not over. Later, another bushwhacker stopped, examined Baker for a moment, then rolled him over on his back. Baker forced himself not to make a sound or move a muscle. He hardly dared breathe as the man leaned over him, pulled out a knife, put the blade deep in Baker's pants pocket, and ripped an eighteen-inch-long gash down his trousers. Finding nothing in that pocket, the man slashed the other one and found it empty. Baker had already been picked clean by experts. The man took Baker's hat, got on his horse, and rode off, leaving the two men alone and bleeding, with their wives still looking on from the house, which stood remarkably untouched. They had persuaded the raiders not to burn it.

The two men lay there for three hours before Quantrill's men left. Thorp was carried inside, where he lingered in intense pain before dying the next day. As for Harlow Baker, he managed to stand up and walk home with help from friends, and, despite his wounds, he lived.

Mayor George Washington Collamore lived not far from the Griswold house. He was high on Quantrill's death list, and a bunch of bushwhackers surrounded his house right away, before he woke up. When he saw them, Collamore knew he had no way to escape. All he could do was hide and pray they would not find him. He dressed quickly and, together with Patrick Keith, his hired hand, headed downstairs and through the kitchen to the tiny well house connected to the back of the house. They lowered themselves to the bottom of the shaft and waited in the darkness for faces to appear in the circle of light far above them.

The raiders stormed through the house and demanded that

the mayor's wife, Julia, tell them where he was. Neither she nor her children told them anything, and they searched everywhere for him except the well. They were furious at not finding him and ransacked the house, stealing everything they wanted, then set the place on fire. They waited out on the lawn, hoping that if Collamore was hiding inside, the smoke would force him out.

The flames leapt higher, up to the roof, and spread to the back, to the kitchen and the well house. The walls and ceiling crashed down amid showers of sparks and flaming timbers, forcing heat and smoke into the well, suffocating both men. Well-aimed bullets would have brought easier deaths than waiting, trapped and helpless, below the surface of the earth while all the oxygen around them was sucked up into the sky and replaced by dense, gagging, choking clouds of smoke.

Later, after Quantrill's men left Lawrence and the fire burned down, the well claimed another life. Joseph Lowe, a friend of the mayor's, volunteered to bring up the bodies. No one could find any rope, because the fire had destroyed everything, and Lowe had to improvise with a length of thin cord. He tied it around his body and started down the well while two men held the cord from the top. He got about two-thirds of the way to the bottom, at which point he evidently reached the level of the toxic smoke. He tugged on the cord to signal the men above to haul him up, but they yanked the twine too sharply. It snapped, and Lowe fell to his death.

Arthur Spicer was terrified. He knew he should never have drawn attention to himself at the Eldridge House by reminding Quantrill that he had known him as Charley Hart. Although Spicer had never taken any action against Hart, his brother had been a law officer and more than once had tried to nab Hart. After Quantrill fixed Spicer with that menacing stare, Spicer managed to keep out of the guerrilla leader's way. He had begun to believe Quantrill had forgotten about him when two of the scruffiest bushwhackers came for him. They took him to Quantrill, who asked if his brother was in town. He was not pleased when Spicer said his brother was away, on duty with the Union army.

Quantrill turned to a squad of his men and told them to take Spicer with them as a guide, to help them find some of those on the death list. He added that if Spicer misled them in any way, they were to shoot him on the spot. If he did his job well, "they must bring him back unharmed as he had an account to settle with him and he wished to deal with him himself." Either way, the prospects for Arthur Spicer were none too bright.

The raiders took Spicer all over town, seeking out the homes of a number of prominent people, all of whom he knew. He dared not give the bushwhackers false information, and so he led them where they wanted to go. Fortunately for those on Quantrill's list whom these raiders were seeking, and perhaps for Spicer's conscience as well, no one he led the raiders to that day was found. They had all either escaped earlier or were so well hidden in their homes as to evade detection.

Still, Spicer's life remained in the balance virtually every minute. More than once, he heard the sounds of revolvers being cocked behind him. For two hours, he led them around the carnage taking place in Lawrence, until, finally, his end seemed certain. He got confused when they asked him where the powder magazine was. When they found it was not where he said it was, they pulled out their pistols again and took aim.

He was saved at the last second by George Todd, who cussed them out for almost killing him. Todd sent him to Nathan Stone's City Hotel, where Quantrill had made his headquarters. Quantrill had been there most of the morning, enjoying a hearty breakfast while his men carried out his private war against Lawrence, killing his real and imagined enemies. He met Spicer in front of the hotel and told him to wait inside. Spicer went in the front door and out the back. He never saw Charley Hart again.

The first name on Quantrill's death list—the man he hated more than any other, the first person Arthur Spicer was ordered to find—was Senator Jim Lane. He had been awakened when a black man—perhaps one of the recruits fleeing their camp downtown—ran past his house yelling that "the Secesh" were coming. Lane jumped out of bed, ran in his nightshirt to the front door, and pried his nameplate off while his wife and children searched for two guns he had hidden. Lane had hidden the weapons so well, they could not be found. In desperation, he grabbed his ceremonial saber, ready to repel all invaders.

He dropped the sword the instant he saw a squad of bushwhackers led by Arthur Spicer. Lane, barefoot and still in his nightshirt, leapt from a rear window and disappeared into a twelve-foot-high patch of corn behind his house. He raced through the sixty-acre field and ran for more than a mile, until he reached a farmhouse. The farmer, a short, fat man, gave him a pair of pants, which looked comical on the six-foot Lane, along with a shabby hat and an old pair of ill-fitting shoes. Lane made his way to another farm, where he was given an old plow horse. He loped slowly along on it to the southwest, spreading the alarm.

Lane's wife, Mary, opened the door to the raiders and told them politely that the senator was not at home. If they could not have Lane, then, by God, they would have his house, the finest in Lawrence, and everything in it. The home was beautifully furnished, most of the items stolen from homes in Missouri on Lane's Jayhawker raids. Now Missourians were taking revenge, and they relished the destruction, smashing china, mirrors, fine furniture, and the piano. They took the rings off the fingers of Mary and her daughter and announced they would burn the house to the ground. Jim Lane might live, but he would have no home to come back to.

They set fire to the house twice, lighting matches to the curtains and anything else that would burn, but each time Mary and her children put the blaze out. On the third try, the fire took hold, and Lane's family was forced to flee. The mansion was destroyed. Even with that, old Jim Lane was a lucky man. Had he been caught, Quantrill had reserved an especially horrible fate for him—nothing so easy as a bullet for the likes of Jim Lane. Two years later, when Quantrill lay dying, he revealed what he had planned for Lane that day.

"You want to know what would have been done with Jim Lane
had he been captured?" As Quantrill asked this question, his
eyes flashed fire, it seemed, his nostrils were distended, and although unable to move, he looked the fiend incarnate as he
almost hissed the answer between his clenched teeth: "I would
have burned him at the stake!"

Charles Robinson, the first governor of Kansas when it was still
a territory, was also lucky that day. Strongly pro-Union, the former agent of the much-hated New England Emigrant Aid Society survived to return to an intact house. He had left home at 4:45
that morning, a half hour before the raiders struck, to go to his
barn on Mount Oread. He planned to get his horses, then take
them over the river to cut hay. He stayed at the barn and watched
the sacking of Lawrence. Returning to town would have served
no purpose and probably would have cost him his life. And from
his vantage point high above the town, he could see that his
house was safe. It remained untouched because of the presence
of Lieutenant Ellis, who had replaced Lieutenant Hadley, and his
handful of soldiers sitting impotently across the river.

Robinson's wife, Sara, was at home, along with two guests,
Lizzie Leonard, just returned from a trip to Europe, and the
aging and ailing Gen. George Deitzler. Precisely at 5:15 in the
morning, the household was awakened when Robert, the general's hired servant, shouted a warning from outside.

"Quantrill has come!"

Everybody got dressed as fast as they could. Sara put on a pink
calico dress, while Lizzie packed her great steamer trunks and
pulled on a traveling dress and a bonnet, looking as if she was
ready to embark on another long journey. General Deitzler told
the housekeeper to leave the blinds closed and not to light the
fire in the kitchen. If the house looked unoccupied, perhaps the
bushwhackers would leave it alone.

They did not leave it alone. Two of them rode up to the back
of the house. From an upstairs window, the general tried to
steady his pistol to get off a good shot at the men, hoping to hit
at least one, but Sara would not allow it.

"Oh! don't," she pleaded.

Years later, writing about that day, she said Deitzler had often reminded her of that moment. "There might have been one bushwhacker less but for you," he would say. And she always answered, "And quite a number of other people likewise, with no roof over them."

They need not have worried. The location of their house, the last one on Massachusetts Street before the river, saved them. As soon as the raiders appeared at the rear of the house, Lieutenant Ellis's men, happy to have someone to shoot at finally, fired a volley at them. The guerrillas took off, never to return, and all of their comrades were careful to keep their distance from the river.

Peter Ridenour, Harlow Baker's partner in the grocery store, was awakened by the sound of gunshots a few blocks away. He and his wife, Sarah Louise, got dressed while more shots rang out. Ridenour suspected the worst: that a band of guerrillas had slipped past General Ewing's string of outposts and was attacking the town. The shooting continued and appeared to be spreading to other parts of Lawrence. Ridenour believed his neighbors must have gotten their guns and were fighting back. They would need help. He started for the warehouse where government-issue weapons were stored.

He had barely left his front porch when he saw George Bell. The county clerk, armed with a rifle, had rushed from his home on Mount Oread spoiling for a fight. Bell was about two blocks away. Ridenour followed him and watched as he suddenly dropped the rifle and ducked into an unfinished house with another man. A bushwhacker went in after them. A minute or two later, Ridenour saw Bell and the other man come out. They were shot down in cold blood by a gang of raiders who had just ridden up.

Ridenour wisely lost all thought of taking up arms against the raiders. He turned and ran to his house, spurred on by the sight of another killing. He saw his neighbor across the street, Bill Lamar, who was being pursued by several guerrillas, run to his house. Lamar started to climb over the fence into his yard but was hit before he reached safety. Ridenour saw Lamar fall over the fence. Then the raiders turned on him.

Ridenour bolted for the house and slammed the door, relieved that the guerrillas chose to pass on down the street rather than come after him. He and Sarah Louise talked over their situation and concluded they were in no real danger as long as they stayed indoors. The bushwhackers, they believed, were shooting only at those who ventured outside.

That complacent feeling changed when Mrs. Allen, a neighbor, knocked on the door. She said the raiders had searched her house, looking for men, and that they had told her they were killing every man they could find. She advised Ridenour to flee; if they found him, he was done for. No sooner had she said that than bushwhackers pounded on the front door. Ridenour slipped out the back and hid among the potato vines behind the house.

Sarah Louise told them her husband had gone east to buy goods for the store, so they contented themselves with taking her money and jewelry, then ordered her to cook breakfast for them. She refused, and they said they would return in a half hour. She left as soon as they did and went to the top of a hill two blocks away where a number of women had gathered. From there, she watched the gang return, carry out a lot of clothes and other valuables, and set fire to her house.

All the while, Ridenour lay among the potato vines, hugging the earth so closely "that a plantain leaf would have covered him." Several times, raiders peered over his backyard fence, and each time he was certain they had spotted him. But they rode away and he stayed there until the whole bunch left town at nine o'clock. He got up, surveyed the charred ruins of his house, then walked downtown and surveyed the charred ruins of his store. He had lost everything he owned, but at least he was alive.

George Holt and J. L. Crane owned a shoe store on Vermont Street, one block behind Massachusetts Street in the downtown business district. They lived in an apartment above the store and were awakened by the sounds of dozens of bushwhackers blast-

ing away with their revolvers. One band yelled up at them to surrender, but they made no reply, and the men rode on. Not long
after, a lone guerrilla returned and said that they would be safe
if they gave themselves up.

They agreed and were immediately robbed by the lone gun-
man, who ordered them into the street, where a second raider
appeared. The new man took charge and listened impatiently
when he was told the two had surrendered. What should he do
with them? the first man asked. They should be shot immediately
was the reply; "they had been in Missouri killing our people."
Holt protested that they had never harmed a soul in Missouri,
but they were shot almost before the words were out. Crane died
instantly; Holt lived, despite a bullet hole a half inch below his
right eye. The store and their home above it were looted and set
on fire.

Lemuel Fillmore, who lived near the ravine on the north side
of town, wanted to save his horse. He managed to lead it into the
brush before raiders showed up at his house. He should have
stayed hidden away with his horse, but instead, he went home,
got his gun, and headed toward the business district. Apparently,
he was intent on trying to save the town, but some bushwhackers stopped him and took away his gun.

They marched him toward Massachusetts Street, but as they
led him past the ravine with its thick belt of trees and undergrowth, one of his captors spoke to him quietly, as if he did not
want the others to hear.

"Now is your time to make your escape—now is your time to
run."

Fillmore darted for the nearest trees but got no farther than
a dozen yards before his captor shot him in the back.

In the western part of town, old Mr. Murphy stood in front of
his house, watching the excitement. A lone bushwhacker rode
up and asked him for a drink of water. Murphy went inside and
came back with a cup, which he handed to the rider. The guerrilla took the cup in his left hand and calmly shot the old man
with the gun in his right. No man was safe anywhere that morning.

THE BUSINESS DISTRICT was a roaring inferno. Two walls of flame enclosed Massachusetts Street like giant, flickering red fences. In the still morning air, each flaming building sent up its own column of thick black smoke like so many pillars supporting an overhanging pall of gray cloud.

Along the walks, almost every step, lay the dead; some bodies half burned up, other so crisped and blackened that their nearest friends could not identify them. Some had evidently been only seriously wounded and so disabled that they could not drag themselves from the vicinity of the burning buildings.

People had burned to death where they lay.

The Eldridge House, stripped of everything that could be carted away, was set on fire at several places on the ground floor. While the fires were being started, a woman screamed that a black baby had been left somewhere inside the building. The raiders did not even pause.

"Burn the God damn little brat," they said as they went on about their work.

In short order, fire was dancing as high as the roof, with sharp tongues of flame leaping from every window. For the second time in its life, the hotel was completely gutted. The courthouse burned down, taking with it all the county records. Denver's Ice Cream Saloon went, along with every other store in the district. The bushwhackers, festooned with stolen jewelry, rode up and down the streets, sweating in the heat of the flames, wearing new clothes pilfered from shops, drinking beer, fine wines, and champagne, smoking cigars, and gobbling down exotic foods.

Many of the merchants were dead by bullet or fire. A German man named Pollock who owned a clothing store, one of the array of fine shops in the hotel, had been robbed of all his merchandise and shot. Addison Waugh, a clerk who slept in Dr. Griswold's drugstore, had been ordered to open the safe. When he told the gunmen he could not, that Dr. Griswold had the only key, they told him to go and get it. A guard was sent along, but he was too impatient to wait. He shot the boy as soon as they left the store. His body was later found on the sidewalk, burned almost beyond recognition.

William Hazeltine lived next door above his small grocery store and bakery. He ran out the back, raced across Vermont Street, and headed toward the safety of the ravine while a half a dozen raiders behind him fired as they ran. Miraculously, he reached the trees untouched, then tripped and fell down the sloping hill to the bottom of the gorge. He was unhurt. His pursuers cheered when he fell, thinking they had hit him, and they went on their way.

Eldridge and Ford, the largest clothing store in town, was broken into early. Two boys who worked there, James Eldridge and James Perrine, both about seventeen, slept in the store. They were ordered to open the safe. When they explained that Mr. Ford had the only key, they were told their lives would be spared if they got it. Eldridge was taken to Ford's house, where he retrieved the key. Once the safe was emptied of its money, the boys were forced to wait on a steady stream of bushwhackers, outfitting them in the latest men's fashions. They worked frantically to please their customers and when they were done, when there were no more clothes to give away, they were shot and the store set on fire over their bodies.

The offices of the *Lawrence Tribune,* owned by John Speer, stood across the street from the Eldridge House. Speer and all three of his sons, the youngest only fifteen, were on the death list. John Speer, Jr., age nineteen, slept in the office along with two printers. Both of them made good their escape and lived, but John junior was not so lucky. He ran out the back door but got only a block away when he had the misfortune to meet the savage former Baptist minister, Larkin Skaggs.

Skaggs demanded his money, then shot the boy when he handed it over. John junior was still alive, though wounded so badly that he could not move, even when the heat from a building set afire only ten feet away became severe. He begged some passing guerrillas to move him, not to let him burn alive. They responded by shooting him dead and then walking on.

His father was at home on the east side of town when Quantrill's men came for him. He ran to safety in a nearby cornfield while his wife put out the fire the raiders set in their house. When the bushwhackers rode up, Speer's youngest son, fifteen-year-old Billy, had walked casually out the front door. One of the raiders stopped him and asked his name.

"Billy Smith," he said.

The guerrilla ran his eye down the list, found no one by that name, and allowed the boy to pass. He had not gone far when he decided it would be prudent to get out of sight. There were too many bands of men riding around town taking potshots at anyone they saw. He crawled beneath a wooden sidewalk and stayed there for a while, but he realized they would kill him for sure if they found him hiding.

He came out just as another band killed a man nearby and dismounted to burn down his house. If he ran, they would shoot him, so he offered to hold their horses while they torched the home. When they finished their work, they beat him badly, but he got away and later took his revenge on the man who had shot his eldest brother.

Speer's son Robert, age seventeen, worked as a printer for another newspaper, the *Lawrence Republican*. He and another printer slept in the offices and were there when it was burned down. Both were killed, but the fire was so intense that no trace of either body was ever found. His mother set a place for him at the dinner table for the rest of her life, hoping he would return.

While the business district was going up in flames, bands of bushwhackers continued to terrorize the residential areas. Many homes had already been torched, but there were more to burn, and more men to kill. Quantrill was not through with Lawrence yet.

Judge Louis Carpenter was a young man of prominence who lived on New Hampshire Street with Mary, his wife of less than a year, and his sister, Abigail. A number of guerrilla bands came to his house that morning, pounding on the door and demanding entry. Each group robbed and plundered, but none of them shot Carpenter or reached for their matches. It was his bearing that saved him, "his coolness and self possession, his genial manner and tact every time diverted them, and they left him unharmed and his house unburned."

He managed to turn away the wrath of every group that came to his house—except the last one. These raiders were drunk and were not deflected by his charm. They were out to kill. He greeted them as pleasantly as he had the previous groups, but they had no time for pleasantries. They asked him where he was from.

"New York," he replied.

"Oh it's you New York fellows who are doing all the mischief."

The man who spoke drew his gun, and Carpenter ran back inside the house as the bushwhacker fired wildly behind him. Carpenter ran upstairs, then came back down and made for the cellar. He was badly wounded by then, and blood formed in a pool at his feet as he pressed himself against the dirt wall.

The drunken raider started down the steps to the cellar. Carpenter drew on his last reserves of strength and ran out in the yard, where he was shot again. He collapsed to the ground and Mary threw herself over him to protect him with her body. The bushwhacker leaned down, pulled her arm away, "thrust his revolver under it, and fired so that she saw the charge enter her husband's head." Carpenter was not on Quantrill's death list. He had done nothing to provoke the men. His only crime was that he lived in Lawrence.

Edward Fitch lived a few blocks away from Judge Carpenter. He answered the pounding on his door and was shot the instant he opened it. Not a word had been spoken. He appeared to be dead, but just to make sure, one of the bushwhackers shot him seven more times. The gang raced through the house, taking what they wanted, then set it on fire.

His wife, Sarah, tried to drag his body away from the flames, but they would not let her. She reached for her husband's picture on the wall, but they stopped her again. She stood dazed, unable to move, remaining rigid, with her three children huddled around her as the fire spread. They might have all died there if one of the men who had started the fire had not dragged them outside.

> She then took her three little ones a short distance away, and sat down on the grass and watched the flames consume her husband who still lay in the doorway of his home. While she sat looking on, one of the ruffians went up to the door, and drew the boots off Mr. Fitch's feet, and put them on himself, and walked away.

Edward Fitch was not on Quantrill's death list, nor had he offered any resistance. The only apparent reason for the brutality displayed toward him and his wife was the presence out in back of a little toy Union flag his children had raised on top of a shed. They played underneath it, pretending to be Yankee soldiers. The flag was hardly bigger than a few inches square.

A man named Burt was in front of his house when a band rode up and demanded all of his money. He handed them what he had with him. One of the raiders took it in one hand and shot him with the other. A German man, Albach, was sick in his bed when the raiders stormed through his house. They told his family to take him outside because they were about to burn the place down. They carried him out into the front yard, mattress and all. When the bushwhackers had the fire going, they walked by the ailing Albach and shot him dead where he lay.

The Reverend Hugh Fisher was high on Quantrill's death list. Back in 1861, when Jim Lane led a band of Jayhawkers into Missouri, Fisher had gone along as a self-appointed chaplain. It is not known how much praying he did, but by all accounts he joined in the orgy of looting that took place when the Jayhawkers fell upon the town of Osceola. They broke open safes, plundered homes, shops, warehouses, and barns, and took enough wagons and carriages to carry their plunder back home to Lawrence. Osceola was set on fire and left a smoldering ruin, very much as Lawrence was now being left. The difference was that no one had been killed in Osceola.

So Fisher, like Jim Lane, had that to pay for, but he had also helped to relocate runaway slaves in Kansas and elsewhere and lured them away from their masters in Missouri. He was clearly a man who deserved to die, as far as Quantrill was concerned.

"Pa, get up!," Fisher's wife, Elizabeth, yelled about 5:15 that morning. "There is a company of soldiers coming into town. I believe it is Quantrill and his men!"

That got the minister's attention. He glanced out his bedroom window in time to see the Reverend S. S. Snyder shot while milking his cow, and he knew he was in trouble. He thought it best to get away from the house before Quantrill's men found him there. He talked it over with Elizabeth and decided to try to reach Mount Oread with their two older sons, ages ten and twelve. Elizabeth would stay at home with the three younger children, including a six-month-old baby.

Fisher did not get far before he knew he had made a mistake. He had been seriously ill with a throat infection that left him weak and unable to run far or fast. Then, too, as he looked up the hill to Mount Oread, he saw guerrillas every hundred yards or so on picket duty. He knew he could never get by them, even if he had been in good health. But the boys could. They were small enough to slip through the bushes and gullies, so he sent them on while he went back home.

His oldest boy, Willie, ran into a friend from school who happened to be wearing a blue shirt and pants his mother had made out of his father's old army uniform. One of the pickets spotted a figure in blue running, took aim, and shot him in the head. The boy was hit right next to Willie, "his brains and blood spattering in Willie's face, frightening him almost to death and so terrorizing him that he has never fully recovered his nervous vigor," the Reverend Hugh Fisher wrote thirty-three years later. Both of his boys escaped physical harm, though they were shot at several times before coming to rest in a cemetery two and a half miles away from town.

Fisher made it back to his house and hid in the small eight-by-fourteen-foot cellar he had dug himself. His wife told him to trust in the Lord and pray. He had to pray pretty fast, for a band of bushwhackers came in the house moments after he returned. They stood directly over his head and he heard every footstep and every word they said. They asked Mrs. Fisher if he was home.

"Do you think that he would be fool enough to stay about the house and you killing everybody you can? No, sir; he left with the little boys when you first came into town."

"I know a damned sight better," one of the raiders said, "he's in the cellar. Where is it?"

"The cellar is open," Mrs. Fisher said. "If you think he is there go look for yourselves."

She was taking a big gamble, hoping that by inviting them to check the cellar, by almost daring them to, they would conclude that her husband was not there. They called her bluff, however, and demanded a lamp. She gave them an oil lamp, then lied by saying they had ruined it by turning the wick down into the bowl of oil. It would take at least a half hour, she said, for the wick to dry out enough to light again, hoping they would lose interest with that long a wait in store.

They spent the time ransacking the house for valuables before one of them had the idea to ask for another lamp. It was upstairs, she told them, protesting that she could not get it and hold the baby at the same time. One raider took the baby carefully in his arms, made cooing sounds, and walked him around the room while waiting for a light so he could kill the child's father. Finally, Elizabeth could delay them no longer, and three of them started down the cellar steps, revolvers cocked, ready to shoot on sight.

Fisher crawled behind a loosely packed bank of dirt. His left foot shook so badly, he had to put his other foot on it to keep it still. All three bushwhackers crowded into the small, dark cellar. "I could see them plainly," Fisher said, "could even have reached over and touched the leader on the shoulder. But they did not see me and I was saved." The men went back upstairs to Mrs. Fisher, who had stood stock-still, with her baby pressed to one ear and her hand to the other to mask the shots and screams she expected to hear.

But now, Hugh Fisher faced a new danger. The raiders set the house on fire and left one man behind to make sure Elizabeth Fisher did not put it out. He offered to help her save anything of value, but she declined. If he really wanted to do something for her, she said, he could help her extinguish the fire.

"It would cost me my life to do that," he told her.

"If you can't help me put out the fire, just get on your horse and ride off, telling them that it was burning when you left and I'll soon put it out myself."

He agreed, but he warned her that others would come because her house was on the list of those to be burned. After he left, she managed to put out the fire, carrying bucket after bucket of water up to the second floor. No sooner had she done that, however, when three more raiders stormed into the house, made kindling of much of the furniture and shutters, and set a stronger blaze going. Two of them rode off, again leaving one behind to make sure the house burned down this time. This raider was drunk, and he swore he would kill her if she tried to put out the fire. Elizabeth Fisher slammed the door in his face and started filling buckets and pots and pans and anything else that would hold water.

She fought the fire until much of the second story collapsed. It was beyond anyone's control now, and the first floor was burning through to the cellar when she yelled to her husband to get out. He came up the steps to the blazing kitchen. His resourceful wife threw a dress over his head, then a carpet, and told him to stoop over and stay underneath the carpet as she dragged it outside.

She got him as far as a large bush and draped the carpet over it while he huddled beneath it. She and a neighbor woman retrieved some chairs and other items from the ruins of her home and piled them around the carpet. Four guerrillas watched with guns drawn but suspected nothing. Fisher stayed under the carpet while his wife stood guard until the bushwhackers finally left town.

Samuel Riggs, the local district attorney, left his house when the shooting started but was stopped out front by one of Quantrill's men on horseback. Mrs. Riggs ran to her husband's side as soon as she saw what had happened. When the raider raised his gun and took aim, Riggs knocked it aside and ran. The raider whirled around and galloped after Riggs. Mrs. Riggs "seized hold of the bridle rein and clung to it till she was dragged round a house, over a wood pile, and through the yard back on to the street again."

Riggs was not out of danger yet; he was still in the open, still an easy target. The guerrilla took aim and was about to squeeze the trigger when Mrs. Riggs grabbed hold of the other rein and spun the horse around, ruining his shot. She held on to both reins with all her strength, all the while being struck by the raider, until her husband was out of sight. The raider threatened to shoot her, but he did not, and her husband lived.

One woman, whose name has been lost to history, saved as

many as ten men. In the center of town, not far from the Johnson House, was a cyclone cellar, an underground shelter exca-
vated in the dirt, whose entrance was hidden by a patch of tall
weeds. The woman stationed herself not far from the entrance
and directed those being chased by bushwhackers into the
refuge. The guerrillas were puzzled at where the men had gone
and began to suspect she had something to do with their disap-
pearance. They pointed their guns at her and demanded she tell
them where the men were.

"Tell me or I will shoot you," one said.

She looked him in the eye and refused.

"You may shoot me if you will," she said, "but you will not find
out where the men are."

They were furious with her, but they could not bring themselves to shoot a woman, and they rode off, leaving her there to
save more lives.

Fred Read looked out an upstairs window when the raiders
came into Lawrence. He moved fast when a bullet hit the win-
dowsill not six inches from his right eye, then hid when the first
band of bushwhackers forced its way inside. There would be a
total of seven groups who invaded the Read house that day. The
home was set afire four times, and each time Mrs. Read put out
the flames.

The first band came for money and jewelry. They did not ask
where Read was; they had come only to steal. In the back of a bureau drawer, Larkin Skaggs found some gold and coral jewelry
that had belonged to the Reads' baby, who had died a few months
before. Mrs. Read begged him not to take the items. They were
the only reminders she had of her dead child.

"Damn your dead baby," Skaggs yelled, "she'll never need
them again."

The next bunch sliced open a mattress and put a match to it.
It was stuffed with hair, though, and would not burn, so they
threw some clothes in a pile, lit them, and left. Mrs. Read quickly
extinguished the blaze. Another group rode up to the house, but
this time only one man went in. He looked around—there was

not much left of any real value by then—and yanked the cover off of the piano.

"This is all I want, Madame," he said.

He took it outside, removed his saddle, and put the piano cover on his horse to serve as a saddle blanket. The next group was drunk, and the men demanded to know who had put the fire out. When Mrs. Read said that she had and would do it again, one of them grabbed her by her wrists while the others piled up bedclothes and books on a cotton lounge and set it afire.

The smoke got so thick, they had to go out on the porch, and they dragged Mrs. Read along and continued to hold her until the curtains caught on fire and flames leapt out from the top of the window.

"Damn you," one yelled at her, "you can have your home now, if you will put it out."

As soon as they left, she raced back into the fire and smoke-filled room, grabbed two pillows to protect her hands, and pushed the flaming window sash outside, saving her house once again.

The next group was led by someone whom she said behaved like an officer, and he asked where her husband was. When she told him he was back east on a buying trip, the raider asked where their store was. She pointed to a blazing drugstore nearby, which actually belonged to someone else. The man looked down at a sheet of paper he was carrying and told the others that what she had said about her husband was true. Someone from that store had gone east. Indeed, a clerk from the gutted store she had pointed to had done so weeks earlier, which showed how well informed Quantrill's men were.

Mrs. Read gestured to her ransacked and partially burned house and the wrecked store and said that she had been punished enough. The man agreed, ordered the others to leave her house alone, and remained outside for a half hour to keep other bands from stopping. Mr. Read stayed safely in his hiding place upstairs until after all of Quantrill's men left town.

* * *

The Bullene family lived not far from the Reads on New Hampshire Street. Mr. Bullene was in New York City buying goods for his store. When the raiders came, his wife and children and his wife's sister and invalid mother were at home. George Todd chose their house for his headquarters and ordered Mrs. Bullene to prepare breakfast for him and his men. In return, he promised their house would be spared. The women cooked all morning for one group after another, until their food was gone. One raider demanded a glass of milk and insisted they taste it first to prove it had not been poisoned.

Twice, when Todd was away, the guerrillas threatened to burn the house. Once, Mrs. Bullene begged them to help carry out her elderly mother before setting the place on fire. When they saw the old woman, they changed their minds and rode off. She persuaded a second group to leave by telling them Captain Todd had said the house was to be spared.

"In that case we will not burn it," the leader said. "We obey orders."

By the end of the day, the Bullene house was the only one in that part of town left standing.

Young Billy Bullene, playing in the front yard, unaware of the danger he was in, watched nine men die. One was John Speer, Jr. Billy also helped a man escape. A Union army recruiting office was located across the street, and the officer in charge found himself trapped there, in uniform, when Quantrill's men rode into town.

When they started burning stores, he knew he could not remain there, and it was equally clear he could not show himself in uniform. He stripped to his shirt and shorts and dashed across the street, dodging a hail of bullets. He reached the Bullene place, where Billy led him inside and gave him some women's clothes to put on.

A block away on New Hampshire Street, raiders carefully carried a piano out of the house, set it down in the yard, and returned to George Sargeant's house to set it afire. Sargeant and his wife, along with two other men who lived there, watched the flames consume their home. Another band of raiders rode by and shot into the group. One man was killed instantly; another, untouched, dropped to the ground and pretended to be dead. Sargeant was wounded.

Mrs. Sargeant fell to her knees beside him to shield him from further shots, begging the men to spare him. One guerrilla dismounted, steadied his revolver above her shoulder, and fired a ball into Mr. Sargeant's head. The shot was so close, it burned her neck. Her husband died of his wounds eleven days later.

John Bergen saved himself by burying his head beneath a corpse. He was one of several men who were gunned down together while fleeing the guerrillas. The others were killed, but Bergen pretended to be dead whenever a pack of guerrillas rode past. One bushwhacker saw he was still alive and took a shot at him. Bergen felt the ball go by. When the man rode off, Bergen burrowed under one of the bodies and lay still.

He remained there until the mother of the young man above him came out to retrieve her son's body. Quietly, he asked her to please leave her son's body alone; it was his only hope of living. She agreed, and he remained beneath the corpse until the bushwhackers left town.

Mr. Winchell, chased by several bushwhackers, dashed into the home of Dr. Charles Reynolds, rector of the Episcopal church. Reynolds was not home—he was serving as chaplain with the Union army—but his wife and two women friends were there. They reacted with speed, imagination, and daring when poor Winchell showed up. They shaved off his beard, wrapped a shawl around him, placed a frilly mobcap on his head, and pushed him into a chair beside a table littered with medicine bottles, cups, and spoons.

When a gang of Quantrill's men forced their way into the house, the ladies told them to take anything they wanted but to please be quiet so as not to disturb poor old Aunt Betsie, who was ailing and not long for this world. One of the ladies sat beside Aunt Betsie's chair, fanning her and looking the picture of concern. The men ransacked the house and, it was said, gave

Aunt Betsie several suspicious glances, but they left without disturbing her or burning down the house.

The Rankin cousins—John, a lieutenant, and Bill, a captain in the Union army—were home on leave, up before dawn to take a stroll. They had violated Mayor Collamore's edict and had their revolvers with them. When they turned a corner, they saw two horsemen shoot an unarmed man who was lying in a yard.

The Rankin men drew their guns and ran toward the raiders just as four others rode up behind the cousins. They all started shooting at once, until John and Bill had emptied their guns. Bill's last shot never left the barrel; a raider's bullet hit the muzzle of his gun as he fired. For some reason, perhaps because they did not like to deal with people who shot back, the bushwhackers rode away and the Rankins lived to return to the war.

There were other cases in which the guerrillas left people alone who fought back, or even threatened to. An old man, A. K. Allen, kept his revolver in his house, and he was ready to use it when four of Quantrill's men pounded on his door. They said they would kill everybody inside if they offered any resistance but that no one would be hurt if they all surrendered.

Mr. Allen, who lived alone, did not believe their assurances of safe passage. With his revolver cocked and ready, he shouted through the closed door for them to come and get him if they felt up to it.

"If you want anything of me, come where I am—I am good for five of you."

The bushwhackers thought better of it and rode off to find easier pickings. They apparently spread the word to others about that stone house down on Kentucky Street, because no one else approached Allen's home.

Lieutenant Ellis, whose men were camped over the river, lived on Massachusetts Street in a boardinghouse across from the stable. He was a law-abiding sort and had left his revolver in camp. So there he was, unarmed, dressed in a blue uniform, in a house that was surrounded. He realized there was no way to slip out of the place unseen and no possibility of staying there, either, as he watched one building after another set afire.

He figured he had only one chance. If he could get across the street and past the stable, he could find a hiding place among the tall weeds and old buildings. He ran out the front door of his boardinghouse and into the middle of a large column of raiders, catching them by surprise. "He grasped the bridles of their horses, whirled them around, dodged under their necks and rushed past them. The boldness of the move undoubtedly astonished the bushwhackers. They did not, however, forget to shoot."

Ellis got safely inside the stable, ran through the stalls, leapt atop one of the partitions, and pulled himself into the loft. Quantrill's men were right behind him, firing as they ran. They missed him but killed the horse in the stall beneath him. They ordered him to come down, insisting they would not harm him. Ellis found a short piece of wood, held it like a club, and yelled for them to come up and get him.

None of them was willing to do that, so they set fire to the stable and waited for the smoke and flames to drive him out. While they kept their guns on the openings along the top story, Ellis slipped down from the loft and made his way out the rear door to an overgrown garden across the street from Nathan Stone's City Hotel. He hid himself among the tangle of vines and reeds, counting seven bullet holes in his uniform.

Larkin Skaggs was among the worst of a bad lot. A cold-blooded killer, he had lost track of the number of men he had murdered that morning. The onetime servant of God had no room in his heart for compassion or mercy or remorse for his victims. He was a rough, fearsome bear of a man, large, muscular, and powerful, with long unkempt hair and a scraggly beard. He was vicious and cruel at the best of times, and liquor intensified his savagery.

He swaggered into Nathan Stone's hotel, where his gaze settled on Stone's daughter, Lydia. But it was not her appearance that caught his attention; it was her large diamond ring, which

Quantrill had given her three years before. He strode over to her and pulled it off her finger without a word.

She said nothing—anyone could tell by looking at Skaggs that that would not be wise—but she told Quantrill about it when he returned to the hotel. Quantrill found Skaggs threatening the prisoners from the Eldridge House and had a few words with him. Even in his drunken state, Skaggs knew better than to argue with Quantrill, and he sullenly returned the ring to Lydia Stone.

"I'll make you rue this," Skaggs told her.

John Thornton hid upstairs when the bushwhackers came to his house. His wife, Nancy, put out the first fire they set, but she was dragged outside when the home was set aflame a second time. She could do nothing but watch and think of her husband being burned to death as the fire raced up to the second floor. Thornton stood it as long as he dared, then ran downstairs and outside, where the raiders were waiting for him.

The first three bullets struck him in the hip, but he kept on running. The fourth bullet hit him in the head, and the fifth struck behind his shoulder, passing all the way down his back and exiting at the hip. He fell to the ground. Nancy ran to him and shielded him with her body. One of the raiders stood over her, looking for a chance to shoot him again. Finally, he managed to get his revolver between the two of them, and he shot Thornton through the face. But he was still alive, which infuriated the bushwhacker.

"Damn your Kansas hide," he yelled. "I can kill you another way."

He beat Thornton over his head with the butt of his gun time and time again until he was exhausted. He turned his gun around, ready to shoot Thornton again, but Nancy pushed it aside and shrieked at him to leave her husband alone, that he was already dead. The man got back on his horse and rode away, looking for more victims, more unarmed men like John Thornton to kill.

But Thornton was still alive, despite six bullets and repeated blows to his head. He lived on for many years, crippled and in great pain. Doctors had to leave two of the bullets in his hip joints.

Otis Lonley was a quiet, peaceful, kindly man of sixty years who lived with his wife on a little farm a mile southwest of town. He had remained neutral in the border wars, being neither for nor against slavery. He got along well with everyone, regardless of their views on that explosive issue. But his age, manner, and neutrality were no help when two of Quantrill's pickets stationed outside of town came to his house. They had their guns drawn and they talked of death. Mrs. Lonley begged them to show some mercy, some pity.

"We are old people," she said, "and cannot live long at the best."

They answered her by shooting down her husband in front of her. He collapsed to the ground but was still alive, and so they kept shooting him until he died. Then they set fire to the house, but Mrs. Lonley put it out after they left.

The difference between life and death was often a random thing, as unpredictable as where a twister will touch down, destroying one house and leaving its neighbor unharmed. A fraction of an inch in the passage of a bullet, a stone house with closed shutters, a cornfield next door, a safe hiding place where prying eyes or groping fire could not reach, a determined wife, even a raider with a streak of compassion buried deep but not yet extinct could make the difference. On the basis of such vagaries, some died and some saw the sunrise the next day and lived on to wonder why they had been spared when so many others had died, and to experience the joy, the exultation, and the guilt at having survived.

The Reverend Richard Cordley walked quietly through the streets of Lawrence with his wife and child and a friend. No one shot at them or stopped them and they got as far as the tall reeds along the riverbank. Cordley looked across the river and must have felt as if he beheld a miracle. There, on the opposite bank, was an old friend. The man gathered up his courage and rowed a little skiff over, thus saving the lives of the Cordleys and their friend. Not even the soldiers on the far bank had tried to cross the river. But the man who knew Cordley and who had happened to look across the river at the same instant the minister glanced over did.

Another man whose name is unknown sat quietly outside, in plain view, holding an umbrella over the heads of his wife and child to protect them from the hot sun. How many bushwhackers rode by them that morning and did not rob or kill him? Why were they left alone and the family a block away or two houses down assaulted and their lives changed forever? What was there about them? Was it the sheer ludicrousness of the picture they presented, the father holding an umbrella over his family while bullets flew everywhere? There is no answer, but they were not touched.

A woman tacked a piece of cardboard on her front door with the word SOUTHERN printed on it in large letters, and nobody pounded on her door. Survival could be that simple. A man paid a band of bushwhackers one thousand dollars to spare his life and his house; both were intact at the end of the day. Another man paid the same amount; the guerrillas took his money and honored the bargain, but another bushwhacker came along and shot him dead.

Some men hid in a large cornfield west of town. Bands of raiders rode up to the edge of the field, but none ventured in. A woman who lived nearby carried water to the men; she said it was the hottest place she could ever imagine being in. Presently, a bushwhacker asked her what was out there in the cornfield.

"Go and see," she said, "and you will find it the hottest place you were ever in."

She meant it literally, but the raiders thought she meant that the field was dangerous, that armed men were hiding there. None of the guerrillas dared probe the cornfield, and every man hiding there survived, all because of a misunderstanding.

A man was shot as he ran from a gang of raiders and fell into a gutter. As the killers rode away, his wife screamed and knelt beside him.

"Don't take on so, wife. I don't know as I am hit at all," he said. He was right.

Cole Younger killed more men than he could remember, but on at least two occasions he saved lives. Rampaging through one house, he found a man hiding in a closet and pulled him out.

"Please don't kill him," his wife pleaded. "He has asthma."

The news evidently startled Younger.

"Has asthma?" he asked.

"Yes," she said. "He has it so bad that he hasn't slept in a bed for nine years."

"I wouldn't kill anyone with asthma," Younger said, and he left the man untouched.

He entered another house with three other raiders and found three elderly men, long past the age of military service. The others were ready to kill them, but Cole Younger ordered the raiders out of the house. Before he left, he assigned a man he trusted to guard the place to keep anyone else from going inside. Then he went down the street to find others to kill.

There were other acts of kindness. Not all of Quantrill's men were as savage as he had ordered them to be. A few did not rob or plunder, burn or murder. Stories later emerged of raiders who allowed women to save their valuables before their houses were set on fire. Others helped women carry out treasured pieces of furniture.

Some expressed regret and apologized for burning houses, saying they would be punished if they failed to follow orders. Some were dazzled by the trappings of wealth and could not bring themselves to despoil such splendor and opulence. And a few told men to hide, lest some other raider find them and kill them. Once or twice, a bushwhacker discovered a man shaking in a closet or behind a couch or in a cellar, then moved on, saying nothing to his comrades, who were searching for the man. Two young guerrillas showed one Lawrence family their revolvers, proudly pointing to the caps that showed no signs of powder soot on them. They had refused to fire their weapons all morning.

There is no evidence that Quantrill fired his weapons. There are no reports of Quantrill killing anyone, or burning down a house, or robbing any resident. Perhaps he preferred the image of military leader, no longer a murderer or common thief, as the people of Lawrence had known him before the war. In his own mind, he was no longer Charley Hart, wanted outlaw, but a respected captain of the Partisan Rangers. Or was it colonel? While he gave the orders that led to such brutality and rode around town in his stolen buggy, watching his men commit atrocities, he evidently committed none himself.

Gordon Grovenor was shot at twice from only ten feet away, but both times the raider's gun jammed. Several other raiders rode up and their leader told the first bushwhacker to stop shooting. Grovenor had no idea why his life was spared or why the leader then instructed him to hide. He did as he was told, remaining in the cellar of his house, beneath the kitchen, while the rest of the place was burned down.

The guerrillas ordered Mrs. Grovenor to draw water from the well for them and their horses. One man dismounted, took the bucket from her, and volunteered to do it, saying it was too hard a job for a lady. While he was winching up the bucket, he told her he had no idea the raid on Lawrence would become so brutal.

"They told me they were only coming up to recover some stolen horses," he explained to Mrs. Grovenor. "I have not killed a man nor burnt a house yet, and I do not mean to."

Col. John Holt of the Confederate army, who had brought his 104 recruits with Quantrill to christen them in battle, took no part in the killings. He spent most of the morning at the home of Henry Clarke, to the relief of Clarke, who had been robbed earlier by two of Quantrill's men and had seen Judge Carpenter killed. When Colonel Holt appeared, Clarke offered him breakfast, hoping the colonel's presence would save both his life and his house.

At first, Holt was suspicious, and he ordered Clarke to eat some of the food to prove it was not poisoned. The colonel ate on horseback at the front gate, and the sight of him enjoying his breakfast prompted other bushwhackers to stop. Before the food ran out, Mrs. Clarke fed twenty men. The last one complimented her on how tasty her cold potatoes were; by then, that was all she had left.

A guerrilla rode by and aimed his revolver at Clarke, but Holt ordered the man not to shoot. When the colonel finally departed, he told Clarke's wife and sister to keep Clarke indoors, for he would surely be killed if he stayed outside. Years later, Clarke and Holt corresponded about that morning when the colonel saved Clarke's life.

Such acts of kindness were few. More typical was what happened to Dan Palmer and his friend. Palmer was a gunsmith who owned a shop at the end of the business district, so small that the raiders ignored it. When the shooting and burning had all but ended, Palmer and his friend stood in the doorway, looking at the ruins of their city.

A band of guerrillas on their way out of town spied the two men. The bushwhackers were drunk and decided to have one more bit of fun. They shot Palmer and his friend, wounding them both. They dismounted, set fire to the shop, bound the men together with rope, and threw them into the burning building. Palmer and his friend got to their feet, still bound together, and hobbled outside, shouting for mercy. The bushwhackers laughed and tossed them back into the inferno. As the flames burned through the rope, Palmer struggled to his feet. "Oh God, save us!" he screamed. "He raised his hands above his head, and as the flames wrapped him in a sheet of fire he sank back, on his face a look of indescribable agony." The raiders cheered as Palmer's shrieks died away, then mounted their horses and rode on, laughing as they trotted down the street.

At nine o'clock in the morning, one of Quantrill's lookouts on Mount Oread spotted a column of men in blue. It was Maj. Preston Plumb, General Ewing's chief of staff, with thirty troopers. They had been riding hard for eight hours since leaving Kansas

City at one o'clock in the morning. Seven miles behind them, too far to be seen from Mount Oread, Capt. Charles Coleman led the incompetent Capt. Joshua Pike and 180 men, following Quantrill's trail. Coleman had left his border outpost at Little Sante Fe at nine o'clock the previous night.

The lookout raced down the hill and reported the sighting to Quantrill, who summoned Bill Gregg and the other officers. He ordered Gregg to stay behind in Lawrence with twenty men to round up stragglers. Quantrill looked around and picked out a big white house on a hill, beyond the Wakarusa River. That would be their rendezvous. He would wait there for Gregg for one hour, no more.

Quantrill rode to the City Hotel to say good-bye to his friend Nathan Stone. He said he hoped they would meet again in happier times. He added that the women of Lawrence had been brave that day, but the men had been cowards. Then he rode away, leading his men south out of Lawrence.

Gregg had some difficulty rounding up the stragglers, most of whom were roaring drunk. When he was sure he had them all—or at least as many as he was willing to take the time to find, what with the Yankees getting closer by the minute—he headed for the big white house on the hill.

One man remained in town, Larkin Skaggs, smarting over Quantrill's order to return the diamond ring to Lydia Stone. He had warned her she would be sorry she had told Quantrill. Now it was payback time. Skaggs rode up to the City Hotel with both guns drawn.

"All you God damned sons of bitches come in front! Come right out here!"

A number of the hotel's residents and guests filed out, though many, including Lydia Stone, hid inside or ran out the back door. Skaggs ordered them to form two lines, women on one side, men on the other. He asked one man where he was from. Ohio was the answer. Skaggs opined that Ohio was even worse than Kansas, and he shot him.

He fired several shots into the hotel lobby, which brought Nathan Stone out to protest that Quantrill had pledged protection. Skaggs shot him in the stomach, killing him.

Skaggs wheeled his horse around, swaying in the saddle as he did so, and rode out of town, so drunk that he headed in the wrong direction. It was not until he saw some farmers approaching that he realized his mistake. He turned and raced back to Lawrence.

Billy Speer, age fifteen, had returned home to his weeping mother, who told him his brothers John and Robert were missing. She gave him an old rifle and begged him to kill any bushwhackers he could find. The first one Billy saw was Skaggs. Billy hid behind a hedge, poked his rifle barrel through the leaves, took careful aim, and fired. The shot struck Skaggs in the shoulder, toppling him off his horse.

White Turkey, the Delaware Indian who had once faced down Charley Hart over a stolen pony, watched Skaggs fall.

"Him kill everybody," he said. "Me kill him." And he shot Larkin Skaggs through the heart.

Some townspeople ran up and tied a rope around Skaggs's neck. Led by a black man singing "John Brown's Body," they slowly dragged Skaggs through town. A crowd gathered behind, tossing stones at the corpse as it was hauled off to the park. A group of former slaves tried, unsuccessfully, to burn it. The body was stripped and thrown naked into a ravine, where it rotted for several months. Boys cut the rings off the fingers and were none too careful about it. Larkin Skaggs, Baptist minister in his better days, was never buried.

Ten miles south of Lawrence, a gang of bushwhackers rode up to a farmhouse and ordered the women to cook them breakfast. Old Mr. Rothrock, who owned the farm, did not think he was in danger, so he remained in the house, making no attempt to hide. While the raiders were eating his food, they asked the women who the old man was. A Dunkard preacher, they said.

"Oh," one guerrilla said, "we intend to kill all the damned preachers."

They shot Rothrock several times, finished their meal, and rode off. Rothrock was the last man killed in the Lawrence raid.

12

LET US FOLLOW THEM, BOYS

Down the Fort Scott Road they came. Some were riding fresh mounts and leading their old, while most made do with the same poor beast that had brought them [to Lawrence]. Many were drunk and reeling. All were very tired. And all had some form of plunder either hanging from saddle horns or strapped on packhorses—boots, shoes and coats, fancy lace shawls, bolts of cloth, silverware, tea services, picture frames, clocks, gadgets of all kinds, even ladies' sidesaddles. Most wore new hats, shirts, and trousers. Many had pockets stuffed with paper, jewelry, and gold. All had a share according to his taste.

They crossed the Wakarusa River, waited for Bill Gregg and his men to catch up, then headed south, kicking up an enormous cloud of dust that followed them relentlessly, like a giant finger pointing accusingly from the clear blue sky. Outriders on both sides of the main column set fire to everything that would burn—homes, barns, dry crops, and stored grain. Slivers of black smoke formed a broad border on both sides of their dust-cloud trail.

They stopped in the tiny town of Brooklyn, twelve miles south of Lawrence. The place was deserted; the residents had fled when farmers to the north came running, spreading the news that Quantrill was coming. Quantrill stopped to figure out the best escape route. He thought it wise not to go due east, back the way they had come. Surely, the Yankees would be swarming all over the border region by now, expecting them to come that way.

He decided to head southeast, toward Osawatomie and the deep, tangled forests along the Marais des Cygnes, where no large body of troops could ever hope to track them. From there, he would lead them due south until he had gotten so far ahead of any pursuers that he could safely cross back over into Missouri. And he would leave a trail of destruction along the way. By God, the people would know that William Clarke Quantrill had come through. They would tremble at the mention of his name for as long as they lived.

Burn everything, he told his men. Spread out and leave a path of fire and destruction a mile wide and fifty miles long. Leave nothing standing. The men cheered, then began setting fire to Brooklyn when someone noticed a cloud of dust closing on them from the north. Quantrill had no idea of who it was or how large was the force, and he was not about to stay around to find out. He ordered his men to saddle up and move out.

The rapidly approaching dust cloud was raised by Senator Jim Lane and a ragtag force of thirty-five farmers, clerks, and boys. Lane, dressed in a faded borrowed shirt and ridiculously short pants, was mounted on an old mare with no saddle. He had come dashing into Lawrence with about a dozen farmers not long after Quantrill had left. He took one look at what was left of his city and called for volunteers to hunt Quantrill down.

"Let us follow them, boys," he yelled. "Let us follow them."

About a dozen of the dazed survivors in Lawrence went with him, and he picked up more men on his way south. It was a motley, almost comical posse. If Quantrill's men could have seen them then, they would have had a good laugh before cutting them down.

Some rode mules. Others tried to keep up on worn-out horses Quantrill's men had abandoned in Lawrence, or on broodmares, whose colts ambled along after them. A few lucky riders had saddles; others rode bareback. None of them had a decent weapon, only shotguns, squirrel rifles, obsolete muskets, cumbersome .26-caliber pepperbox pistols. A few had no guns at all, only knives. But they rode as fast as their sorry nags could go, and they caught up with the last of Quantrill's men lingering and looting in Brooklyn.

The bushwhackers did not stay when they saw Lane's men approaching the town. They lit out without firing a shot and caught up with the main body of guerrillas. Lane watched them ride four abreast cavalry-style down the Fort Scott Road. He stopped briefly in Brooklyn to figure out what to do next. He knew it would be madness to attack a force ten times larger than his own, so he decided to stalk them and wait for reinforcements. There had to be militia and home guard outfits out looking for Quantrill, along with regular army units. Sooner or later, they would show up, and Lane would be there to lead them.

He sent a man back to Lawrence to round up more riders, guns, and ammunition. He chose Lt. John Rankin, one of the two cousins home on leave when Quantrill struck, to lead the men south. Lane told them to keep on the guerrillas' left flank and to stay close enough to keep them in sight, but not so close as to be caught in a gunfight. Lane's only hope was to join up with some larger unit farther down the road. But in the meantime, his and Rankin's persistence in trailing Quantrill's men kept them from setting any more fires.

Several miles behind Lane's makeshift army, Maj. Preston Plumb raised his own small dust cloud with the thirty troopers he had led out of Kansas City at one o'clock that morning. They had reached Olathe at dawn, where they were told by the residents that Quantrill had passed through at midnight, heading toward Lawrence. Plumb glanced toward the west and was appalled to see a giant thunderhead of black smoke boiling up into the sky.

"Quantrill is in Lawrence," he shouted, and he led his men toward the distant smoke.

They rode as hard as the horses would permit. At 10:30, they saw a larger band of riders in the distance and quickly closed with them. It was Captain Coleman and his 180 men, along with Captain Pike. Coleman had been riding for over thirteen hours, since leaving his border outpost at Little Sante Fe at nine o'clock the previous night. The two forces joined along the Wakarusa River, some six miles southeast of Lawrence.

Plumb took command of Coleman's outfit and considered his next course of action. The sky was still black over Lawrence, but there were also columns of smoke rising from the south away from town. Obviously, Quantrill had left Lawrence, and Plumb decided to try to intercept him before he could get back over the border into Missouri, providing their exhausted horses did not give out first.

By one o'clock, Plumb's command had covered eight miles, still following the trail of smoke. The men grabbed whatever food and water they could from farmers grateful to see them. Some horses dropped dead in their tracks, others were obviously weakening, but Plumb pushed his column onward, tracking Quantrill on the guerrilla leader's right flank, west of the Fort Scott Road.

Lane and his men were opposite Plumb on Quantrill's left flank. Neither Lane nor Plumb knew of the existence of the other force until a farmer told Lane that a large body of cavalry led by Major Plumb was no more than a half mile away. The impulsive Lane decided this could be his moment of glory. He would attack.

What he did was order Lieutenant Rankin to attack. A good general, after all, had to be in command of all his men, not just those at hand but also the ones in blue across the way. Lane was not about to let anyone forget—certainly not a mere major—that he had been a major general in the Free State Militia. He told the farmer to carry an order to Major Plumb.

"Tell Major Plumb, Quantrill is just on the other side of this cornfield. We will attack him at once. Tell him to come forward as quickly as possible."

Rankin led his men—no one knows how many there were—

on a mad charge. His horse was the best of the lot, and he galloped far out in front of the others. Their mules and tired nags could not keep up. When he had ridden a half mile, Rankin turned in his saddle and discovered that he was alone. The others were a quarter of a mile behind. Deciding that this was not a good idea, the lieutenant turned around and headed back.

Quantrill had seen the Yankees gaining on him, and he stopped for a moment to ponder his situation. One thing was clear: He was not about to stand and fight, not knowing the size of the enemy force. And who knew how many more might be coming up on the heels of those he could see? He spotted a narrow trail leading through a cornfield off the Fort Scott Road and ordered his men to head that way.

They lightened their loads, throwing away much of their plunder, and headed through the field. Quantrill told George Todd to take sixty of the best men and fight a rear-guard action while the rest got away.

Jim Lane rode over to Major Plumb's outfit and announced that he would take command of the operation. Plumb refused, not about to be outranked by some general of militia. The two men shouted insults at each other, Lane showering the major with an impressive set of expletives. The troops looking on were amused; it was always good fun to watch officers battle each other. But while they were yelling, Quantrill was getting away.

Major Plumb ordered Captain Coleman to charge the rear of Quantrill's column with two companies, while he led the rest of the men south to try to cut the guerrillas off at Ottawa Creek. Jim Lane tagged along after Plumb, still arguing for command of the outfit but being ignored by the exasperated major. Coleman led his men down the road, followed by an enthusiastic group of farmers and local militia that had been following behind Plumb's command. They passed Lieutenant Rankin as he headed back from his solitary charge against Quantrill. The intrepid lieutenant whirled his horse around and galloped after them.

Up ahead, on the Fort Scott Road, George Todd and the sixty men of his rear guard saw the Federals riding hard their way. He called to his men: "Boys, let down those rail fences, part of you go up one side through the corn and part of you follow me right up the lane and by God we'll charge them! We've got to check them or the whole outfit is lost!" They tore down the fence and raced toward the approaching troopers.

Lieutenant Rankin caught up with the charging Union cavalry as they ran headlong into the bushwhackers. In the first volley, the Yankees suffered heavy casualties.

Todd's horse, with the unlikely name of Sam Gaty, was hit, but Todd fell clear of him. He stood up and stripped off the luxurious blue uniform coat he had taken from Captain Banks, the Union officer who had surrendered the Eldridge House. He did not want to be mistaken for a Yankee by his own men. It was not until after the fight that Todd remembered the stolen four thousand dollars he had stuffed into one of the coat pockets.

Lieutenant Rankin tried to rally the troopers.

"Throw the fence and charge," he called. "Throw the fence and charge."

The men jumped from their horses, tore apart the rail fence, and prepared to fire. Before they could get off a volley, Todd's men came swooping down on them, firing their big Navy Colt revolvers and shouting that terrifying, spine-tingling rebel yell. The Union horses stampeded, and their riders were not far behind. The Union line broke, and the men ran back the way they had come. It was a rout. They tore madly through the tall corn, with Todd and his men close behind, yelling and firing like demons with four to eight revolvers apiece.

Jim Lane was out there in the cornfield, having hurried ahead of Plumb when the major turned his men toward the sounds of battle. Lane found himself alone, facing the guerrillas, unaware of the panic that had gripped the men behind him. He zigzagged through the field, ducking his head, hunching and running as fast as he could.

The bushwhackers stopped the chase and pulled back when they saw Plumb's command ride up. The fleeing troops saw them, too, and they stopped running when they reached the rail fence where they had entered the field with so much confidence. Not a man had been hit during the retreat, but many were badly scratched from the tall corn. They were a lot less confident than they had been five minutes before. When they looked back through the field of damaged corn, they saw Todd's men, safely out of range, laughing and taunting them, "waving their hats mockingly in the air."

The pursuit of Quantrill and his army continued the rest of the day.

"The sweating bodies of the raiders ached with fatigue, their faces were grimy with dirt and smoke. An intense physical and emotional letdown had set in after the wild excitement of the massacre. The only thing that kept many of them going was fear of capture and desire to reach Missouri and safety." They were wilting under the broiling August sun. There was no relief from it, or from the hunger and thirst that was weakening their bodies, or the physical exhaustion that threatened to lower their alertness. "It really looked as though we were doomed," Bill Gregg wrote. "The whole earth was 'blue' behind us."

Major Plumb's men were not in much better shape. Most had been in the saddle since the night before, and they, too, were parched and hungry. Their horses were exhausted, able to move no faster than a slow walk. There was no way the command could keep up with Quantrill. But shortly after the battle in the cornfield, eighty fresh men and horses arrived to join the chase. They were farmers mostly, boiling mad when they heard about the massacre at Lawrence, along with a militia company from the town of Black Jack. They might not have been as well trained as the troopers, but they were fresh and rested, and so were their horses.

One of Plumb's officers, Lt. Cyrus Leland, Jr., was granted permission to take those eighty men, plus about the same number of troopers whose horses were in relatively better shape than the others, and go after the bushwhackers. Leland argued that if they kept after them constantly, harassing them and forcing their rear guard to stop and fight, they could keep them from burning any more homes or towns.

A monotonous rhythm of attack and defense developed. Leland's men charged and Todd's weary band held them off in brief firefights. Four raiders were killed. The nasty little battles always ended when Plumb and the main Yankee force rode into view. Then, the rear guard rode off to catch up with Quantrill and form a new defensive line, while the rest of the bushwhackers continued south.

Both the rear guard and the main force of guerrillas stayed intact, displaying a remarkable degree of discipline for a gang of bushwhackers on the run. Only one man, Joab Perry, panicked. At four o'clock that afternoon he fled, "his long hair standing out in the Kansas breeze."

Some of the men wanted to kill him, while others said "no, he will get it soon enough," but he made it through to Missouri unscathed so far as bullets were concerned. However, he was horseless, bootless, coatless, and with only one revolver out of six, the remainder of his clothing torn into shreds, his flesh terribly mutilated by brush and briar.

At 5:00 p.m., Lt. Col. Charles Clark reached the town of Paola, thirty-five miles south of Lawrence. Clark had ridden more than fifty miles since leaving Coldwater Grove at three o'clock that morning. When Clark reached Gardner during the night, he learned that he was a good half day's ride behind Quantrill. Realizing there was no hope of catching up with Quantrill, he decided to try to cut off his escape route, which he guessed, correctly, would be due south through the forests of the Marais des Cygnes.

When Clark reached Paola, he found the townspeople alerted and armed. He also learned that Quantrill was less than five miles away and heading for town. He established a defensive position on Paola's western edge and set a trap for the bushwhackers along a creek where he figured they would stop to water their horses. Since it was the first creek the raiders would encounter in many miles, there would be no way to keep the horses from plunging into the water. Clark told his men to hold their fire until the rebels were in the middle of the creek, trapped in their saddles on horses parched from the long day's ride.

Quantrill halted his men along the top of a ridge close by the summit of Big Hill. The ridge sloped to the creek where Clark's men were waiting. Not far behind, Lt. Cyrus Leland, his force down to forty men, the rest having dropped out from exhaustion, drove forward. He saw soldiers in Paola in the fading light of dusk and decided that if he attacked Quantrill now, the fresh troops would come to his aid.

Leland's band drove in Quantrill's rear guard toward the main body of bushwhackers. Quantrill saw him coming. He knew about the troops in Paola, and he also knew that he had to take drastic action to stop his pursuers. If he could beat back this attack, the Yankees would not have enough time to launch another before dark. If he could last another half hour or so, then there was a good chance they could make it back to Missouri.

"Halt!" Quantrill shouted. "Face about!"

His men waited in silence until Leland and his troops were no more than sixty yards away.

"Steady men," Quantrill said. "Charge!"

Leland's force dismounted and held their ground for all of ten minutes. The raiders, ten times their number, forced them to fall back. As soon as the federal line broke, Quantrill halted his charge and led his men south as fast as his horses could take them.

Clark's men waited at the ambush site as dusk settled over the creek. They waited for an hour after the sounds of gunshots faded away. Finally, one of their scouts returned with the news that Quantrill was on his way. Moments later, they heard hundreds of horses approaching. As soon as the parched horses smelled the water, they stampeded to the creek. They smashed through the undergrowth, with their riders cursing but unable to rein them in until they plunged into the water and stopped to drink.

The officer in charge was about to give the signal to open fire on the mass of horses and riders trapped in the water below. He stopped when he heard a familiar voice.

"Is that you, Plumb?" he called.

It was, indeed, Major Plumb and his command, a second or two from annihilation. Quantrill had bypassed the ambush site and was now several miles beyond it. The two Union forces rode into Paola, where Colonel Clark assumed command of the pursuit, which immediately ground to a halt for the night.

Clark would not be moved. As General Ewing later wrote in his official report of the operation, "He was slow in ordering pursuit." The little town of Paola was overrun with armed men. More than one thousand soldiers, militia, and citizens lighted fires for dinner and laid down to sleep wherever they could find room. Major Plumb and his men were worn-out. They had been riding nineteen hours and had covered more than seventy miles without pause for rest or food. Many of their horses had broken down, and all were in such bad condition that most died within the next two days. Captain Coleman's outfit had ridden more than one hundred miles and had been in the saddle for over twenty-four hours. Neither unit could expect to keep moving without rest.

However, other outfits, particularly the local militias, were rested and ready to ride, and they grew restless as evening turned to night and no orders were given. At 1:00 A.M., scouts rode into town with news that Quantrill was camped only five miles away. Word spread through town in minutes, and the militia units assembled their gear and prepared to move out.

When the officers went to Colonel Clark for orders, he told them to stay put. The officers were stunned and angry. Intemperate words were exchanged, but Clark was adamant. He refused to break camp until his regular army units had more rest. The militia commanders argued that the guerrillas would surely escape if they did not leave now, but Clark refused. His army would not march until he decided it was ready.

Some men offered to go ahead on their own to confront Quantrill, but Clark would not permit it, and when a new unit arrived in town, he told the men to unsaddle their horses, stack

their arms, and get some rest. It began to look as if they were settling in for a long stay.

While the Yankees slept, Quantrill's men were on the move.
After the battle at Big Hill, Quantrill led them east to Bull Creek.
The sanctuary of the Marais des Cygnes was not far on the other
side, but Quantrill chose to go several miles north to cross the
creek. Perhaps he suspected that the Federals would be waiting
for him on the other side, believing he would go that way. After
Quantrill crossed the creek, they made camp and stopped to
rest. That was the camp Clark's scouts had found, but by midnight it was deserted, well before the scouts reached Paola with
the news.

Quantrill's men had to be forced to get up. Stuporous from
lack of sleep, they reeled like a bunch of drunks. They had been
in the saddle a lot longer than their pursuers, and Quantrill
knew they could not afford the luxury of more rest. They
mounted up and rode east, and Quantrill told them they would
stop for nothing until they crossed the border into Missouri. He
expected to be there not long after daybreak.

Colonel Clark finally resumed the chase at three o'clock on
the morning of August twenty-second, a full ten hours after setting up camp in Paola. There was no denying that the rest was
much needed, particularly by Coleman's and Plumb's com-
mands, but the stop put them so far behind Quantrill that they
had no chance of catching him. Still, they had to try. Captain
Coleman departed first with a force of 140 men, regulars and
militia. He led them north until he found the bushwhackers'
trail, then turned east and headed toward Missouri. Clark left
Paola a little later with the rest of the men. Other units, including some from Missouri, were also looking for Quantrill. Some
were behind the raiders, others ahead, riding for the same spot
where Quantrill was preparing to cross the border.

A Missouri militia unit caught up with Quantrill's rear guard.
They captured three bushwhackers and turned them over to a
guard detail commanded by Capt. George Hoyt, a lawyer who

had defended John Brown at his trial after the Harpers Ferry raid. Hoyt, an abolitionist and former horse thief, had no sympathy for guerrillas, and he watched impassively as one of the prisoners was relieved of the loot he had stolen at Lawrence. It was a pile of cheap goods—marbles, mouth organs, toys, shoestrings, buttons. Hoyt stared at the plunder in disgust and pulled out his pistol.

"I will just kill you for being a damned fool," he said.

Hoyt shot all three bushwhackers. He was in no mood for forgiveness.

Quantrill led his men into Missouri a few miles south of where he had crossed two days before.

"Boys, we are back home!" he told them. "Not all the troops in Kansas can catch us now."

They rode on for four miles and set up camp in a clearing along the Grand River. The men needed rest, but even more they needed food. Quantrill sent out details to take food from nearby farms. While waiting for them to return, he and his officers divided up the loot. Each private was given twenty dollars and the officers shared the rest; the precise amount is not known. They also parceled out other valuables such as watches, clothing, and jewelry.

Just as Quantrill's men returned with food, a farmer rode up with the news that a Yankee force of twelve hundred was positioned on the far side of a divide four miles to the east. Quantrill quickly mounted his horse and told his men to saddle up. They refused, insisting they would not leave until they had a chance to eat.

"The Kansans are coming," Quantrill said, hoping that would be sufficient to spur them. He did not tell them about the Federals four miles away.

"Damn the Kansans," one man said. "We whipped them yesterday, we can whip them today. We are not going to leave here till we get something to eat."

"I know you can whip the Kansans," Quantrill said, "but what are you going to do about the twelve hundred fresh Missouri troops awaiting us just over the divide?"

"Well," another said, according to Bill Gregg's account, "that is a horse of another color. We will saddle up."

Most of them did, but some could not; their horses were done for. Bill Gregg knew his mare could not go another mile, even without a rider. Quantrill ordered Gregg and the others without mounts to hide in the woods and hope for the best.

More than one hundred of the raiders, including some who had horses, decided to take their chances on their own. Some had farms not too far away, to which they now headed, either alone or in small groups. Others, too exhausted or too scared to risk a fight with twelve hundred Yankees, took to the woods for shelter. Some found deserted cabins, others hid in caves, and some crawled inside rotting logs. They settled down to sleep, hoping that when they woke up, it would not be to the sight of a blue uniform standing over them.

Three other men had to be left behind: a guerrilla named Jim Bledsoe and two of Colonel Holt's recruits. They had been wounded and carried along in a carriage but could no longer keep up the pace. The carriage with the men inside was pushed deep into the brush, where it was hoped no one would see it.

Much later, when the Kansans reached the abandoned camp-site along the Grand River, White Turkey, the Delaware Indian from Lawrence who had killed Larkin Skaggs, and Pelathe, the Shawnee who had tried to warn the people of Lawrence, found the wagon. The recruits begged for mercy, but Bledsoe would have none of it.

"Stop it!" he shouted. "We are not entitled to mercy! We spare none and do not expect to be spared!"

Bledsoe confronted the Kansas troops waiting to kill them.

"Just take us out of this trap and put us on our knees facing you and shoot us. We are not able to stand on our feet. Let us see you. Do not shoot us from behind."

The troopers did as he asked. After the raiders were dead, the Indians scalped them.

Other raiders who tried to hide in the woods were tracked

down and killed. Capt. George Hoyt was a particularly diligent executioner. He led a band of like-minded vengeance seekers through the woods and murdered every guerrilla he found, as well as some farmers who had given them shelter.

No one was safe if Hoyt thought they had the slightest connection with the rebels. He shot most of his captives on the spot and hanged others from stout branches so high off the ground that no one could cut down their bodies. The corpses hung in the trees for months, rotting and twisting in the wind.

Bill Gregg and the six men with him ran several miles to a farmhouse, where they hoped to find food and shelter. Gregg questioned the farmer, trying to determine his sympathies, whether or not he was sound on the goose. The man turned out to be a friend of Gregg's father. He cooked his guests a hearty meal and stood guard while they slept. That night, he sent them on their way with a reliable guide who led them back to their refuge in Sni-A-Bar.

Quantrill led the rest of his men, now numbering around three hundred, east toward the twelve hundred Missouri troops the farmer had told him about. The man's count was off. There were only 320, but they were fresh, rested, and riding good horses, more than a match for Quantrill's tired men. The soldiers belonged to the First Missouri State Militia Cavalry, Lt. Col. Bazel Lazear commanding. They were the only troops in Quantrill's path, the only barrier to his escape, and they were moving westward toward him.

Lazear led his troops across Big Creek. He spotted a long column of horsemen a half mile away and waved his men to a halt. The horsemen were riding in a column of fours. Some were dressed in blue. Lazear knew there were a lot of Union cavalry about, but he was wary of this lot, and he signaled his men to approach slowly. As he watched, the horsemen stopped along the top of a ridge and formed into a battle line. That told Lazear all he needed to know. He had found the bushwhackers.

He ordered some of his men to dismount and send their

horses to the rear. They moved forward on foot in a skirmish line, with the rest of Lazear's cavalry following. Quantrill, watching intently, had been hoping to see this classic maneuver right out of the cavalry training manual. With only a portion of the Yankee force on horseback and capable of pursuing him, he led his men off and was a half mile away before Lazear was able to follow.

The Yankees chased Quantrill and his men up a hill. When the Federals galloped over the top, they found themselves facing a line of rebels who opened fire with their Navy Colts. The cavalry returned fire with their long-range carbines, sending the raiders fleeing for the tree line. At least five bushwhackers were killed and several wounded; the Yankees finished those off where they fell.

Lazear led his men into the woods, where they killed five more of Quantrill's men. Then, incredibly, Lazear halted. He announced that the chase was over and declared the battle a victory. Even though the raiders were disorganized and on the run, even though Lazear's troopers and horses were still fresh, he ordered them to make camp, insisting they deserved a rest.

Had Lazear pushed on, he might have captured Quantrill and the rest of his band, but as it was, most of the men who had massacred the residents of Lawrence and sacked the town survived—to kill another day, to revel in the glory of their deeds, to enjoy the adulation of legions of Southerners. They had earned a place in history. The name William Clarke Quantrill would never be forgotten. He had planned and executed one of the most audacious raids of the war, and he had gotten away with it.

Gen. Thomas Ewing had had two bad days. The message Major Plumb, his chief of staff, had sent did not reach the general until 10:45 on the morning of the twenty-first. By then, Quantrill had already left Lawrence.

Ewing must have been shocked to learn that eight hundred guerrillas had penetrated his string of supposedly impenetrable border outposts, and that the information was already more than ten hours old. How far had the raiders gone—and where—since the message was sent? A second message informed him that the bushwhackers had passed through Gardner and were heading west. Ewing, the man who would be blamed for allowing the Lawrence massacre to occur, knew nothing more. Worse, there was no way he could reach his troops because he did not know where they were.

The only way for him to redeem himself and save his reputation and his job was to find his men and lead the pursuit. He rallied the few hundred troops at Leavenworth, men who were in the process of being equipped for service out west against the Indians, but they were not ready to march until one o'clock that afternoon. Most had not yet been issued weapons or horses.

When Ewing and his men reached the Kansas River, they were delayed for five hours, waiting to be ferried across. Ewing was so impatient that he pushed on, leaving one-third of his men on the north bank of the river. He called a halt at DeSoto for men and horses to eat and told the troops they could sleep until dawn. But Ewing was eager to be on the move, and he roused them in the middle of the night. Pvt. Hervey Johnson wrote, "We started about three in the morning, riding like maniacs; several horses stumbled and threw their riders and dragged them in the dust, but no one was hurt much."

Ewing pushed his troops through the blistering morning heat. Horses died and men collapsed from sunstroke. One officer died, but Ewing rode on, allowing no more than a minute or two of rest every hour. "I never saw as hot a day in my life," Private Johnson wrote. "Men and horses were completely wearied out. . . . The men appeared to care for nothing." Soldiers who could not keep up were left behind to fend for themselves.

In the afternoon, Ewing quickened the pace. Weary men slept in the saddle and fell from their horses. Many more dropped out. The grueling march took its toll, but Ewing did not slow. By late afternoon, he decided to go on alone, feeling that the bulk of the men were holding him back. Only a few could keep up with him. The rest were told to manage as best they could.

Clearly exhausted and frantic with worry about being out of touch during the biggest guerrilla raid of the war, Ewing reached

Clark's camp on the Grand River at nightfall. Quantrill had long since escaped. For all his effort, Ewing was too late. But there would be no rest for him. He was confronted, loudly and savagely, by Jim Lane, the most powerful man in all of Kansas, mad as a hornet whose nest had been set afire. Senator Lane, smarting over not being given command of the troops during the pursuit, embarrassed at being forced to flee in his nightshirt, and furious at the loss of his home and his town, vented his anger on the hapless General Ewing.

Lane threatened that when he got to Washington, he would see that Ewing was removed from command. Because of his own ambitions, the general was unable to challenge Lane. As much as he detested the senator, Ewing had to appease him if he wanted a political career after the war. Lane was too influential to antagonize. No one could advance politically in Kansas without Lane's endorsement and support.

Ewing asked Lane what he could do to save his job. The answer was simple. Ewing would have to issue the order he had already considered and abandoned as unnecessarily harsh: the depopulation of a large area of the Missouri border region. Lane wanted the forcible removal of several thousand people and the burning of their homes, barns, and crops. This action would leave Quantrill's guerrillas with no sanctuary, no food, no fresh horses, and no shelter. They would have to move on, far away from Jim Lane's territory. If Ewing issued that order, Lane would make no complaint against the general in Washington.

Ewing's choice was brutally clear. He would have to issue the order if he wished to retain his command and plan a postwar political career. If he refused to issue the order, he would suffer the disgrace of dismissal and the end of his dreams of political glory. A Kansas lieutenant overheard Lane threaten Ewing, saying, "You are a dead dog if you fail to issue that order."

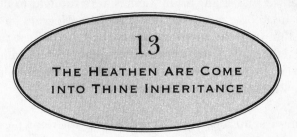

THE SKY OVER Lawrence was black with a funereal pall of thick, choking smoke oozing out of the ruins. The businesses along Massachusetts Street smoldered for the rest of the day, as did many of the homes. Seventy-five buildings in the business district had been destroyed, along with more than one hundred houses. Many of the buildings left standing had been partially burned, and almost all had been ransacked and vandalized. One of the few buildings not damaged was the armory; inside it, the town militia's weapons remained neatly stacked.

Two of every three residents had no place to live; many had no more clothing than what they had hastily put on that morning when the raiders came. Most were penniless, robbed of their money and valuables. Even for those who had hidden their money from the raiders, there was nothing to buy. There was barely enough food in town to last two days, and the only edible goods in the one remaining store were four bags of flour.

The human toll was staggering. No one could avoid the sight and smell of the dead: 185 men and boys, charred and broken corpses. At first, many of the victims were thought to be black men, and people wondered where so many Negroes had come from. But when the survivors approached the bodies, they discovered the truth. These were their neighbors, white men whose shriveled, incinerated bodies were nearly unrecognizable.

The Reverend Richard Cordley wrote:

> Going over the town one saw the dead everywhere, on the sidewalks, in the streets, among the weeds in the gardens, and in the few remaining homes. . . . Now and then one came across a group, a mother and her children watching their dead beside the ashes of their home. A little later there could be seen a woman sitting among the ashes of a building, holding in her hands a blackened skull, fondling it and kissing it, and crying piteously over it.

The people who were able set to work, gathering up the corpses and the wounded, carrying them to the Methodist church, now serving as hospital and morgue. The dead were laid out in neat rows. The town's two remaining doctors tended to the wounded with penknives or improvised other surgical instruments; scraps of petticoats and shirts were used for bandages. They had nothing to give their moaning patients to dull the pain of the probing blades.

The dead had to be buried quickly or the searing heat would add pestilence and plague to the list of calamities that had befallen the people of Lawrence. But there were no coffins and few carpenters to build them. Most craftsmen had lost their tools when their shops were set afire. Enterprising men searched the lumberyards for timber and sifted through the ashes of the hardware stores, unearthing piles of burned nails, some fused into lumps by the heat of the fires.

They sawed the wood into boards and nailed them together to form rough boxes, but there was not enough lumber to accommodate all the dead. Some bodies were interred wrapped only in sheets and blankets. Many were laid to rest in the town cemetery in their family plots, but fifty-three others, still in their tattered clothing, were laid side by side in a single long trench gouged out of the black earth. Still others were buried on their own land, alongside the remains of their homes.

It took a week for the townspeople of Lawrence to find all the dead. Funerals were held every day until the last victim was found, Edward Fitch, who had been shot down in the doorway of his home. A young woman who lived with the Fitches had searched the rubble every day for Mr. Fitch's remains. And every night, she came away from the ruins in tears, having found nothing. "One day she found the charred bones among the hot ashes. She got down into the cellar and took them out with her hands one by one, and tenderly laid them together. They were so hot that her hands were all burned and blistered when her sad work was done."

Editor John Speer spent days raking the ashes of the newspaper office looking for the body of his seventeen-year-old son, Robert. He would stop passersby, begging for their assistance. "I want you to help me find my boy. They have killed one, and the other I cannot find."

When darkness fell the first night after the raiders left, an eerie glow from the smoldering fires illuminated the clouds above Lawrence. Throughout the night, dogs howled mournfully for their dead masters.

The next day in Lawrence, the survivors hanged a man. His name was Jake Callew, and no one seemed to know much about him. He wandered into town that Saturday for reasons he never had a chance to explain. The rumors started: Someone said he looked like a proslavery man. Another denounced him for having been involved in the bloody border conflicts before the war. Someone else said he must be a spy for that devil Quantrill. There was only one way to deal with his sort.

In minutes, an angry mob surrounded Jake Callew. Like all mobs, it was mindless, without conscience, scruples, or compassion. Like some great, dumb, cornered beast, it acted on instinct alone, lashing out to kill, to take revenge for the horror it had just suffered, not caring who was killed so long as there was blood for blood.

The citizenry went through the motions of a trial, convening an impromptu court in the street, but the verdict, never in question, was pronounced in the absence of any evidence to support the charge that Callew was a spy for the bushwhackers. No one asked why a spy would show up after the town was attacked and not before. No one wanted answers to such confusing questions.

"You have heard the verdict," the judge said. "Now what will you do with the prisoner?"

"Hang him," the mob roared.

Callew was led to the river, where a rope was made ready. The judge called for a clergyman; even a no-good spy should have a chance to get right with his Maker.

"You had better make your peace with God," the minister told the condemned man, "for you don't stand much chance with this crowd."

"You needn't trouble yourself about my soul," Callew answered.

The rope was looped around his neck and he was hoisted off the ground. The last sound Callew heard was the voice of the hangman.

"How do you like that, old fellow," the hangman said, yanking the body higher for all to see.

Four other strangers—unsuspecting, unwitting, and no more guilty than Jake Callew—visited Lawrence that day, and the mob went after them, too. Cooler heads prevailed, perhaps shamed by the memory of Callew's twitching body, and the visitors were jailed and not hanged. They were later released.

One of the townspeople almost became a victim of the mob. Sally Young, the seamstress at the Eldridge House, was taunted and jeered by some who had seen her riding around town behind the raiders. A cry went up: She had to be one of them, doing the bushwhackers' dirty work, pointing out the homes of the people on Quantrill's death list. Sally Young was arrested and held in jail, for transfer to Fort Leavenworth for trial by the army, but when the crowd's anger abated, she was released.

Many other people who flooded into Lawrence after the attack met with a more grateful reception. Even while the fires were still burning, farmers from miles around loaded their wagons with food and drove to town. They gave the stuff away; no one would think of charging a neighbor in need.

As word of the disaster spread to other towns—to Leavenworth, Kansas City, Wyandotte, and Topeka—people filled their wagons with produce and meat, with clothing, medicine, and blankets, whatever they thought would help. Folks in Leavenworth collected all the coffins in town and sent them on their way. Cities collected money to help the residents of Lawrence rebuild their homes and businesses. St. Louis raised ten thousand dollars to be dispensed as no-interest loans to citizens who had lost everything.

The day after they hanged Jake Callew, the survivors of Quantrill's raid went to church to pray. The Sunday service was held in the old Congregational church. The blistering heat of the August morning was aggravated by the smoking fires. The air caught the sweet smell of death and decay. There was no breeze to sweep the stench away.

The church was crowded, but the worn wooden pews were filled mostly with women and children, many newly widowed and orphaned. A number were still dressed in the clothes they had been wearing when Quantrill came, all the finery they had left. Grieving women covered their heads with sunbonnets, hoods, shawls, or loosely draped handkerchiefs. The few men among them wore their work clothes, stained and soiled.

The Reverend Richard Cordley officiated, assisted by the Reverend Morse, who had come from Emporia to bury his brother-in-law, Judge Carpenter. Cordley made no remarks and offered no sermon. No one was in the mood for much talk. He offered up a prayer for the souls of the departed and read the Seventy-ninth Psalm. The simple words were chilling, sounding as though they had been written specifically for this time and this place.

O God, the heathen are come into Thine inheritance;
They have laid Jerusalem in heaps.

The dead bodies of Thy servants have they given to be meat
unto the fowls of the heaven, and the flesh of Thy saints unto
the beasts of the earth.
Their blood have shed they like water round about Jerusalem,
and there was none to bury them.

After a moment of silence, everyone filed out into the rancid, foul heat to get on with the job of rebuilding. They wondered where God had been two days before.

That evening, it seemed certain God had deserted them a second time, or perhaps was punishing them for something. The people of Lawrence were exhausted at the end of another day spent searching for bodies, burying friends and relatives, sifting through the rubble of their lives for some treasured memento to link them to their lost past. Some people were still in shock, able to do little but weep or sit silently on porch stoops, rocking back and forth, their faces frozen in despair, unable to comprehend the enormity of events, unable to grasp that their lives had changed forever.

Toward dusk, a farmer on Mount Oread happened to glance southward, toward the Wakarusa River, where Quantrill's men had last been seen after they left town. The farmer was startled to see the awful specter of smoke and flame, no more than three miles from Lawrence. Something was burning, and that could mean only one thing: Quantrill and his men were rampaging again. The farmer jumped on his horse and raced down the hill, shouting a warning.

"They are coming again, they are coming again! Run for your lives, run for your lives."

Isadora Johnson, resting at a friend's house, was awakened by the clattering hooves and the alarmed cries of her neighbors. She did not want to disturb her baby, who had finally fallen asleep after hours of fretting, but she had no choice once the shouts became clear.

"Quantrill is coming," voices yelled, "killing and burning everything as he goes!"

Mrs. Johnson and her neighbors gathered up their children and ran for the cornfields. On the way, one woman's elderly mother stopped, announcing that she had to return home to get her mother's teaspoons.

"Never mind the spoons, Mother. We have no time to get them."

The old lady glared at her daughter.

"Your grandmother's spoons that I brought from Scotland with me must be saved."

Ignoring the threat of the bushwhackers, the woman went back to her house, retrieved the spoons, and hurried to the cornfields, which were rapidly filling with terrified residents, panic-stricken at the thought of Quantrill's return. When he had arrived two days ago, they had not known what to expect. Robbery, of course, but surely not cold-blooded killing. Now they knew better; "reserves cracked, then crumbled, and suddenly there was nothing left."

The Reverend Hugh Fisher and his family, living above the stables beside the ruins of their house, watched their neighbors fleeing on foot and on horseback. He managed to stop one man long enough to ask what was going on.

"Run for your life, Mr. Fisher," the man warned. "Quantrill is coming back and will kill all of us."

Soon the exodus out of town became a stampede. Women who had proved so courageous during the first attack ran shrieking into the cornfields and to the river. Men did the same, and some paused long enough to don dresses and sunbonnets as a disguise. Within minutes, the town appeared deserted. The only people left were the wounded in the Methodist church, abandoned to lie helpless on the floor, at the mercy of the guerrillas, with no way of escaping and no weapons with which to defend themselves.

For the first time in many weeks, it started to rain. The temperature dropped sharply in the cornfields and the underbrush and the gardens, soaking and chilling the residents as the winds blew fiercely, the rain turned to stinging hail, and lightning cracked ominously overhead. Hundreds of people stayed hidden throughout the night, wet, miserable, and frightened, not daring to venture out until noon the next day.

Where was Quantrill and his army? Why hadn't they come? Did the storm keep them away? Were they still out there beyond the Wakarusa, preparing to attack? It was unbearable, the waiting, the uncertainty, the anticipation. The Reverend Richard Cordley observed:

> The horror of that Sunday night was in some respects worse than the raid itself. At the raid there was no panic and no outcry. . . . There had been no warning and there was no escape. But this night alarm gave room for the wildest imaginations and the most exaggerated fears. It unnerved the bravest with its undefined dread. In some respects, panic is worse than peril. People who passed through the raid without flinching, were utterly unstrung and demoralized by this Sunday night panic.

It had all been a mistake. A few days later, it was learned that the fires the farmer spotted from Mount Oread had been caused by the accidental burning of haystacks near Eudora. Quantrill was miles away, back in Missouri, but in the minds of the frightened people of Lawrence, he was lurking in every patch of woods, watching under cover of night, stalking them, ready to ride down on them whenever he chose.

The panic and despondency did not last long; there was too much to do. The citizens of Lawrence quickly began what had seemed an impossibility only three days before: to clear away the rubble and rebuild their town and their lives. Three reporters from the *Missouri Democrat* wired to their newspaper a story reflecting the city's mood.

> Up to this morning 183 bodies were buried in Lawrence. . . . One hundred and eighty-two buildings were burned; 80 of

them were brick; 65 of them were on Massachusetts street. There are 85 widows and 240 orphans made by Quantrill's raid. [Senator] Lane has commenced rebuilding his house. Three men have subscribed $100,000 to rebuild the . . . Eldridge Hotel. Several merchants have commenced rebuilding. All the laboring men in town will be set to work to-morrow to clear off the ruins. In spite of the terrible calamity, the people are in good spirits. All the towns in the State have sent in large sums of money. Even the men burned out on Quantrill's retreat have sent in loads of vegetables and provisions.

People set to work with the same kind of determination, will, and sense of purpose that brought them out west in the first place and enabled them to survive and prosper. Once the initial shock dissipated, they were not about to let the near destruction of their town defeat them. Few were more vigorous and stalwart in aiding the comeback of Lawrence, Kansas, than Peter Ridenour.

Ridenour's house was gone, his partner, Harlow Baker, lay near death. Their store, the successful R&Bs, was in ruins. Ridenour spent Saturday and Sunday helping to bury the dead and sitting patiently by the bedside of his friend. Baker was not expected to survive his wounds.

On Monday, Ridenour picked his way through the rubble of the store and dug out their safe. Inside, he found his account books and papers intact and $610 in checks and currency. That was all he had left.

He paid off some creditors with six hundred dollars and put ten dollars in his pocket, using it to start his business anew. He went out into the street and approached men who looked lost and dazed, mostly clerks and other merchants put out of business, and asked if they wanted to work. He paid them out of his remaining ten dollars. There were many eager takers. Ridenour told them to scrounge wheelbarrows and shovels and clear out the store site, where the walls, flooring, roof, plus the inventory and furnishings, had collapsed into the cellar.

Behind the store, an old corncrib had escaped the fire, and it was there R&Bs reopened. Ridenour hoisted an American flag on a pole stuck in the ground, constructed a lean-to shelter over the corncrib from spare lumber, and sold out the first shipment of salt he received after the attack. Ridenour spent every day at the store, selling, supervising, sawing, hammering, dreaming of his future.

He wrote to his creditors in Fort Leavenworth, St. Louis, and New York, explaining his situation, promising that the business would continue. He expected to repay his debts in full, but it might take a long time. They all responded with new shipments of goods and assured him that his credit was good.

One creditor, who was owed fifteen hundred dollars, believed Ridenour and Baker had been killed in Quantrill's raid. Before he received Ridenour's letter pledging payment, he had wired a banker in Leavenworth, instructing him to give the Ridenour and Baker families whatever money they needed, drawing it from his account. When he learned the men had survived and that Ridenour had reopened the store, the creditor offered to lend them more money at a low rate of interest. He also insisted that they forget about repaying the original debt until the business was fully functioning. The man had never met Ridenour or Baker, nor had he ever set foot in Lawrence. R&Bs did business with him for a long time after that.

At night, after closing the store, Ridenour would sit by Baker's bedside, talking to him to cheer him up, discussing everything but business. One evening about two weeks after the raid, Ridenour came to the sickroom, to find Baker alert and smiling.

"Now tell me what you are doing," Baker said, and for the first time, Ridenour described how matters were progressing.

"That is all right," Baker said. "I hope to be out soon to help you."

Four weeks later, Harlow Baker managed to walk unaided to the corncrib and the site of the new building. R&Bs' partners were back in business.

Homes were being rebuilt with the same determination. The Reverend Hugh Fisher and his family lived in the hayloft of the stable, cooking and eating their meals in the shade of a tree in their backyard. Years later, recalling that time, Fisher wrote:

The first week after the raid, while the fire was still smoulder-ing, I hired carpenters and contracted for lumber to rebuild my house, for the [stone] walls stood like walls of iron. We cut trees in the woods, loaded them from the stump, and they never touched the ground until the joists were laid down at the door. In a short time the roof was on and the plasterers were at work completing the house for occupancy. It still stands, a monumental reminder of what was and what is.

Gen. Thomas Ewing was in big trouble. His career and his fu-ture, once deemed so promising, appeared to have reached an ignominious end. So far, Jim Lane was keeping his part of the bargain. Lane had not criticized Ewing publicly because Lane was sure Ewing would issue the order to depopulate Missouri's border region. But Lane was about the only person in Kansas, and elsewhere, who had refrained from chastising the general.

"Ewing is frightened," ran a story in the *Missouri Democrat,* "and in the chase after Quantrill was in a complete quandary. He is looked upon as being a general without heart and brains." A report from Fort Leavenworth, published in *The New York Times* on August 23, 1864, was also critical of Ewing, and it carried the general's embarrassment to the national level.

The feeling among all classes of citizens here is very bitter against the commanders of this Department and District for being so wholly unprepared to meet such an emergency. The commanding General was absent from his headquarters at the time the raid occurred, and did not know of the invasion until the destruction of Lawrence was complete.

Disturbed by what he called the "horrors of the massacre," Ewing adopted the tone, in a letter to his superior, of being of-fended by unjust criticism. To Maj. Gen. John M. Schofield, commander of the Department of the Missouri, Ewing wrote, "My political enemies are fanning the flames, and wish me for a burnt-offering to satisfy the just passion of the people. . . . It is all mere mob clamor." He asked General Schofield whether he should request a court of inquiry to clear his name, at the same time insisting he had done nothing wrong.

> I have not the slightest doubt that any fair court would not only acquit me of all suspicion of negligence, but also give me credit for great precaution and some skill in my adjustment of troops. I assure you, general, I would quit the service at once if I were accused, after candid investigation, of the slightest negligence or of a want of average skill in the command of the forces you have given me.

General Ewing had no intention of quitting the service, and he was sure he would not have to, once he set in motion the plan to depopulate the border region, the plan Jim Lane had forced on him. That action would allay the criticism he was getting from Kansans, who hated Missourians with a passion born of years of bloody fighting. To Kansans, the Missourians who lived along the border were as responsible as Quantrill for the Lawrence massacre. If they had not been there, Quantrill and his men would not have been able to flourish all these years. They had to go, and the quicker the better.

On August twenty-fourth, Kansas governor Thomas Carney sent a message to Schofield calling for the clearing of the border region and threatening that the people of his state would take matters into their own hands, invading Missouri if the army did not act.

> I must hold Missouri responsible for this fearful, fiendish raid. No body of men large as that commanded by Quantrill could have been gathered together without the people residing in Western Missouri knowing everything about it. Such people

cannot be considered loyal, and should not be treated as loyal citizens; for while they conceal the movements of desperadoes like Quantrill and his followers, they are, in the worst sense of the word, their aiders and abettors, and should be held equally guilty.

The following day, General Schofield told Ewing that he was "pretty much convinced that the mode of carrying on the war on the border during the past two years has produced such a state of feeling that nothing short of total devastation of the districts which are made the haunts of guerrillas will be sufficient to put a stop to the evil."

On that same day, August twenty-fifth, four days after the Lawrence raid, General Ewing issued General Orders Number 11, judged by one historian to be the "harshest military measure directed against civilians during the Civil War." Another called it "perhaps the harshest act of the U.S. government against its own people in American history."

The orders led to the ruin of thousands of lives and created a wasteland eighty-five miles long and fifty miles wide, from the Missouri River in the north to the Osage in the south. General Orders Number 11 decreed that everyone living within those boundaries had to leave the area within fifteen days. The only exceptions permitted were homes located within one mile of a town in which Union troops were stationed and whose residents could prove their loyalty to the Union cause. Not many people could offer such proof.

Everyone else was banished. All their property and all possessions they could not carry away were to be destroyed. Every home, barn, and outbuilding was to be burned to the ground, and every bit of food appropriated or destroyed, along with the livestock left behind. Nothing was to remain that could provide sustenance for the bushwhackers. Anyone who did not leave in fifteen days would be forcibly removed by Union troops. As to where they were supposed to go, that was entirely their problem. No assistance would be forthcoming.

Some twenty thousand families in four counties were forced

to flee their homes. Soon the trails, the roads, and the open prairie were filled with caravans of the dispossessed stretching for miles. The travelers were mostly women, children, and old men. The more fortunate ones among them had decrepit mules or oxen to haul the wagons in which they piled their household goods. Many people had no means of transporting their furniture and had to leave everything behind. Some had a cow or a few sheep, but most of the livestock and horses had been confiscated by the Yankees. Hardly anyone remained in the wasteland. It was difficult to prove one's loyalty to the Union, and the officers examining such entreaties were none too compassionate.

Many of the refugees headed north, to other counties in Missouri, but federal authorities there, trying to cope with their own bushwhacker problems, refused to let them stay, forcing them to move on. Others headed south into the Confederacy, a land already impoverished, drained of food and livestock to feed the rebel army.

Descriptions of the trek are soul-searing: "Barefooted and bareheaded women and children, stripped of every article of clothing except a scant covering for their bodies, exposed to the heat of an August sun and struggling through the dust on foot." A Kansas City resident saw large numbers of

> poor people, widows and children, who, with little bundles of clothing, are crossing the river to be subsisted by the charities of the people amongst whom they might find shelter. . . . hundreds of fleeing families . . . toiling slowly and painfully southward. Tender and gentle women . . . driving oxen and riding upon miserable broken-down horses without saddles.

To add to their misery, many people were harassed and molested by Union soldiers, mostly Kansans who had no sympathy for anyone from Missouri, no matter how desperate their plight or how pitiful their appearance. General Ewing, to his credit, ordered his troops not to harm the refugees, but some soldiers disregarded his authority. They stopped every band of refugees, looking for weapons, pawing through wagons, stealing whatever took their fancy.

Gangs of Kansas Jayhawkers out for revenge broke into the homes of people who had not yet left and threw them out on the spot. They set fire to the houses and refused to allow the owners to save anything. Jayhawkers, and even some Union troops, killed anyone who protested this treatment, or just because they felt like it.

Near the town of Lone Jack, a squad of soldiers approached several families who were loading their wagons. They interrogated the men about their loyalties and permitted two of them to leave with the women and children. Six men—the youngest seventeen, the oldest seventy-five—were detained for what the families were told was further questioning. When the families had gone some distance, they heard shots. They ventured back and found all six men dead.

One house not yet vacated belonged to the Younger family. Bersheba Younger, Cole's mother, knew she had to leave, but her two younger sons, twelve-year-old John and ten-year-old Bob, refused to go. They took turns watching at the windows, ready to take on the whole Yankee army with old muskets as big as they were. Jim Younger, at fifteen the oldest boy living at home, had gone off to search for a place the family could move to. Mrs. Younger was so agitated with worry that she became ill. Her condition upset the boys, and they agreed to leave as soon as Jim returned.

Union troops came to the door before Jim returned, and the officer in charge went inside to see Mrs. Younger, who had taken to her bed.

"Mrs. Younger," the Yankee asked, "why haven't you complied with Order Number Eleven?"

"I am sick," she said. "I have no place to go, and it seems impossible for me to leave."

The officer said they were going to burn the house and barn, so she had better prepare to leave. She asked him to spare the farm, but he refused. He had his orders. She continued to plead until he agreed that she and the boys could stay the night, but only if she promised to set the place afire the next morning.

Cole Younger recalled:

> On the following day my mother had the Negroes place a bed
> in a farm wagon and carry her out of the house. She set it afire
> with her own hands. She was placed on the bed in the wagon.
> They drove away, my mother, four children, and two Negroes.
> Seven persons were in that wagon; not one among them had
> ever done anyone a wrong in their lives.

They were as innocent of harming others as were most of the other residents of Lawrence.

Within two weeks, all of central-western Missouri was desolated and virtually deserted. In Cass County, only six hundred people remained out of a population of ten thousand, and other counties had even fewer people. For hundreds of miles, blackened stone chimneys like tall, thin tombstones were the only sign that people had once lived there. For years after, the place was called "the Burnt District."

A few of the Federals were moved by the plight of the displaced Missourians. Lt. Col. Bazel Lazear, commander of the last Union force to battle Quantrill during his escape, conveyed his feelings in a letter to his wife: "It is heart-sickening to see what I have seen since I have been back here. A desolated country and men & women and children, some of them almost naked. Some on foot and some in old wagons. Oh God."

George Caleb Bingham—the prominent Missouri artist who owned the Kansas City building that had collapsed, killing the women prisoners—was outraged when he saw the refugees fleeing their homes. He stomped into General Ewing's office and lost no time making known his feelings about General Orders Number 11.

"I don't approve of your order," he told the startled general, "and I sincerely believe it is unjust and will cause much suffering among innocent people."

WILLIAM CLARKE
QUANTRILL

•

*Kansas Collection,
University of
Kansas Libraries*

FREE STATE
CONVENTION!

All persons who are favorable to a union of effort, and a permanent organization of all the Free State elements of Kansas Territory, and who wish to secure upon the broadest platform the co-operation of all who agree upon this point, are requested to meet at their several places of holding elections, in their respective districts on the 25th of August, instant, at one o'clock, P. M., and appoint five delegates to each representative to which they were entitled in the Legislative Assembly, who shall meet in general Convention at

Big Springs, Wednesday, Sept. 5th '55,

at 10 o'clock A. M., for the purpose of adopting a Platform upon which all may act harmoniously who prefer Freedom to Slavery.
The nomination of a Delegate to Congress, will also come up before the General Convention.
Let no sectional or party issue distract or prevent the perfect co-operation of Free State men. Union and harmony are absolutely necessary to success. The pro-slavery party are fully and effectually organized. No jars nor minor issues divide them. And to contend against them successfully, we also must be united.— Without prudence and harmony of action we are certain to fail. Let every man then do his duty and we are certain of victory.
All Free State men, without distinction, are earnestly requested to take immediate and effective steps to insure a full and correct representation for every District in the Territory. "United we stand; divided we fall."
By order of the Executive Committee of the Free State Party of the Territory of Kansas, as per resolution of the Mass Convention in session at Lawrence, Aug 15th and 16th, 1855.

J. K. GOODIN, Sec'y.   **C. ROBINSON, Chairman.**
                                              Herald of Freedom, Print.

ANNOUNCEMENT OF A FREE STATE
CONVENTION FOR KANSAS TERRITORY

•

Kansas State Historical Society

James H. Lane
•
*Kansas State
Historical Society*

John Brown
•
*Kansas Collection,
University of Kansas
Libraries*

GOVERNOR
CHARLES
ROBINSON

•

*Kansas State
Historical Society*

JAYHAWKER
CHARLES
JENNISON

•

*Kansas State
Historical Society*

"BLOODY BILL"
ANDERSON

•

State Historical Society
of Missouri, Columbia

GEORGE TODD

•

State Historical Society
of Missouri, Columbia

"LITTLE ARCHIE"
CLEMENTS
•
*State Historical Society of
Missouri, Columbia*

FLETCH TAYLOR,
FRANK JAMES, AND
JESSE JAMES
•
*State Historical Society of
Missouri, Columbia*

COLE YOUNGER
•
State Historical
Society of Missouri,
Columbia

GENERAL
JAMES BLUNT
•
Kansas State
Historical Society

GENERAL THOMAS
EWING, JR.
•
*Kansas State
Historical Society*

CAPTAIN
JOSHUA PIKE
•
*Kansas State
Historical Society*

CAPTAIN CHARLES
COLEMAN
•
*Kansas State
Historical Society*

MASSACHUSETTS
STREET, LAWRENCE,
KANSAS, 1863
•
*Kansas State
Historical Society*

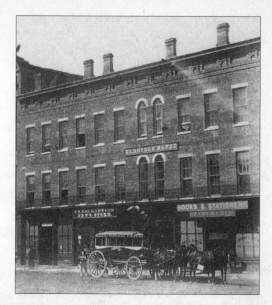

The Lawrence Massacre BY LAURETTA LOUISE FOX FISK

•

The Ruins of Lawrence,
Harper's Weekly,
SEPTEMBER 19, 1863
●
Kansas State Historical Society

FROM *The New York Times,*
AUGUST 23, 1863
●
*Copyright 1863 by
The New York Times Co.
Reprinted by permission.*

VOL. XII—NO. 3717.

THE INVASION OF KANSAS.

Particulars of the Destruction of Lawrence by Quantrell.

Dreadful Scenes of Pillage and Murder.

Citizens Shot Without Mercy in the Midst of their Families.

The Mayor and His Son and a Large Number of Prominent Men Killed.

ABOUT 180 MURDERED

The Pecuniary Loss About Two Millions.

ESCAPE OF GENERAL LANE.

LEAVENWORTH, Saturday, Aug. 22.

From citizens of Lawrence, Kansas, who have arrived here for supplies and medicines, I have

THE

The

CHATTA

The *G*
ROSECRAN
BURNSIDE
Both ar
The for
to Knoxv
The tre

DEP
IMPORTA

HEADQ
GENER
desire of
as well as
all possib
they shou
and civil
and of th
II. Sin
Middle T
army; th
are in da
for theft,
guerrilla
To pre
country,
all such
course.

DR. J. F. GRISWOLD.

H. W. BAKER.

JOSIAH C. TRASK.

S. M. THORPE.

QUANTRILL RAID VICTIMS SHOT DOWN TOGETHER.

Quantrill raid victims Griswold,
Baker, Trask, and Thorpe

•

SALLY YOUNG

•

*Kansas State
Historical Society*

THE REVEREND
HUGH D. FISHER

•

*Kansas State
Historical Society*

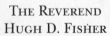

GEORGE CALEB BINGHAM PAINTING, *Order Number 11*

•

State Historical Society of Missouri, Columbia

MASSACHUSETTS
STREET, REVIVED
•
*Kansas State
Historical Society*

GENERAL SAMUEL
CURTIS
•
*State Historical Society
of Missouri, Columbia*

"Bloody Bill"
Anderson in
death

•

*State Historical
Society of Missouri,
Columbia*

Monument to the victims of
Quantrill's raid

•

Kansas Collection, University of Kansas Libraries

653 Remaining Pioneers of Quantrell's Band

REUNION OF QUANTRILL'S
RAIDERS, 1912
•
*State Historical Society of
Missouri, Columbia*

Ewing admitted he did not like the order either but said there was no alternative if Quantrill was to be prevented from making raids like the one that had devastated Lawrence. The two men argued for a few minutes, and Bingham demanded that Ewing rescind the order. The enraged Ewing shouted at his visitor.

"Rescind it! Rescind it! That is impossible. I wouldn't if I could. It is a preposterous request and reveals a lack of knowledge of the military requirements of this department."

"I do not take issue," Bingham said, "on whether I lack or possess any military knowledge, but I do not lack a sense of what is just and right, and that order is neither."

Their argument grew more heated. Bingham called the action "stupid and outrageous," insisting it would lead to more trouble along the border. He accused Ewing of issuing the order solely because he had been unable to prevent Quantrill from raiding in Kansas—or to catch him once he had—and to satisfy his political ambitions.

"I will say now," Bingham added, "and continue to say that Order Number Eleven is nothing but a revenge move on your part to pacify the people of Kansas who, you hope, some day after the war may have an opportunity to vote for you in preference to Jim Lane."

Ewing was livid.

"Mister Bingham, you can get out of here."

"Then you absolutely refuse to rescind the order?"

"It will not be rescinded except on the orders of my superior."

Bingham reached over the general's desk and shook his finger in Ewing's face.

"If you persist in executing this order," Bingham warned, "I shall make you infamous with my pen and brush so far as I am able."

Ewing smiled. What possible harm could some painting do him? But Bingham turned out to have the last laugh and the ultimate revenge. His painting entitled *Order Number Eleven* depicted General Ewing looking on while his troops evict a family from its home. In the work, which has been described as "mediocre art but superb propaganda," the soldiers are shown murdering two men. A woman kneels on the ground, begging for mercy as her house is pillaged.

Fourteen years later, in 1877, when Ewing was running for governor of Ohio, Bingham exhibited the painting throughout the state. Ewing lost the election, which put an end to his political aspirations.

Many years later, Ewing admitted to a friend that his General Orders Number 11 changed the lives of a lot of people. "It changed mine, I know," he commented. "It is in the past now, but I sometimes wonder if I had not issued that order . . . what might have happened." In 1896, Ewing died after being hit by a streetcar near his New York City law office.

Ewing also had a problem with Jim Lane. Lane had promised Ewing he would not cause any trouble if Ewing issued the depopulation order. Obviously, that was a promise he did not intend to keep, because he was threatening to amass a private avenging army of his own and lead it into Missouri to kill every rebel in sight.

When he returned to Lawrence after failing to take command of the forces pursuing Quantrill, Lane sensed the strong need among the survivors for revenge. The people wanted to ride into western Missouri, recover their stolen property, and take vengeance on the populace there. Always a persuasive speaker, Lane assured them he had already taken care of their concerns by forcing Ewing to issue his depopulation order.

To Lane's surprise, his announcement did not assuage the people. They had no confidence that Ewing would do the job properly. And even if the order was carried out fully, it merely meant the Missourians would be forced from their homes, free to take away their plunder from Lawrence and carry on their guerrilla warfare elsewhere. It was "a pardon to Rebels, not a punishment." The people of Lawrence demanded death; expulsion was not enough.

Ever the politician, Lane shifted his position from touting Ewing's plan to promoting one of his own. He would channel the

Kansans' hatred into an army under his command, an action that would guarantee him votes in Kansas for a generation. As a bonus, Lane's plan would ensure that Ewing would not become a hero and siphon off those future votes.

With all the furious energy of a demagogue, Lane embarked on his mission to enlist all Kansas in his crusade to punish Missouri. The fervor, fire, and thirst for vengeance were particularly keen in Fort Leavenworth, whose residents were convinced they were Quantrill's next target. On the night of August twenty-seventh, two days after General Ewing issued General Orders Number 11, a torchlit rally drew an angry crowd of ten thousand people, ready to ride, to follow Jim Lane into Missouri.

Other speakers roused the people to greater hatred: Charles Jennison, the notorious Jayhawker leader; Capt. George Hoyt, who shot and hanged his way through the border region during the pursuit of Quantrill; and Dan Anthony, Leavenworth's firebrand mayor and younger brother of the suffragist Susan B. Anthony.

For several hours, they harangued the crowd, calling for the destruction of western Missouri and warming up the mob for the master rabble-rouser, Jim Lane. For two hours, Lane held them spellbound with his inflammatory, theatrical oratory. He called for the extermination of the residents of the first tier of Missouri counties along the border. And if that did not work, if Kansas was still open to attack by bushwhackers, then they would exterminate the second tier of counties, and the third, and, if necessary, the entire state.

Lane called for five thousand men to march with him into Missouri to kill and scorch and burn, to turn the state into a desert. The crowd roared its approval; Lane could have twice that number of volunteers, an army of ten thousand. Lane announced he would assemble the invasion force September eighth in Paola, fifty miles southeast of Lawrence, ten miles from the border.

When General Schofield learned of this "Paola movement," as he called it, he vowed to stop it. There would be no army of vigilantes led by the likes of Jim Lane to spread murder and terror in his department. He left his St. Louis headquarters four days after Lane's mass meeting to put an end to the plan before it gathered more momentum. He had sent telegrams in advance of his arrival to Lane and the other leaders, forbidding any armed movement across the border. After Schofield's warning was read to the Leavenworth crowds, it was booed, jeered, and shouted down.

When Schofield met with Lane, the senator proposed that his army be placed under General Ewing's command—since Lane knew he had a hold over Ewing—a suggestion promptly denied by Schofield, who was not about to give official sanction to Lane's crusade. Schofield reiterated his unalterable opposition to the Paola movement, but Lane, unfazed, threatened to go over his head. Schofield later wrote: "If I decided not to allow the people the 'right' which they claimed, [Lane said] he would appeal to the President," whom Lane insisted was an old friend.

When Lane saw his threat had no effect, he switched tactics, offering to let Schofield command his army. He suggested none too subtly that doing so would win for Schofield considerable support among Kansans. Schofield cared no more for that enticement than for Lane's boast that he would take his case to Abraham Lincoln. To take command of a vigilante mob, Schofield later wrote, would mean that "I, of course, would be held responsible for the murder and robbery which must necessarily ensue."

General Schofield was proving tougher and more unyielding in dealing with Lane than Ewing had been. He told the senator that no armed mob would be allowed to cross the border as long as he was in command; he was prepared to meet such a mob with troops. On September fourth, he made that warning official with General Orders Number 92, which declared, "No armed bodies of men, not belonging to the United States troops . . . will be permitted, under any pretext whatever, to pass from one State to the other." Schofield reinforced the order by stationing more troops along the border, making sure their presence was highly visible to the people of Kansas.

Jim Lane had met his match. He knew he dared not violate Schofield's order, and he sensed that many Kansans were having second thoughts about invading Missouri to seek vengeance. Word was spreading that Ewing's depopulation order was proving effective in clearing out the border counties, and growing numbers of Kansans seemed content to let the army get on with its job. If Ewing's troops were successful in ridding the border region of Missourians, then there was no need for Kansans to cross over and do it themselves.

A couple of hundred armed men did show up in Paola on September eighth, far fewer than the five thousand Lane had called for. They were eager enough, however, and they whistled and cheered when Lane mounted the platform. He was always good for a show. Just as Lane started to speak, it began to rain, and showers continued for the next three hours while Lane worked the crowd.

He ranted, raved, threatened, and condemned Quantrill, Ewing, Schofield, and everybody else he could think of, but he barely mentioned his plan to invade Missouri, which was the reason the men had come to Paola. They cheered the few times he made reference to crossing the border, but he always passed quickly over that point to move on to another topic.

The crowd grew impatient standing in the pouring rain, and several yelled that it was time to get started. Lane tried to quiet their passion, and finally he told them that the United States Army would not let them cross the border.

With that, the fervor died, and people began drifting away. The meeting ended with the onlookers shouting their approval of a few meaningless resolutions condemning the residents of Missouri. The Paola movement was over, and with it went much of Jim Lane's influence and political power.

In 1866, a year after the Civil War had ended, Lane began to show signs of mental derangement. He sought rest and treatment at a government asylum outside Leavenworth. John Speer, the Lawrence newspaper editor, who later wrote a biography of Lane, went to visit him.

"The pitcher is broken at the fountain," Lane told Speer enigmatically. "My life is ended; I want you to do my memory justice; I ask nothing more."

Two days later, Lane went riding in a carriage with two orderlies. As they got out to open a gate, Lane also stepped out.

"Good-bye, Mac," he called to one of them.

He pulled a revolver from his pocket, placed it in his mouth, and fired one bullet through his brain. Gravely wounded, he lingered for several days. When the Reverend Hugh Fisher from Lawrence came to visit Lane on his deathbed, Lane took Fisher's hand in his, placed it on his bandaged head, and said, "Bad, bad." Soon afterward, Lane died.

14

IT WAS A FEARFUL SIGHT

BY THE MIDDLE of September, the border region lay desolate and barren. Not a house, barn, or haystack remained. A passerby might well think he had wandered to the end of the world and was the only person left alive. Stark chimneys, remnants of a lost civilization, broke the flat prairie landscape, and the stench of dead livestock and burned wood tainted the sweet air.

Ewing had succeeded in creating a desert out of a lush, rich garden, but "those whom his order was designed to destroy, the bushwhackers, were least injured of all by it. In fact, its immediate effect on them was practically nil. To quote one of Ewing's Missouri critics, they 'laughed at it.' "

It was true Quantrill could no longer operate so freely. Ewing had ordered cavalry patrols to scour the area, chase the raiders down, and take no prisoners. But the Federals, seeing bushwhackers waiting in ambush in every gully and wood, stuck to the main roads and open country, where Quantrill's men could see them a mile or two away. Still, there were enough Yankee soldiers around that Quantrill thought it wise to hide during daylight hours and come out only at night to find food. Sufficient numbers of chickens and cows had been left, enough to keep them well fed, at least for a few weeks.

Quantrill kept moving his camp; there was no use in tempting fate. With so many federal troops inundating the region, more than western Missouri had ever seen at one time, they might come across him by accident. Capt. Charles Coleman was out there searching for him, and Lt. Col. Bazel Lazear, along with many other officers, each longing to be the one to run Quantrill down. Lazear had close to one thousand men in his command. It was best to keep moving, Quantrill knew.

On September fifteenth, a cavalry patrol led by Captain Coleman surprised Quantrill in his main camp. They swooped down on the bushwhackers, killing two. Quantrill and his men fled to the gorges and thickets of the Sni-A-Bar. The soldiers captured forty horses and confiscated a huge supply of ammunition, clothing, and food.

Quantrill moved back to the area around Blue Springs to set up a new camp at the Stanley farm. His wife, Kate, joined him there. They lived in close quarters in a one-room log cabin, together with George Todd and his mistress. A few days later, a picket brought word that a Union patrol was closing in. Quantrill and Todd saddled horses for the women and told them to ride hard. Risking their own lives was one thing, but they were not about to take unnecessary chances with their women.

Quantrill ordered his men to break camp. He was not prepared to do battle with the Union patrol because he did not know the size of the enemy force. It was time to hide, not fight, and so he led his men deeper into the tangled forests. He chose a new campsite at the Dillingham farm, southwest of Blue Springs. It was an excellent hiding place, deep in the woods, with only one trail leading to it. Even if the Yankees chanced upon it and were foolish enough to ride in, he could hold them off for days with a small force while the rest of the raiders escaped in a region they knew as well as their own homes.

By the end of September, Quantrill decided it was time to head south to Texas, as he did every winter to escape the cold and leafless forests that provided so little cover. This year, there were too many Yankees about to risk further raiding, and too little food to be found in the scorched countryside. Also, bad weather was settling in earlier than usual. He sent out word for his men, who had scattered into smaller bands, to assemble at Captain Perdee's farm on the Blackwater River, where they had gathered so many times before.

Bloody Bill Anderson's group met Quantrill there, along with Colonel Holt's recruits and other smaller outfits. Kate Quantrill came to say good-bye to her husband. She planned to spend the winter with her father, to wait for Quantrill's return in the spring. About four hundred men assembled at Perdee's place, and on October first, Quantrill led them out.

They crossed the border into Kansas near Baxter Springs, in the southeast corner of the state. They were no more than five miles from Indian Territory, the region that later became Oklahoma, having traveled more than 120 miles in five days. On the morning of October sixth, Dave Pool led the advance party. At a river ford, they captured a wagon loaded with lumber, driven by two teamsters, who told Pool they were on their way to a Union encampment at Baxter Springs, which was news to Pool. He had no idea Union troops were in the area.

Pool killed the teamsters and rode ahead to scout the size of the Union force, leaving one man behind to tell Quantrill. When Quantrill heard about the Federals, he sent Bill Gregg with a detachment to reinforce Pool, then led the rest of his men through the forest to approach the Yankee troops from the north.

John McCorkle, who was with the advance party, wrote, "We all then rushed up the creek and to our utter surprise, we found a fort at Baxter Springs. None of us had ever heard that there was a fort there with a command of troops stationed in it."

It was not much of a fort, a three-sided embankment four feet high built of dirt and logs. A few log cabins stood outside the enclosure, and a cooking and eating camp was two hundred feet away. The fort was too small for its detachment of 150 Negro troops to be quartered inside. Their commanding officer, Lt. James Pond, had arrived only two days before. Sixty of his men were out on a foraging expedition, and most of the remaining Union soldiers were in the cooking camp awaiting the noon meal. They did not have their weapons with them because they knew there were no rebels about for miles. Lieutenant Pond was in his tent nearby. It was twelve o'clock.

Dave Pool and Bill Gregg led their men in a charge, yelling and firing their Colts. Pool's men raced between the troops and the fort, hoping to cut them off and run them down while they were out in the open. The black soldiers ran for the fort, through the mounted guerrillas. Some were hit, but most made it to the safety of the walls, with the bushwhackers right behind them. Some even rode inside the fort.

Lieutenant Pond reached the fort safely and headed for a small howitzer, the detachment's only artillery piece. He had never fired a howitzer before, but he manhandled it into position and managed to get off three rounds. He did not hit any of the rebels, but the cannon's sharp report took them by surprise. They lost their momentum and their courage, and soon they made a disorderly retreat. By then, the black troops had retrieved their weapons and were firing back at the enemy from strong defensive positions behind the dirt and log walls. Nine men had been killed and ten wounded, but the rest would live that day. Pond later received the Medal of Honor for his actions.

Quantrill did not participate in the brief battle at the fort. He had ridden at a leisurely pace through the woods and across the open prairie a few hundred yards from the fighting. As he gazed down the Fort Scott Road, he saw a sight that caused him to rein in his horse and order his men to form a battle line. Two hundred yards away stood a column of wagons with a cavalry escort. They were Yankees, and they, too, were formed in a line of battle.

Maj. Gen. James Blunt was pleased to see the large number of what appeared to be blue-uniformed cavalry up ahead. He assumed it was a welcoming party sent out by the commander of the fort at Baxter Springs. A quirk of topography, a long high ridge, had prevented him from hearing the battle. As far as he was concerned, the cavalry two hundred yards down the road was there to honor a visitor wearing two stars.

Blunt, the coarse, unscrupulous, brash former doctor and protégé of Jim Lane, had lost his command in eastern Kansas to Thomas Ewing and had been sent in disgrace to the western part of the state. He had performed better there, where he did not have Quantrill to contend with, and was on his way to a new assignment, with headquarters at Fort Gibson, Indian Territory. It was pure chance and Blunt's bad luck that he approached Baxter Springs at the moment four hundred bushwhackers were attacking it. Blunt was leading a column of eight wagons, with an assortment of staff officers, a few civilians, including one woman, his brass band, of which he was inordinately proud, and an escort of one hundred cavalry.

As Blunt stared at the welcoming party, he became increasingly suspicious. He saw some of them riding up and down the line of men, who milled about in some confusion. If they were Union troops, they were not very well trained or disciplined. He sent two officers forward to take a closer look. They raced back with the news that the men were guerrillas. Blunt was not worried. He was far from Quantrill country, and he knew bushwhackers that far south were no threat to him.

"Oh," he said, laughing, "it is just a few of Jackman's guerrillas from South Missouri. Give them a few rounds and they will run off to cover."

Quantrill rode behind the whole length of the line, getting his men in formation, ready to attack. Then he took off his hat, stuffed it inside his coat, and spurred his horse forward.

"Come on, boys," he shouted.

The raiders charged at the same time Blunt led his men forward. "I turned toward my escort to give the command to fire," Blunt wrote in his report, "when I discovered the line broken, and all of them in full gallop over the prairie, completely panic-stricken." Blunt was alone, facing four hundred charging bushwhackers. He had no choice but to turn tail and ride after his men. He yelled and cursed. He called them cowards and tried to get them to stop and form a defensive line, but it was hopeless. No one was willing to stand and fight a force four times larger than their own.

When Blunt reached the wagons, he got his civilian passenger, twenty-two-year-old Mrs. Chester Thomas, out of his buggy and onto one of his fastest horses. There was no time for decorum, and the young woman mounted the horse astride on a regular saddle, a position unheard of for a lady, who always rode sidesaddle. Blunt and the woman rode off, the general calling to her to hold on to the saddle horn for dear life.

John McCorkle and a few other raiders spied the bulky general and went after him, knowing he would be a prize catch, but Blunt and Mrs. Thomas had better horses and quickly outdistanced their pursuers with a final leap over a gorge. Blunt was fortunate that he was accompanied by a woman, because otherwise the rebels would have shot him down. "Several of us boys tried to catch them," McCorkle said, "and followed them about a mile and of course, we would not shoot at them on account of the woman." The general survived the day, but he had suffered the most humiliating defeat of his career. He died in an insane asylum sixteen years later.

The bushwhackers took no prisoners among the soldiers. One by one, the troops were run down and slaughtered, most at a ravine their horses were not able to leap. "We followed these soldiers for about three miles," John McCorkle recalled, "leaving most of them on the prairie and there were only a few of them that ever returned our fire."

Most of Blunt's one-hundred-man escort was killed. Lt. Col. Charles Blair wrote, "It was a fearful sight; some 85 bodies, nearly all shot through the head, most of them shot from five to seven times each, horribly mangled. . . . The wounded, who numbered six or seven, were all shot at least six times."

Maj. Benjamin Henning, another of Blunt's officers, reported that the men were told they would be treated as prisoners of war if they agreed to surrender, but as soon as they raised their hands to do so, they were then shot down.

Sgt. Jack Splane put up his hands to surrender and was shot five times. He survived, recalling that the man who shot him shouted as he pulled the trigger: "Tell old God that the last man you saw on earth was Quantrill." Pvt. Jesse Smith was shot several times but remained conscious, lying facedown in the grass. He later told Major Henning that "the rebel who shot him . . . jumped upon his back and essayed to dance, uttering the most vile imprecations."

Greater savagery was reserved for a wagonload of men trying to escape. Aboard the wagon were the driver, fourteen musicians of General Blunt's band and their twelve-year-old drummer boy, and a civilian reporter, James O'Neal of *Frank Leslie's Weekly*. Bill Bledsoe rode up to the wagon and demanded the men surrender. Someone aboard took a shot at him, and Bledsoe fell off his horse, mortally wounded. The driver whipped his team of mules, urging them on as fast as they would go.

"Fletch," Bledsoe called to his friend Fletch Taylor, "that outfit have shot and killed me; take my two pistols and kill all of them."

Taylor took off after the wagon, with several other guerrillas close behind. The mules kept up a good pace until the wagon's left front wheel fell off, tumbling the men out onto the ground. They gestured that they would surrender, but they were shot down, even the drummer boy and the reporter, who may have been the only Civil War correspondent to be killed in battle.

The wagon was set afire, and the bushwhackers hurled the bandsmen's bodies into the flames. Major Henning saw the corpses afterward and described the terrible fate of the young drummer boy; he was still alive when Quantrill's men tossed him into the blazing wagon. "When the fire reached his clothes it must have brought returned consciousness, as he had crawled a distance of 30 yards, marking the course by bits of burning clothes and scorched grass, and was found dead with all his clothes burned off except the portion between his back and the ground."

The bushwhackers took two civilian prisoners, both black men. One had a stroke of good fortune; the other did not. Rube was the lucky one. He was driving General Blunt's buggy when George Maddox captured him. Maddox raised his gun, about to pull the trigger.

"Before you shoot me," Rube said, "I want to ask you a question."

Amazed at the man's nerve, Maddox allowed him to speak. Rube asked if George Todd was with the gang.

"Please don't shoot me until I see him," Rube said.

Maddox yelled for Todd to come over.

"By God, it's Rube!" Todd said, recognizing the prisoner.

He shook Rube's hand, greeting him like a long-lost brother. Then he confronted his men, gesturing at Rube with his thumb.

"Boys, the first man that hurts this nigger, I will kill."

Rube, a freed black, had saved George Todd's life back when Rube had a barbershop in Kansas City. While cutting a Yankee officer's hair, Rube overheard the officer and a friend discussing their plan to capture that no-good bushwhacker George Todd, who was visiting his father in town. Rube told Todd's father about the Yankee plan and offered to hide George in the cellar of his house. George Todd stayed with Rube for ten days, until Rube could arrange for Todd to escape. Now Todd was pleased to return the favor, and Rube was taken with the guerrillas to Texas, where he took up his old trade, giving haircuts to the bushwhackers.

The other black prisoner, Jack Mann, was well known to the guerrillas. They hated him, particularly George Maddox. In 1861, Mann had run away from his owner in Missouri and come to Kansas, where he joined the Jayhawkers, serving as a guide on a number of raids into Missouri. Worse, in the eyes of Southerners, Jack Mann had insulted white women, including Maddox's wife.

Mann had led a gang of Kansans to the Maddox house. While looting the home, Mann found Maddox's wedding suit. He undressed in front of Mrs. Maddox, a sin in itself, put on her husband's suit, and asked how she liked the way he looked. The odds against his surviving capture were not high. Maddox wanted to shoot him on sight, but Quantrill said they would take care of him later. First, they had some looting of their own to do.

In addition to the usual plunder—food, weapons, ammunition, and clothing—Quantrill's men found an expensive saddle and saber belonging to General Blunt, as well as his ornate personal flag. Opening one of many trunks, John McCorkle found a colonel's new tailored uniform, along with expensive boots, six fine shirts, and a pair of Colt revolvers.

What interested the men most was what they found in the dead Yankees' canteens: whiskey! Before long, most of them were drunk and reeling about while feasting on tins of fine delicacies Blunt had been carrying. Riley Crawford picked up a Union cavalry saber and flailed it about. He stopped next to one of the dead federal soldiers and struck him with the flat of the sword.

"Get up, you Federal son of a bitch."

To everyone's astonishment, the dead soldier stood up like a ghost rising from the grave. He had been pretending to be wounded, hoping to save himself, but apparently he figured that now his ruse had been uncovered. Riley Crawford shot him without a word.

Quantrill found his own private stash, a five-gallon demijohn of brandy that was part of General Blunt's personal stock. Quantrill liberated it with enthusiasm. It was the only time any of his men, including his closest lieutenants, had ever seen him drunk. He wandered around the battlefield drinking and boasting about his success.

"By God," he shouted, "Shelby could not whip Blunt; neither could Marmaduke, but I whipped him."

He spied John McCorkle and decided to have some fun at his

expense. McCorkle had been with the advance party, whose discovery of the Union troops had led to the battle. Forward scouts were sometimes referred to as "pilots" because they guided the main body.

"John," Quantrill said harshly, "I thought you always knew that whenever a pilot led me into trouble, I always shoot him."

McCorkle knew that when Quantrill talked about killing, he meant what he said. And now that he was drunk, who knew what he might do? McCorkle pulled out his Navy Colt.

"If you can shoot quicker than I can, shoot."

Quantrill broke out laughing.

"Put that thing up, you damned fool," he said. "I'm going to shoot you in the neck."

Quantrill handed the bottle to a much-relieved McCorkle, who took a long drink from it. Being shot in the neck was a slang expression for having a drink.

George Todd and Bloody Bill Anderson wanted to attack the fort, but Quantrill was not interested. He may have been drunk, but he was not foolish enough to assault well-armed troops with stout walls in front of them.

"No," he said, "there is nothing to be gained by taking it. Beside, we would probably lose fifteen or twenty men, and, I would not give the life of one of my men for the whole business."

They left Baxter Springs at five o'clock that afternoon, taking Blunt's ambulance for Bill Bledsoe's body and a wounded man, John Koger. The other two wounded were able to ride their horses. The casualties among Quantrill's force had once again been extremely light, out of proportion to the Union losses. In assaulting the fort, one man was killed and two wounded; Bledsoe was killed and Koger wounded in the fight with Blunt's soldiers. Rube, whom McCorkle dubbed "Todd's pet nigger," drove the ambulance, and Jack Mann was brought along under tight guard.

They had gone about ten miles when Koger complained that Bledsoe was starting to smell bad, and they stopped to bury him.

None of them had any shovels, so they carried Bledsoe's body to an abandoned house. The garden had been recently plowed. Using boards and a stick, the men scooped out a shallow grave.

Will McGuire was detached to stand guard over Jack Mann. Perhaps Mann wanted to get the inevitable over with, for he surely knew they would never let him go. But whatever his intent, he began to insult McGuire. McGuire tolerated the stream of abuse as long as he could, then shot Mann directly between the eyes. George Maddox was furious that he had been deprived of the chance to kill Mann himself. He pulled out his gun and turned on McGuire. The others restrained him in time.

At dusk, they chanced upon a wagon train with twelve Creek Indians; it was thought that they favored the Union cause and had ridden with Kansas Jayhawkers. No one knew that for certain, but suspicion alone was reason enough for conviction. They were captured easily without a fight, then slaughtered to a man. As John McCorkle put it, "In a short time, they were all good Indians." It had been quite a day.

The bushwhackers continued south into Indian Territory. On October twelfth, they stopped at an encampment of Confederate troops. Here, Quantrill wrote his one and only official military report of the war. He sent it to Maj. Gen. Sterling Price, the fifty-three-year-old former governor of Missouri who commanded an army made up mostly of Missourians. Called "Old Pap" by his men, Price, who had fought in the Mexican War, had little regard for West Pointers. He took great pleasure in boasting, once in a newspaper interview, that he had no military training. He was then headquartered at Camp Bragg, Arkansas, not far from the Texas border.

Quantrill wrote a vague description of the fight at Fort Baxter, and with General Blunt's troops. He reported that Blunt was among those killed, which he knew was not true. He also wildly exaggerated his accomplishments during the march south from Baxter Springs, claiming to have killed 150 Indians and Negroes. "We caught about 150 Federal Indians and negroes in the [Indian] Nation gathering ponies. We brought none of them through."

Along with his report, he sent, as gifts to General Price, Blunt's elaborate saber, flag, commission, and all his official papers. He brazenly signed the document, "Colonel, Commanding." He apparently thought that after "whipping Blunt," which Confederate generals had been unable to do, he damned well deserved to be colonel. If Richmond would not recognize his contributions by giving him the rank, then he would appropriate it for himself. A singular omission from his long report was any mention whatsoever of Lawrence. He noted, however, that "At some future day I will send you a complete report of my summer's campaign on the Missouri River." He never sent such a report, not to Price or to anyone else.

A few days later, Quantrill led his men farther south, across the Red River twelve miles into Texas, where they established their winter camp at Mineral Springs, northwest of the town of Sherman. There they built rough log cabins to keep out the winter cold and laid in a supply of deer meat. Quantrill sold Blunt's ambulance and mule team for enough money to buy a rare item of luxury in the Confederacy at that stage of the war: four hundred pounds of real coffee.

According to John McCorkle, the guerrillas were welcomed royally in Sherman and invited to any number of dances and parties that winter, including a lavish Christmas ball. The reality was apparently quite different; "it was not a pleasant winter for the people of Sherman." Quantrill's men had a grand time at the town's expense.

They rode into town bent on hell-raising every day. At the local track, they engaged in raucous horse races, which Quantrill almost always won. His horse, Old Charley, was the fastest one around, and also the meanest to anyone other than him. If someone else so much as walked too close, Old Charley, whom Quantrill had captured from a Yankee officer in Independence, would kick and bite. Yet with him, the horse was as tame and gentle as could be.

What was much worse for the residents of Sherman were the

bushwhackers' drunken rampages. On Christmas Day, they rode their horses into the Christian Hotel and shot the tassels and ornaments off the hat of an elderly woman while she was wearing it. They shot holes in the church steeples, and doorknobs off doors. They had a very merry Christmas.

Another bunch of Quantrill's men went to have their pictures taken by the town photographer. They posed on horseback with guns drawn, but they did not like the way the photographs turned out. They smashed the photographer's camera and ransacked his shop, leaving it a wreck.

Quantrill did not go along on those drunken sprees, and he was angry when Ben Christian, the hotel owner, sent word to him about what his men had done. He rode into town with the guerrillas who were sober, carted off the drunks, and apologized to the residents. The next day, he made those who had vandalized the photographer's studio pay for the damage. Quantrill's boys were not good neighbors when they got drunk, and that was often.

Some of his men had opportunities for romance. Cole Younger's mother had moved to nearby Scyene, Texas, after being forced to burn her home and flee the border region of Missouri under Ewing's General Orders Number 11. While visiting her, Cole met an old friend from Missouri, John Shirley, who owned a saloon in town. Mr. Shirley had a daughter, Myra Maebelle, who took a fancy to Cole. Myra was described as "a fairly good-looking girl of sixteen with unusually black hair and black eyes. She didn't have to be too ravishing to intrigue Cole, who had seen few girls since he had taken to the brush. Cole found her definitely interesting."

Myra Maebelle was charming, vivacious, and an accomplished pianist who had attended a finishing school back east. She flirted with the guerrillas, including Frank and Jesse James, but Cole Younger was her favorite. She claimed to be in love with him and later insisted he was the father of her first child. Cole denied it for the rest of his life. After the war, she married Sam Starr, changed her name to Belle, and became as notorious an outlaw as any of the Youngers or the James boys. Among her several later husbands was Cole's uncle, whom she married in 1880. In 1889, she was shot in the back and killed in a dispute with a neighbor.

Bloody Bill Anderson fell in love with a Sherman girl named Bush Smith and announced his intention to marry her at Christmas. Quantrill objected, demanding that Anderson wait until the war was over to get married, even though he had not waited to marry Kate. Anderson defied Quantrill and went ahead with the wedding. (Some of the guerrillas claimed that Anderson and Smith never married but that Smith was a prostitute who became Anderson's mistress.) Anderson soon chose to leave with his band and set up a separate camp nearby.

It was a tense situation, with each man threatening to shoot the other and posting armed guards in case of attack. The residents of Sherman were terrified, fully expecting that Quantrill's and Anderson's bands would settle accounts in a bloody battle in the streets. No shots were fired, but Anderson's defection was the first of many that winter. Eventually, this would lead to Quantrill's downfall as the undisputed leader of the bushwhackers.

Not only were some of Quantrill's own men becoming disaffected with him but so also were some Confederate leaders as word spread of the atrocities at Lawrence and Baxter Springs. Others, however, were lavish in their praise of him on his return to Texas. Gen. Sterling Price was one of those who commended Quantrill for his actions.

Writing to Thomas C. Reynolds, the governor of Missouri, Price enclosed a copy of Quantrill's report to him and strongly endorsed the guerrilla leader. "Colonel Quantrill has now with him some 350 men of that daring and dashing character which has made the name of Quantrill so feared by our enemies, and have aided so much to keep Missouri, though overrun by Federals, identified with the Confederacy."

Maj. Gen. John B. Magruder, commanding the District of Texas, published an order that was distributed throughout his command; he congratulated Colonel Quantrill on his defeat of

General Blunt at Baxter Springs. Other Confederate generals expressed a desire to meet the dashing guerrilla leader when it became known that he was back in Texas.

However, even General Price, Quantrill's most ardent supporter, grew worried as more stories filtered south about the massacre at Lawrence and the wanton killings of members of Blunt's command at Baxter Springs, including those who had surrendered. When Price replied to Quantrill's report to him, he congratulated Quantrill and his "gallant command" on their great successes in battle, but he also requested a full report of Quantrill's summer campaign as soon as possible, so that "your acts should appear in their true light before the world." He wanted to be able to refute the rumors about Quantrill giving no quarter to soldiers and civilians alike.

One Confederate general who saw nothing noble, valiant, or praiseworthy in Quantrill's tactics, and who condemned him as soon as the raiders appeared in Texas, was Brig. Gen. Ben McCulloch, who commanded the District of North Texas. McCulloch's command included the town of Sherman, where the bushwhackers were encamped. McCulloch's headquarters was in Bonham, only a few miles from Sherman. He began hearing stories about the behavior of Quantrill's men soon after they arrived, and he did not like what he heard. On October twenty-second, no more than a week after Quantrill reached Sherman, McCulloch wrote a scathing letter about him to Lt. Gen. Edmund Kirby Smith, commander of the Trans-Mississippi Department, headquartered in Shreveport, Louisiana.

A good many of Colonel Quantrill's command have come into this sub-district, and it is said that he is now within it. He has not reported here, and I do not know what his military status is. I do not know as much about his mode of warfare as others seem to know; but, from all I can learn, it is but little, if at all, removed from that of the wildest savage; so much so, that I do not for a moment believe that our Government can sanction it in one of her officers. Hence, it seems to me if he be an officer of our army, his conduct should be officially noticed,

and if he be not an officer of our army, his acts should be dis-
avowed by our Government, and, as far as practicable, he be
made to understand that we would greatly prefer his remaining away from our army or its vicinity.

I appreciate his services, and am anxious to have them; but
certainly we cannot, as a Christian people, sanction a savage,
inhuman warfare, in which men are to be shot down like dogs,
after throwing down their arms and holding up their hands
supplicating for mercy.

This is a matter to which I wish to call the serious attention
of our commanding generals, and with regard to which I desire their advice and instructions as early as practicable.

Ten days later, McCulloch wrote again to General Smith on a
number of issues, one of which was his continuing disdain for
Quantrill and his quandary over what to do about him. Smith had
not responded to McCulloch's previous request for advice and
instructions. McCulloch wrote, "It may be said that Quantrill will
help you. That may be true in part, but I have but little confidence in men who fight for booty, and whose mode of warfare
is but little, if any, above the uncivilized Indian."

General Smith, a thirty-nine-year-old West Pointer, described as
"Regular Army to the shoesoles," continued to defend Quantrill.
He needed men who would fight hard, and who could keep Yan-
kee forces in Kansas and Missouri so busy that they would stay
out of his territory. And Quantrill had managed to tie up a lot of
Union troops that were chasing after him and guarding the
Kansas border from him.

He wrote to General McCulloch on November second.

Quantrill's Missourians . . . are bold, fearless men, and, more-
over, from all representations, are under very fair discipline.
They are composed, I understand, in a measure of the very best
class of Missourians. They have suffered every outrage in their
person and families at the hands of the Federals, and, being

outlawed and their lives forfeited, have waged a war of no quarter whenever they have come in contact with the enemy.

General Smith obviously had no firsthand knowledge of what Quantrill's men were like. He believed they could be useful in his command, and he suggested that McCulloch employ them to round up several groups of lawless Confederate deserters who were committing mayhem in north Texas. "The best disposition you can make of [Quantrill's men] will be in breaking up and bringing in the bands of deserters in your district," Smith told McCulloch.

General Smith also made it clear, however, that he was not ordering McCulloch to use Quantrill's men for that purpose, or for any purpose, for that matter. If McCulloch did not wish to make use of the guerrillas, then he was instructed to send Quantrill to Shreveport to meet personally with Smith, who would then decide what to do with him.

The choice was an easy one for McCulloch, who not only did not want the guerrillas in his command but also wanted them as far away from north Texas as possible. Let someone else deal with Quantrill and his band of wild savages. He told Quantrill to go to Shreveport. Quantrill met with General Smith there, and he did his best to persuade Smith that he was a well-bred man of honor who had been much misunderstood and unjustly maligned. Apparently, he was at least partially successful.

Smith sent him back to Sherman with orders to McCulloch to employ the bushwhackers in dealing with the roving bands of deserters. However, he cautioned McCulloch to be wary of Quantrill, advice McCulloch clearly did not need. Smith went on to describe Quantrill as a ruthless fighter who could nonetheless be useful to the Confederacy, as long as he was watched carefully. And he was leaving it to McCulloch to do the watching.

Now McCulloch had no choice but to keep Quantrill in his command. However, in late December, an opportunity arose to shift him away from Sherman in order to repel a Union invading force. The Yankees were thirty-five miles west of Sherman, around the town of Gainesville, Texas, and they outnumbered

Quantrill's men by two to one. The bushwhackers marched due west, but by the time they reached Gainesville, the Federals had already crossed the Red River and were heading back north.

The guerrillas returned to their camp, where they received no further orders from McCulloch. Bored and restless, and craving action, they began to roam the countryside and treat the northern part of Texas as though it were Kansas, enemy territory ripe for plunder. They went on bloody raiding parties, sometimes with, but just as often without, Quantrill's authorization. He was losing his control over them.

They robbed farmers and killed those who resisted. They ransacked a distillery, burning the place to the ground and killing one man, then telling the neighbors they would die if they told anybody what had happened. One day, Quantrill, wearing Union blue, led some of his men to the farm of a loyal Confederate family. He gruffly demanded that the women of the house feed his men, which they did promptly with the best food they had. As they left, Quantrill casually tossed a silk handkerchief to a young woman. Then the bushwhackers made off with all the family's horses and cattle. He was Charley Hart again, taking whatever he wanted and fighting for no cause but his own.

Some of his men killed a Confederate officer. When Quantrill heard about it, he promised that the murderers would be court-martialed, but when he found out they were good friends of his, he refused to turn them over to Confederate authorities. Other guerrillas killed a farmer in the area, after robbing him of a considerable sum of money. Another local man was found murdered after playing poker with five of Quantrill's men. The bushwhackers were terrorizing the people of north Texas as if they were the worst of the Jayhawkers up in Kansas. They were out of control, and a far greater threat to the residents than the Yankees, who remained miles away.

General McCulloch was livid when he learned of these outrages. He had warned General Smith about Quantrill's men, and the general had not taken heed. It was time to try again.

Something had to be done about Quantrill and his killers—the "brush crowd," as he called them. Citizens of north Texas were pleading with him for protection from the guerrillas, and Bloody Bill Anderson, still nursing his grievances at Quantrill about his wedding, told McCulloch that Quantrill's men, and not his own, were the ones causing all the trouble.

On February third, McCulloch wrote to his immediate superior, General Magruder, complaining about Quantrill and threatening to arrest him.

> Quantrill will not obey orders, and so much mischief is charged to his command here that I have determined to disarm, arrest, and send his entire command to you or General Smith. This is the only chance to get them out of this section of country, which they have nearly ruined. . . . They regard the life of a man less than you would that of a sheep-killing dog. . . .
>
> Quantrill and his men are determined never to go into the army or fight in any general battle, first, because many of them are deserters from our Confederate ranks, and next, because they are afraid of being captured, and then because it won't pay men who fight for plunder. They will only fight when they have all the advantage and when they can run whenever they find things too hot for them. I regard them as but one shade better than highwaymen, and the community believe that they have committed all the robberies that have been committed about here for some time.

Two days later, McCulloch told General Smith that he had ordered Quantrill and his whole command to be arrested. "They will not obey orders," he wrote to Smith, "and I don't know what else to do. What shall I do with them after arresting them?"

Despite his announced intention to Magruder and Smith to arrest Quantrill and his men, McCulloch took no immediate steps to do so. Instead, he tried a different approach to get rid of them. He attempted to persuade Brig. Gen. H. P. Bee, whose command was far south, along the Texas coast, to take Quantrill's band. Four days after complaining about Quantrill to Smith, he wrote a less than candid letter to General Bee, arguing that Quantrill's men "will do us great good" in the area west of Corpus Christi. Where McCulloch wanted to send the guerrillas was over 420 miles south of Sherman.

He assured Bee that the bushwhackers were "true Southern men" and were not guilty of a fraction of the crimes charged against them. They were victims, he said, of the worst kinds of characters, men who hid in the brush and came out only at night to rob and steal. It was they who had spread "bad tales" about Quantrill's men, only some of which were true. "They are superbly armed and well mounted, and there is no reason that they should not do good service."

It was a valiant try, but it failed. When General Magruder ordered Quantrill south, he refused to go. He said that his commission as a Partisan Ranger came directly from Jefferson Davis, and, as such, he was not answerable to anyone other than the President of the Confederacy.

Now General McCulloch had no choice but to arrest the Confederacy's most daring guerrilla leader, a man hailed and praised all over the South as a hero for taking the war directly to the Yankees in that hotbed of abolitionism, Lawrence, Kansas. On March 30, 1864, Quantrill was ordered to present himself immediately at McCulloch's headquarters in Bonham.

Quantrill knew he was in trouble with McCulloch and that the general wanted to be rid of him, but he obeyed the summons anyway—not, however, without taking precautions. He left George Todd and twelve men behind to guard their camp, then left for Bonham with the rest of the men, who numbered around two hundred at that time. When he arrived at McCulloch's headquarters at the City Hotel in Bonham, he told his men to wait outside, stay alert for any signs of trouble, and keep his horse handy in case he had to make a quick getaway.

As soon as Quantrill entered the general's room, McCulloch told him he was under arrest, then ordered him to remove his sidearms. Quantrill glanced at the two armed guards, threw his two Navy Colts on a cot, and demanded to know why he was being arrested. McCulloch replied that it was noon and time for dinner. He invited Quantrill to go downstairs and eat with him. After dinner, he said, they would discuss the matter.

"No, sir," Quantrill shouted. "I will not go to dinner. By God! I don't care a God damn if I never taste another mouthful on this earth."

McCulloch shrugged and went to the hotel dining room, leaving Quantrill alone with the two guards. Quantrill sat down in a chair in sullen silence for a bit, then asked the guards if it would be all right if he got a drink of water. When they agreed, he walked over to a water jug, filled a cup, then threw it on the floor and grabbed both his revolvers from the cot before the guards had a chance to react.

He disarmed them and locked them in the general's room, taking the key with him. He raced down the single flight of stairs, got the drop on two more guards at the bottom, and ordered them, at gunpoint, to walk through the lobby and go outside.

"Boys," he shouted to his men. "The outfit is under arrest! Let's get out of here!"

He sent one of his men back to camp to tell Todd and his men to get out as fast as they could and to take all the ammunition and other supplies they could carry. They were to meet Quantrill at Colbert's Ferry on the Red River. Meanwhile, McCulloch ordered Colonel J. Martin to take his regiment after Quantrill and bring him back dead or alive. As the troopers started off in pursuit, Bloody Bill Anderson and his men joined the column to help chase down their former commander.

While Quantrill and his main force crossed the Red River, Todd and his men stayed behind as a rear guard. During the afternoon, they skirmished with Anderson's gang, which was scouting ahead for Colonel Martin. Each side had one man hit, but there were no deaths, and the two bands went their separate ways. The next morning, Todd's tiny force confronted Colonel Martin and his whole regiment, which outnumbered them by fifteen or twenty to one. Todd demanded to know what the hell Martin thought he was doing. Martin replied that he had been ordered by General McCulloch to get Quantrill.

"Well," Todd yelled, as if he considered Martin not too bright to be off on such a stupid mission, "don't you know that you're not going to get him? Now you listen to me—you had better get your men together and go back to Bonham and tell General McCulloch that Quantrill said that if he was molested any further he would turn his bushwhackers loose in Texas and he would not be responsible for anything that might happen or what his men did!"

Todd calmly turned his horse around and rode away, confident that his bluff would work. It did. Martin, dumbfounded at being talked to in that manner, led his regiment back to Bonham. A short time later, a thoroughly disgusted McCulloch complained to General Magruder that he could do nothing about Quantrill because he lacked men with sufficient courage to arrest him.

He gave up trying to get rid of Quantrill. All he could do, he realized, was hope for an early spring. Quantrill would head back to Missouri as soon as the grass turned green. That was the only way McCulloch would finally be rid of him. He did not know that Quantrill's men were doing what he had been unable to do. Quantrill's days as their leader were coming to an ignominious end. He would continue to fight—he knew no other way to live—but he would no longer command.

15
DEATH IS COMING

THEY LEFT HIM one by one, like so many leaves falling away from a dying tree. Some left because they were appalled and ashamed at what they had done at Lawrence, gunning down unarmed men and boys, terrorizing women and children, looting and destroying homes. They felt they had gone too far and had become no more than common killers, no longer soldiers. As Bill Gregg put it, "This wholesale killing was repugnant to many of the men."

Others left because they came to believe they had been duped about the reason for the raid on Lawrence. Quantrill had told some of the men that whatever money and other valuables they got at Lawrence would be distributed among the people of the Missouri border region who had helped them. He said he wanted to pay them back for all the aid and comfort they had supplied them. He told Bill Gregg: "I want to compensate the people who have and, still will divide the last biscuit with us."

Some of the men had felt they were going to be modern-day Robin Hoods, stealing from the rich to help the poor. But then, after the raid, they discovered the ugly truth. Quantrill had no

intention of giving the money away. Instead, when it came time
to divide the spoils, Quantrill saw to it that George Todd and a
few of his closest friends got most of it. And they kept it. Nothing more was said about helping those who had helped them.
The men felt deceived and disillusioned.

That realization led some of the men to admit what they may
have tried to hide from themselves earlier, that William Clarke
Quantrill was fighting only for his own greed and glory and his
inherent love of cruelty and killing. Those who truly cared for
the Confederacy finally acknowledged the truth about what
drove Quantrill. He cared nothing for the South or for the
wrongs that had been committed against the people of Missouri
by the Jayhawkers of Kansas, or for any other idea or ideal. He
killed only for the sake of killing and plundered only for the sake
of plunder. They could no longer follow such a man.

In addition, a larger sense of disillusionment drove some men
from Quantrill, the growing conviction that the South was losing
the war. By the winter of 1864, after Gettysburg and Vicksburg,
only the most fanatical could cling to the hope of a Confederate
victory. What was the point of continuing to fight and bleed and
die for a cause that was already lost?

Quantrill fed that sense of despair during the winter when he
told one of his men that the Confederacy had failed, that the war
was as good as lost. Word of his defeatist attitude spread quickly,
and men asked why they should continue to fight for a leader
who had lost his faith. And who could believe in a man who was
so obviously loathed and reviled by many high-ranking Confederate officers, one of whom had tried to arrest him?

And so they left him, one by one.

Bill Gregg was the first to leave. A trusted, loyal lieutenant, Gregg
had been with the guerrillas from the early days and had fought
hard and courageously. His reasons for leaving were as much personal as ideological. He still believed in the Southern confederacy of states and in slavery and thought them worth continuing
to fight for. But Gregg also felt Quantrill favored George Todd,

and he was increasingly jealous of Todd's growing influence over all the guerrillas and over Quantrill.

Gregg also had some trouble with Todd and two of Todd's men over money. Before Lawrence, Gregg had led a raid of his own, taking with him Jim Little and Fletch Taylor, close friends of Todd's. They agreed that any money they got would be divided equally among them, but Little and Taylor decided to keep the huge sum of six thousand dollars they came across. Gregg went to Todd and complained, calling the two men thieves, but Todd defended them, saying they had every right to keep the money. Quantrill supported Todd.

When the bushwhackers arrived in Sherman for the winter, Gregg stayed with friends in town for a couple of weeks. It was during that time that he decided to leave Quantrill and join the Confederate army to fight on until the end. On his way to Quantrill's camp, he ran into Dave Pool and John Jarrette, who told him not to go there, warning him that Todd might try to kill him.

Gregg went anyway, wanting to get a written leave of absence from Quantrill, figuring that he might be liable for court-martial if he left his unit without permission. Before Gregg could say a word, Quantrill advised him to leave camp for good because he had enemies there who might try to kill him. Quantrill told Gregg he had been a good officer and an honest man, perhaps a strange trait for Quantrill to comment on.

Quantrill added that the men Gregg had called thieves were out to get him. Gregg said they were indeed thieves and he had been right to call them so. When Quantrill agreed, Gregg asked why he should be the one to leave. Quantrill replied that the men in question, Little and Taylor, were so close to Todd that ordering them out might offend Todd. And Todd, Quantrill pointed out, was extremely popular with all the men. It was an open admission by Quantrill of how powerful Todd had become, so powerful that Quantrill dared not insult or provoke him. It may have also been an admission that Quantrill, the daring, fearless guerrilla leader, was afraid of George Todd.

Gregg requested a leave of absence, which Quantrill promptly gave him. It was the last time the two men saw each other. As Gregg rode back to Sherman, he was passed by Todd, Little, Taylor, and John Barker, a crony of Todd's who had never liked Gregg. Afraid they would ambush him on the road into town, Gregg spent the night at an inn, then went into Sherman the next morning.

He hitched his horse, walked down the main street, and saw Todd, Taylor, and Barker watching him from a sidewalk. Todd appeared nervous. Gregg did not speak to them as he walked by, but he felt tense and afraid. He knew he stood no chance against them if they drew on him, but he did not know how close he came to being murdered. Fletch Taylor later recalled how Todd tried to persuade him and John Barker to shoot Gregg as he passed them that morning.

"There goes that damned son of a bitch," Todd said. "Now kill him."

"I will not kill Gregg," Taylor said. "He is a Southern man, and he has been a good soldier and officer. If you want him killed you will have to kill him yourself."

Neither Todd nor Barker could bring himself to move against Gregg, and Bill Gregg spent the rest of the war with Gen. Jo Shelby's Missouri Brigade, eventually earning the rank of captain. After the war he became a deputy sheriff in Missouri.

Bloody Bill Anderson was the next to leave, following the argument with Quantrill over Anderson's marriage. He took sixty-five of the toughest raiders with him, men very much in his mold— men who killed as much for the sake of killing as for any cause. They were among the best and most ruthless fighters in Quantrill's band.

Cole Younger also left that winter. The wanton, indiscriminate killing at Lawrence had angered him. He wanted to fight, but not that way, not robbing and murdering civilians. In the spring, he joined a Confederate army expedition to New Mexico to recruit a new regiment of soldiers. The mission was unsuccessful, and Younger believed the cause was lost. He left the army and traveled to Arizona and Mexico. From there, he sailed to San Francisco to live with an uncle and spent the rest of the war in peace.

Two of the more reliable and sober members of the outfit, John Jarrette and Dave Pool, left to join the Confederate army to fight a more conventional war. Forty men went with them. Both Jarrette and Pool eventually attained the rank of captain. Other men wandered off on their own, or in twos and threes, disillusioned with Quantrill or the war, or both. Some returned to their farms in Missouri, others went west in search of adventure, and some joined the Confederate army.

Even those who stayed no longer respected Quantrill as their leader. In that sense, they had left him just as completely as if they'd gone to California or joined the army or ridden off with Bloody Bill. They rejected his leadership, ignored him, and abandoned him. And they humiliated him. Yet, Quantrill stayed on, allowing power and control to shift to George Todd, the illiterate stonemason.

As cruel as Bloody Bill Anderson, the handsome Todd, with his blond hair and cold blue eyes, had always been idolized by the gang's younger members for his fearlessness in battle. Like Quantrill, Todd had robbed and murdered before the war and was deadly accurate with his Navy Colts. He was reputed to be the best shooter in the bunch, with the possible exception of Quantrill. Volatile and hot-tempered, Todd had long harbored a grudge against Quantrill for not supporting him in his bid to be elected first lieutenant when the guerrillas were organized.

As a result, Todd had been elected second lieutenant but felt he deserved more. He and Quantrill had argued about rank then, and Quantrill had ordered him out. Todd then gathered some men of his own and raided independently for several weeks before returning to Quantrill's camp. The two men reconciled, but Todd remained bitter.

Todd's influence over the guerrillas was strong, second only to Quantrill's, and it grew markedly that last winter. Todd retained his belief in the Confederacy's cause—at least he said he did—and that proclamation solidified the allegiance of many who realized that Quantrill was fighting only for himself, not for the South. Todd was a man they could follow and fight for.

Sometime during the winter—the date is not known—the men elected Todd captain, leaving Quantrill with his self-chosen rank of colonel of a regiment that did not really exist. Quantrill became a supernumerary, an actor still on the stage, but one with no lines to speak and no role to play in the drama. Todd's election enhanced his arrogance and belligerence toward Quantrill. He boasted openly about how he feared no man on the face of the earth.

"How about me?" Quantrill asked.

"Oh, well," Todd said, not yet willing to challenge him openly, "you are the only damned man that I ever was afraid of."

That situation would change before long. In late March, shortly before General McCulloch tried to arrest Quantrill, Todd got boisterously drunk and challenged Quantrill openly. Quantrill took a shot at him, missed, and ordered the others to shoot him. They refused and backed off. No one wanted to kill Todd. Only John Barker—curiously, since he was a friend of Todd's—remained at Quantrill's side.

Barker and Quantrill fired and missed Todd again. Perhaps they, too, had been drinking. Todd fired at Barker, sending a bullet through his jacket. Some of the other men finally broke up the fight. Quantrill said he was not trying to kill Todd, and the two men shook hands. Their shaky peace did not last.

Quantrill knew he had lost the allegiance of his men and that operational command of the outfit had shifted to Todd. He also realized it was only through Todd's tacit consent that he was permitted to stay with the band he had led so long. When he finally understood that he had become a vague presence to whom no one paid any heed, he was shattered. His boldness and aggressiveness left him. With Todd, he became "subservient, conciliatory, sometimes pitiably truculent, humble and imploring." Quantrill's glory days were over.

The bushwhackers started north out of Texas in the middle of April in a driving rain that did not let up for days. The journey was slow and difficult. The roads and trails were dark ribbons of mud, pulling at the horses' legs, tugging at the men's boots. The once-mighty guerrilla band, which could assemble two hundred or more men on a few days' notice, now counted no more than fifty raiders. It was not much of an army, and Quantrill could rely on the loyalty of no more than eight.

Everyone was in a foul mood, which was not improved by a stop at the grave of Bill Bledsoe, whom they had buried last October on their way south. All that remained were his bones, naked and exposed on the open ground, picked clean by scavenging animals. The bones of Jack Mann lay there, too, a reminder of the common fate that awaited all, white and black, no matter how they lived or on which side of the struggle they fought.

The rains continued and the rivers rose, and the men groused that they would never dry out or have a warm meal. It was not until they reached Missouri that they had their first decent food. A farmer's wife fixed bacon and biscuits, but that would be the last hospitality they would receive for a while. Yankee troops were swarming over the border region, more than during the previous fall, and they were commanded by new and more aggressive leaders.

Gone was Ewing, of the infamous General Orders Number 11, transferred to St. Louis. Kansas was under the command of Maj. Gen. Samuel Curtis, whose son, a major, had been killed by Quantrill's men at Baxter Springs. Missouri was commanded by Maj. Gen. William Rosecrans. The border region, which used to be Quantrill Country, where his band could hide with impunity, was under the leadership of Brig. Gen. Egbert Brown. Brown allowed many of the refugees who had been forced to flee under General Orders Number 11 to return to their farms. Precious little was left, and nothing to share with the bushwhackers. The farmers were also less willing to help the raiders, having paid such a terrible price for their aid. General Brown was determined to keep the guerrillas out of the border territory.

Todd and Quantrill decided it would not be wise to return to their old haunts, and they moved on to a county beyond the one bordering Kansas to set up their camp. There, one day, the two men sat down to play a fateful game of cards, with the stakes at one hundred dollars a game. Todd cheated, and Quantrill called him on it in full view of the men. Tempers and voices rose. Todd threatened Quantrill. Quantrill said he was not afraid of anyone. Todd drew one of his Navy Colts and challenged Quantrill.

"You are afraid of me, aren't you, Bill?" Todd taunted.

The men backed away as Quantrill tried to stare Todd down. It did not work. Todd's stance was firm, his expression smug. Quantrill knew he had to give in; his life depended on it.

"Yes," he said in a choking voice. "I'm afraid of you."

Todd had won his ultimate prize, shaming Quantrill in front of the men. Todd holstered his revolver and smiled in triumph. Quantrill was silent. He had been beaten and he knew it. He saddled Old Charley and rode away. A half dozen of the older men accompanied him; the rest stayed with Todd.

Quantrill and his group stopped to pick up Kate, and they rode north of the Missouri River, where they remained, removed from the war, for the rest of the summer.

In late September, Quantrill had a final reunion with the men he had once led. It became a disaster for the guerrillas, though that was none of Quantrill's doing. In fact, if the bushwhackers had listened to him, the fiasco would not have occurred, and they would not then have suffered their worst defeat of the war.

Old Pap, Gen. Sterling Price, had planned an invasion of Missouri. In mid-September, his twelve thousand cavalry would sweep north out of Arkansas. If all went well, Price hoped to reach St. Louis and persuade the Missourians that the Union did not control the state. To keep the Union troops in Missouri distracted, Price ordered a major guerrilla uprising in advance of his invasion in order to disrupt communications and destroy railroad lines and bridges, to keep the Federals busy. It was significant that he sent his courier directly to George Todd. Word of Quantrill's downfall had spread.

Todd notified other guerrilla units and on September twentieth joined forces with a band led by John Thrailkill. They rode into the town of Keytesville with 130 men. They quickly surrounded the town, which was garrisoned by a Union force of thirty-five behind the stout, fortified brick walls of the courthouse. Given enough ammunition and sufficient spirit, the garrison could have held off the bushwhackers and inflicted heavy casualties, but the Union officer, Lt. Anthony Pleyer, lacked courage. When Thrailkill rode up carrying a white flag and threatened to burn the town and shoot every soldier, Pleyer surrendered without firing a shot. The raiders paroled the soldiers but set fire to the courthouse, gutting the interior. They looted the houses and shops and marched the sheriff and another man, a strong Union supporter, into the woods and shot them.

Four days later, near the town of Fayette, Todd's men were joined by Dave Pool's band and seven men led by Quantrill, who had decided to rejoin the war. The next morning, they met up with Bloody Bill Anderson and his men, who cheerfully showed off bloody scalps collected in a looting, killing, and drinking spree. Three weeks before, they had ambushed a forty-man Union patrol and scalped five men, one after being hanged, and cut the throats of three others.

They had ransacked a couple of towns and shot up so many Missouri River steamboats that all traffic had been stopped. But a federal patrol killed and scalped six of Anderson's men, and Bloody Bill was thirsting for revenge. They had a new recruit with them, a boy only seventeen. His name was Jesse James, and he was eager to join his brother Frank in battle.

Todd, Anderson, and Quantrill agreed to put past differences aside and unite forces to harass the Federals. This spirit of cooperation quickly broke down in a dispute over whether to attack Fayette. Anderson and Todd were ready to lay waste to the town, but Quantrill argued against it. He said it was too heavily defended and would cost them too many lives.

"We are going into Fayette no matter what," Anderson told Quantrill. "If you want to come along, all right. If not then you can go back into the woods with the rest of the cowards!"

Quantrill told Anderson he would go, but he would fight in the ranks as a private.

Anderson led the charge into Fayette's courthouse square. The raiders immediately drew heavy fire from thirty Union soldiers in well-defended positions inside the brick courthouse and a nearby blockhouse built of railroad ties.

Hamp Watts, one of Anderson's men, wrote, "Now began the wild, wanton, stupid assault. . . . Not one of the enemy could be seen, but the muzzles of muskets protruded from every porthole, belching fire and lead at the charging guerrillas."

It was a turkey shoot. Anderson and Todd led repeated, senseless charges against the blockhouse. Frank James said it was "like charging a stone wall only this stone wall belched forth lead."

When it was over, when Anderson and Todd finally realized it was as futile to continue as it had been to begin the attack, eighteen guerrillas had been killed and forty-two wounded, the highest number of casualties they had ever suffered in one fight. Quantrill rode off, carrying one of his men, who had been shot in the hip. He never saw Todd or Anderson again.

Todd was furious and blamed Quantrill for the defeat. He ordered his men to hunt Quantrill down, but the more levelheaded among them refused, arguing that the assault had not been Quantrill's idea. Todd threatened to go after Quantrill himself, but his men stopped him by appealing to his vanity. Suppose Todd got himself killed going after Quantrill? Who would be left to lead them?

On the morning of September twenty-seventh, Bloody Bill Anderson and eighty men dressed in federal blue uniforms rode into Centralia, Missouri. Anderson was hoping to find a newspaper that would tell him the whereabouts of General Price's Confederate forces. He also wanted to have some fun, to see what he could steal from the town's dozen houses, few stores, and two hotels.

The bushwhackers spread terror among the residents of Centralia, and when they had seized everything they wanted, they began destroying everything else. The raiders broke every piece of china they could get their hands on. They amused themselves by unrolling long bolts of cloth and dragging the fabric through the dusty street. They found a stockpile of new boots, tied the pairs together, and slung them over their saddles. Then they filled the boots with whiskey from a barrel.

At eleven o'clock, the stagecoach from Columbia arrived. The armed guerrillas surrounded it and relieved the seven startled passengers of their money and jewelry. One of the men aboard was a U.S. congressman, James E. Rollins; another was a sheriff. Both were prime targets for a bullet in the head. They successfully concealed their identities, pretending to be as Southern in their sympathies as Jeff Davis himself.

A half hour later, the westbound train from St. Louis chugged into view. When the engineer saw the waiting band of men with drawn guns, he figured they were bushwhackers and opened the throttle all the way, hoping to race through town unscathed. Anderson's men fired wildly at the locomotive, three passenger cars, and the baggage car, then threw railroad ties onto the track. The train might have been able to knock the railroad ties off the rails with its cowcatcher, but the brakeman in the last car panicked and applied the brakes.

The guerrillas swarmed through the cars, firing their revolvers at the ceiling, grabbing the passengers' money, watches, jewelry, and even some of their clothing. Bloody Bill headed straight for the baggage car. He had no trouble persuading the baggage clerk to open the safe, and he scooped out three thousand dollars. Frank James, in what may have been his first train robbery, found a suitcase said to contain several thousand dollars. It was a profitable morning fighting for the noble cause.

The bushwhackers shoved the passengers off the train. Among the riders were twenty-five Union soldiers, on furlough and unarmed. Some were recovering from wounds. Others were ill, and one was on crutches. Anderson ordered them to remove their uniforms; he could always use more Union blue.

"What are you going to do with them fellows, Captain?" Archie Clements asked Anderson.

"Parole them of course," Anderson said, sneering at the word *parole*.

Clements laughed.

"I thought so," he said.

Clements suggested they take one of the soldiers hostage to exchange for one of their men held captive by the Yankees in Columbia. Anderson asked the Yankees if there was a sergeant among them. No one answered. They thought the bushwhackers must be singling out sergeants to be killed and that the rest would be paroled, as Anderson had said.

Anderson asked again. Finally, Sgt. Thomas Goodman stepped forward, as smartly as a man could when attired only in his long underwear. He looked Anderson squarely in the eye and identified himself. Anderson detailed three men to take Goodman away and "protect him." He was kept prisoner for nine days before escaping.

"Arch," Anderson said to Clements, "you take charge of the firing party and when I give the word, pour hell into them."

Some two dozen bushwhackers lined up opposite the soldiers. Some raised their arms in front of their faces, as if that would ward off the bullets. Some pleaded, others fell to their knees and begged, and some stood straight, staring steadily at their killers when Anderson gave the order to fire.

Twelve Union soldiers fell from the first volley. The rest tried to run or crawl away until a pistol shot in the head felled them. Each of the victims took at least three bullets, in full view of the civilian train passengers and the citizens of Centralia. They watched in horror as the raiders methodically slaughtered the surviving soldiers if they showed any sign of life, beating, scalping, and mutilating their victims. One man lay on his back, unconscious, a foot jerking reflexively in a monotonous rhythm.

"He's marking time," Archie Clements said.

One soldier, shot five times, ran past the guerrillas and hid beneath the station platform. Anderson's men dragged him out and shot him in the head. They set fire to the train station and passenger cars, then ordered the engineer to start the train, allowing him to jump off the locomotive before it got out of town. The burning train ran two and a half miles before the steam died and it coasted to a stop.

Sergeant Goodman was tied to a mule and led back to the raiders' camp. The men laughed and joked, saying this had been one of the best days of the war. And it was not over yet.

A half hour after Anderson led his men out of Centralia, Maj. A. V. E. Johnson arrived with 147 men of the Thirty-ninth Missouri State Militia. The men had joined up only a month before. They rode commandeered farm horses and were armed with outdated Enfield muskets. They could not fight as cavalry because their plow horses were not broken to the sounds of battle and because it was difficult to reload a muzzle-loading weapon on horseback. When it came to fighting, which they had yet to do, they were supposed to wage war on foot.

Major Johnson was outraged at the sight of the twenty-four dead Union soldiers, and he vowed to chase down the bushwhackers. The townspeople begged him not to pursue them with his raw troops, but Johnson was determined and cocky. He left thirty-five men in Centralia to restore order. He then rode off with his remaining 112 troops on their cumbersome plow horses to do battle with Anderson's guerrillas.

Bloody Bill and his men were back in camp, which they shared with George Todd's bunch, when scouts rode in to tell of a Yankee column in pursuit. Anderson sent Archie Clements and ten men out to serve as decoys, with instructions to retreat as soon as the Federals saw them, so the Federals would be lured back to the main body of raiders. The rest of the bushwhackers, two hundred strong, formed up in an arc a quarter of a mile wide at the base of a sloping hill, where they would not be seen by the Union troops until they crested the hill.

Major Johnson led his men after Clements's decoys. The Federals raced up the slope and hurriedly reined in just below the ridgeline when they saw the assembled bushwhackers waiting for them. Johnson ordered his troops to dismount, leaving every fourth man behind to hold the horses while the rest formed a tight battle line barely twenty yards wide. That was what the army manual dictated. The guerrillas were dumbfounded when they saw the Yankees dismount.

"Why the fools are going to fight us on foot!" John Koger said. "God help 'em."

"Boys," Anderson shouted, "when we charge, break through the line and keep straight on for their horses."

Anderson rode out to one end of the line, waved his hat in the air, and urged the men forward.

"I can see them now yonder on that ridge," Frank James told a reporter thirty-three years later. James described how the raiders laid low over their horses' necks and how the first and only volley the Yankees were able to fire went mostly over their heads. Only three bushwhackers were hit; two of them—Frank Shepherd and Dick Kinney—were riding on either side of James.

The blood and brains from Shepherd splashed on my pants' leg as he fell from his horse. Kinney was my closest friend. We had ridden together from Texas, fought side by side, slept together, and it hurt me when I heard him say, "Frank, I'm shot." . . .

But we couldn't stop in that terrible charge for anything. Up the hill we went yelling like wild Indians. Such shrieks, young man, you will never hear as broke the stillness of that September afternoon. . . .

On we went up the hill. Almost in the twinkling of an eye we were on the Yankee line. They seemed terrorized. Hypnotized might be a better word. . . . Some of the Yankees were at "fix bayonets," some were biting off their cartridges, preparing to reload. Yelling, shooting our pistols upon them we went. Not a single man of the line escaped. Every one was shot through the head.

Within three minutes, all the Federals on the battle line were dead. Major Johnson, standing straight and firing his revolver to the last, was killed by Jesse James.

The bushwhackers did not stop at the line of dead Yankees; they went on toward the men holding the horses. They chased the survivors all the way into Centralia, where the Yankees joined up with the thirty-five troops there, and pursued them five more miles to the town of Sturgeon.

"Hold on, boys," Frank James yelled when he saw the Sturgeon garrison form a battle line. "We've killed enough of them; let's go back."

Of the men in Major Johnson's command, 131 lay dead or dying. Only sixteen reached safety. Add to that the 24 soldiers from the passenger train and the body count reached 155. No wonder the guerrillas felt like celebrating. They had not had a day like this since Baxter Springs. They ransacked what was left of Centralia, then turned their attention to the Union dead. The bodies were packed so closely together that Dave Pool stepped from one to another without touching the ground. When George Todd asked Pool why he was doing that, Pool said he was counting them.

"But you needn't walk on 'em to count 'em," Todd said. "That's inhuman."

"Aren't they dead?" Pool replied. "And if they're dead I can't hurt them. I cannot count 'em good without stepping on 'em."

The bodies were stripped and some were beheaded. The bushwhackers made a game of switching heads from one body to another and setting some heads up on fence posts. Seventeen soldiers were scalped. Heads were bashed in; a nose was cut off; genitals were severed. Major Johnson's corpse was stripped and scalped, his nose broken.

A month later, on October 26, 1864, Bloody Bill Anderson was ambushed and shot twice in the head while leading a charge against a 150-man Union militia outfit near Richmond, Missouri. The militiamen loaded his body on a wagon and took it into

town, where it was placed on display in the courthouse. Also put
on exhibit were Anderson's six Navy Colts, photographs of Anderson and his wife, six hundred dollars in gold and Union
greenbacks, and a small Confederate flag imprinted with the
words, "Presented to W. L. Anderson by his friend F. M. R. Let
it not be contaminated by Fed. hands."

The celebrating militiamen then cut off Anderson's head,
placed it atop a telegraph pole, and dragged the corpse through
town behind a horse. When they sobered up, they allowed the
townspeople to bury Anderson, head and body together, in an
unmarked grave.

In 1908, Cole Younger passed through Richmond, Missouri,
with his traveling Wild West show and "Hell on the Border" wax
museum. A local man told him Anderson had been buried there
without benefit of clergy, a disgrace Younger was determined to
correct. He persuaded a clergyman to officiate at a formal burial service. Musicians from Younger's show played in the background.

The preacher spoke for twenty minutes, paying tribute to Anderson's courage as a brave soldier of the South to whom it was
time to pay proper honor.

> Taps was sounded, and many a moist eye was in evidence, es-
> pecially those of several old-timers who had known Anderson
> during his hectic career. The rites were concluded with the im-
> pressive draping of the Stars and Stripes with the Stars and
> Bars. There was such a hush that it seemed the warble of a river
> thrush far distant could be heard.

In 1966, Anderson's biographer, Donald Hale, found the
grave site and applied for a government tombstone. The request
was granted under a federal program to provide grave markers
for former military personnel, including Confederate soldiers. In
April 1967, the marker, provided by the government Bloody Bill
Anderson fought against, was set in place. It reads: "William T.
Anderson, Missouri, Capt. Mo. Guerrilla Confederate States
Army, 1840–1864."

*   *   *

George Todd knew he was going to die. After leaving Centralia and splitting up with Anderson's gang, Todd and his men carried out General Price's request. They destroyed railroad bridges, depots, and water tanks and tore down telegraph lines, disrupting Union transportation and communication facilities.

In mid-October, Price ordered Todd and his men to join Gen. Jo Shelby's cavalry division to serve as scouts for the Confederate invasion, which was meeting stiff resistance. While waiting for Shelby to reach their rendezvous point, Todd and his men hid out in the brush. One night, they talked about the war and the possible consequences of Price's invasion. The conversation turned personal.

"Boys," Todd said, "when Price gets here, I will join him and, in the first battle I am in with him, I shall be killed and I want you boys to see that I have a decent burial."

"Well, Captain," John McCorkle said, "if I thought I was going to be killed I would not go into the battle."

"Yes, I am going," Todd said, "and I want you boys to go with me. I know I'll be killed, but it is just as fitting for me to die for my country as any other man. All I ask is that you boys stay with me and see that I get a decent burial."

The next day, October twenty-first, Shelby's cavalrymen reached the Little Blue River east of Independence and fought a battle with the Kansas militia commanded by Gen. James Blunt. Blunt, still smarting over his defeat at Baxter Springs, was beaten again.

Todd and his men, dressed in blue uniforms, followed the path of the retreating troops. They aroused no suspicion when they came across a Union major and several soldiers. They all talked amicably for a bit, until Todd drew his guns. He shot the major while his men disposed of the others. He took the major's horse, which was far better than his own.

The following day, they continued scouting east of Independence. When they reached the Staples's farm, two and a half miles from town, Todd rode ahead of his men to the crest of a hill where he had a clear view of the countryside. He stopped along the ridgeline and rose up in his stirrups to get a better look. A single shot from a Yankee sharpshooter with a Spencer carbine caught Todd in the neck, shattering his throat and leaving him paralyzed.

The bushwhackers rushed Todd into Independence in the hope of finding a doctor, but he died an hour later. Some of the men said he converted to Catholicism just before his death. Determined to give him the decent burial he so much wanted, they brazenly carried the body to the town cemetery and began to dig at the first convenient spot, a plot belonging to the Beatty family. When Mr. Beatty heard what was happening, he rushed to the cemetery and ordered the men to stop.

"I want no such riffraff in my family lot!" he said. "If you bury him here, he won't remain there long, I assure you."

Unaware or unconcerned about the nature of the men he was threatening, he changed his mind quickly enough when Jesse James confronted him.

"If you dare to dig up George's body, old man," James said, "we'll come back here and put you in that empty grave."

George Todd got his decent burial. That night, Gen. Samuel Curtis sent a telegram to his wife: "It is certain that among the rebels killed yesterday the notorious Todd, one of the murderers of our son, was one among many who were killed."

Anderson and Todd were gone within a week of each other. That left only Quantrill.

William Clarke Quantrill believed he had been given another chance for glory, another chance to regain his lost fame and notoriety, the rightful place Todd and Anderson had taken from him. Now they were dead, and there was no one else to challenge him for leadership of the bushwhackers. It could be just like the old days, fighting his personal war in his own way with his own army, answerable to no man and no government.

But Quantrill's war could no longer be fought in Missouri. General Price's twelve-thousand-man invasion force had been defeated. As the weather turned cold and the winds of winter blew down from the north, Old Pap led the remnants of his beaten army south, across the Arkansas River. They made their way through Indian Territory, where starvation and smallpox further reduced their number.

The Civil War in Missouri was over. There would be no more Confederate armies marching north out of Texas. The Confederacy could no longer lay claim to the state, and Southern sympathizers moved away or kept their loyalties private. They knew the war was lost not just in Missouri but everywhere. With such a weakened base among the farmers and other local residents, many bushwhackers moved away also or returned to their farms to try to survive the winter.

Bushwhacking was finished in Missouri but not in neighboring Kentucky. Guerrilla bands still operated freely there, and the state was not overrun with the experienced, battle-tested troops that filled Missouri. Kentucky was defended mostly by small, poorly trained militia units, home guards, scattered throughout the state.

So it was in Kentucky that Quantrill decided to start his new war with his new army, and from there he planned to organize his most daring raid to date, a feat so dazzling and crippling to the enemy that it would, he believed, save the Confederacy and make him the greatest hero the South had ever seen. He thought his name would be honored for generations, that people would speak of him with the same awe as Robert E. Lee. Quantrill decided to lead his men to Washington and assassinate Abraham Lincoln.

Toward the end of October, Quantrill said good-bye to Kate, who would remain in St. Louis, and returned to the Sni-A-Bar region, where he had planned his past successes. He sent out word for the bushwhackers to assemble for a new campaign. It would be a repeat of the days when he rode at the head of a force of several hundred men. He had done it before; he knew he could do it once more.

It took close to a month before his army assembled, and its size must have disappointed him. Only thirty-three men were willing

to ride with Quantrill again. Most were old hands who had been
with him before. John Koger and Jim Little came, along with
John McCorkle, Cole Younger's brother Jim, Frank and Jesse
James, and John Barker. They may have been few in number, but
they were long in experience.

In early December, Quantrill led the group southeast toward
Kentucky. Dressed in Union uniforms—Quantrill outfitted as a
captain—they passed themselves off as part of the Fourth Missouri Cavalry, Captain Clarke commanding, a military unit that
did not exist. They traveled close to one hundred miles without
confronting Yankee troops and crossed the Osage River at the
town of Tuscumbia.

Quantrill and Babe Hudspeth rode into town and asked to see
the federal commander of the garrison. It was a fearless move;
Quantrill had regained his daring. He chatted with the Union
officer and found out all he needed to know about the location
and strength of federal forces in the direction of his route. He
pulled out his revolver and took the startled officer prisoner, forcing him to surrender the garrison. The bushwhackers held the
Yankees under guard and enjoyed a hearty—and free—breakfast
at the local hotel.

Quantrill ordered the garrison's weapons and ammunition
dumped in the river. He paroled all the soldiers except one,
whom he took along as a guide. That night, the guide overheard
one of the raiders mention Quantrill by name. As soon as the soldier saw his chance, he fled into the woods. Quantrill could not
afford the time to track the man down, now that his presence was
known. He had to get to Kentucky fast.

The bushwhackers crossed the Mississippi River into Tennessee
on the night of January 1, 1865. Their band was getting smaller.
By the time they made camp in the little town of Pocahontas, in
Arkansas's northeast corner, Jesse James, John Koger, Babe Hudspeth and his brother Rufus, and two other men decided they
had had enough of the war and told Quantrill they were leaving
for Texas. A seventh man, Vess Akers, wanted to go with them,

but Quantrill talked him out of it. Akers was one of the original gang. Quantrill said he had gotten Akers into the war and wanted to get him safely out of it.

Quantrill and the remaining members of his band headed northwest through western Tennessee, able to obtain all the food they needed for themselves and their horses from obliging federal outposts where the troops believed they were good Union men. Three weeks later, on January twenty-second, Quantrill and his group crossed into Kentucky, stopping at the Yankee garrison at Hartford for a guide. A Lieutenant Barnett volunteered. Two other federal soldiers asked if they could ride along; it was safer to travel with an army outfit than to go alone. Three miles outside of town, Quantrill ordered one soldier hanged. Six miles later, he shot the other one. After Lieutenant Barnett had led them sixteen miles from town, he, too, was shot.

Quantrill's strategy while in Kentucky was to prey on defenseless towns and villages, plundering and burning. By the end of January, after little more than a week, he and his raiders were the subject of increasingly frantic telegrams to headquarters from the officers in command of the isolated Union outposts. "Thirty-five guerrillas, under Captain Clarke, all dressed in Federal uniform and claiming to belong to Fourth Missouri Cavalry, entered Danville yesterday morning. Robbed citizens, & c."

Local militia units were sent in pursuit. An outfit led by Capt. J. H. Bridgewater caught up with some of the guerrillas nine miles from Danville. The bushwhackers had split into three groups, each spending the night at a different house. Bridgewater's militiamen surrounded one of the houses and demanded that the men inside surrender. The twelve raiders tried to fight their way out, but the Yankees killed three and captured the other nine, including Jim Younger and Vess Akers. They told the militia's officers they were heading for Virginia.

In one night, Quantrill had lost nearly half of his outfit, including some of his best men. The ones taken prisoner were lucky. They were transported to Lexington and on three occasions were told they would be hanged, but each time they were returned to their cells. Three months later, eight of Quantrill's men escaped with the help of local residents loyal to the Southern cause.

Quantrill and his remaining men continued their depredations. They burned a railway depot and captured a wagon train, murdering seven men. The persistent Captain Bridgewater caught up with them at two o'clock on the morning of February ninth. They killed four of the bushwhackers, captured thirty-five horses, and ran the rest off into the woods. Bridgewater's official report noted: "Captain Clarke escaped barefooted, but our men in three detachments are hunting for them and with good prospect of finding them as the snow is fresh on the ground."

The net around Quantrill was closing. One Union officer referred directly to Quantrill in his dispatch, rather than to the assumed name, Captain Clarke: "I chased Quantrill all day yesterday from Spencer through Shelby toward the Louisville and Frankfort Railroad; am still after him; will catch him if I can."

A Union general telegraphed a subordinate in pursuit of the raiders: "Order your men not to take any prisoners if they find them. Tell your men to be very careful, as guerrillas are arrayed in Federal uniform."

Quantrill and his men went into hiding to avoid the Union patrols and to obtain new horses and supplies. It was as easy to find shelter in Kentucky as it had been in Missouri; there were many Confederate sympathizers in the area. By the end of February, Quantrill was secluded at the home of Jim Dawson, where he charmed his host's daughter, Nannie.

Nannie asked the man she saw as a gallant fighter for the Confederacy to sign her autograph book. Quantrill wrote down a poem for her, paraphrased from one by the English poet Lord Byron. Quantrill had composed his poem four years before, for another Nannie, the daughter of Morgan Walker of Blue Springs. The lines served him well on both occasions.

> *My horse is at the door,*
> *And the enemy I soon may see;*

But before I go Miss Nannie,
Here's a double health to thee!

Here's a sigh to those who love me,
And a smile to those who hate;
And, whatever sky's above me,
Here's a heart for every fate.

Though the cannons roar around me,
Yet it still shall bear me on;
Though dark clouds are above me,
It hath springs which may be won.

In this verse as with the wine,
The libation I would pour
Should be peace with thine and mine
And a health to thee and all in door.

> *Very respectfully your friend*
> *W. C. Q.*
> *Feb. 26th, 1865*

Nannie Dawson kept Quantrill's poem for twenty-seven years; in 1892, she gave it to Quantrill's mother.

Quantrill and his men remained on the move, hiding out in the area south of Louisville for the rest of the winter. There is no record of his activities or precise location until April thirteenth, the day after Abraham Lincoln was shot.

"Good," Quantrill was reported to have said when he heard the news. "Now I am saved the trouble!"

That night, he and his men turned up drunk at the home of a local judge, a proslavery man.

"Excuse us, ladies," Quantrill said. "We are a little in our cups today. The grand-daddy of all the greenbacks, Abraham Lincoln, was shot in a theatre at Washington last night."

The judge brought out glasses and a toast was offered by one of Quantrill's men.

"Here's to the death of Abraham Lincoln, hoping that his bones may serve in hell as a gridiron to fry Yankees on."

As the weather turned warmer, Quantrill's band resumed their raids, and federal authorities intensified their efforts to catch him. The Union commander in Kentucky, Maj. Gen. John Palmer, decided that a guerrilla outfit might best be hunted by its own kind. He established a band of Yankee guerrillas under the command of Capt. Edwin Terrill, a nineteen-year-old firebrand who had once fought for the South but deserted and became a bushwhacker in Kentucky. A killer, like Quantrill, though on a smaller scale, Terrill was given a free hand to organize and lead a band of thirty men. They had one mission: to get Quantrill dead or alive.

Terrill tracked Quantrill down quickly enough. Their first confrontation was on April thirteenth; Terrill's men killed two bushwhackers and wounded three, without suffering casualties themselves. Terrill pursued them for the rest of April and into May, preventing Quantrill from making any more raids. Quantrill had become the prey.

During the first week of May, Quantrill had a premonition that soon he would die. His horse, Old Charley, who meant more to him than most people, developed a loose shoe. Quantrill took him to a blacksmith in Canton. Old Charley shied from the man, jerking backward and injuring himself severely. It was clear the horse would have to be put down. Stricken, Quantrill turned deathly pale.

"That means my work is done," he said. "My career is run. Death is coming, and my end is near."

Edwin Terrill came for Quantrill on May tenth. Quantrill and about a dozen men were staying at John Wakefield's farm. Terrill's men surrounded the farm, trapping them in the barn. Minutes before, they had been tossing corncobs at one another like boys at play while Quantrill slept in the hayloft.

The soldiers shouted for the men to surrender. Bullets tore through the flimsy walls of the barn; horses whinnied in terror.

Quantrill's men panicked. They did not even have the presence of mind to shoot back. Some raced for their horses and got away. Quantrill tried to mount his new horse, but it reared and bucked; Old Charley wouldn't have done that. But Old Charley was gone, and Quantrill found himself on foot, abandoned by his men. He ran from the barn, calling for his men to wait. Dick Glassock and Clark Hockensmith heard him and reined in. They turned in their saddles and fired at the pursuing Yankees while Quantrill sprinted to catch up with them.

He reached Glassock's horse just as it was hit and went down. As he ran to Hockensmith, he took a bullet in the back. It struck his spinal cord, paralyzing him from the waist down. He pitched face forward into the mud and was nearly trampled by the Union horses. One of Terrill's men stopped and shot off Quantrill's trigger finger.

"It is useless to shoot me any more," Quantrill told him. "I am now a dying man."

Glassock and Hockensmith were gunned down and killed. They probably would have escaped had they not stopped to help Quantrill.

Union soldiers took Quantrill's Navy Colts and boots. They carried him into the parlor of the Wakefield house and laid him on the couch. Edwin Terrill asked him who he was. Quantrill gave his name as Captain Clarke of the Fourth Missouri Cavalry. Thus, Terrill did not yet know he had caught the man who had eluded Union forces for almost three years, whose true name struck terror in the hearts of Union supporters in three states.

Quantrill gave Terrill a gold watch and five hundred dollars to be allowed to stay at the Wakefield house. Terrill agreed. He said he would hold John Wakefield responsible if Captain Clarke did not remain there until he returned with a wagon to take him to a hospital. Quantrill gave his word that he would not allow anyone to move him. Terrill began to ransack the house, but after Wakefield gave him twenty dollars and a jug of whiskey, he left.

Wakefield summoned the local doctor, who examined the wound and pronounced it fatal, as Quantrill already suspected. During the night, Frank James and three other raiders slipped back to the house and offered to take Quantrill away, but he declined.

"Boys," he said, "it is impossible for me to get well. The war is over and I am in reality a dying man, so let me alone. Good-bye."

Two days later, Terrill returned with a wagon to take Quantrill to Louisville. By then, he knew who his prisoner was. The wagon was filled with straw, and Quantrill was gently placed inside. He thanked John Wakefield for his care and said he would send a letter from Louisville with instructions for providing money for his mother and sister. Wakefield never heard from him again. Quantrill's mother never received any money from her son, and Quantrill's sister, Mary, had died two years before.

Terrill was solicitous of Quantrill's needs during the two-day trip to Louisville, proceeding slowly so as not to jar the ailing man more than necessary. He stopped along the way to have local doctors examine him. Quantrill was taken to the hospital of Louisville's military prison, where he lingered in great pain for nearly a month. Nursed by a Catholic priest, toward the end he confessed his sins and was baptized into the Catholic faith. Quantrill told the priest he had four thousand dollars. Just before he died, he gave half of the money to the priest for a headstone and asked him to send the other half to his wife, Kate, in St. Louis. Legend has it that Kate used her share to start a highly successful brothel. He sent nothing to his mother, not even a note.

William Clarke Quantrill, alias Charley Hart, alias Captain Clarke, died at four o'clock in the afternoon on June 6, 1865, two months after the Civil War ended. Quantrill's war, which he had waged since he was a boy, was over as well. He was buried in Louisville, in the Old Portland Catholic Cemetery. The priest who officiated at the burial refused to erect a tombstone at the grave site as Quantrill had requested, fearing someone might steal the body. He ordered the custodians to empty their dishwater and slops over the grave to wipe out all traces of it.

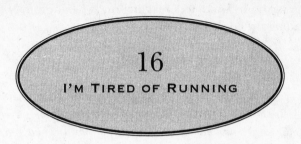

16

I'M TIRED OF RUNNING

QUANTRILL'S BUSHWHACKERS continued their grisly, merciless war for more than a month after Robert E. Lee surrendered. Many of the guerrillas were in Texas when the war ended. Some decided to stay there, but about one hundred men headed home, back to Quantrill Country in Missouri. Dave Pool was among the group that rode north, along with Jesse James and the savage Archie Clements. Together, they murdered a Union militiaman; James and two others held him down while Clements cut his throat and scalped him. Peace had not yet come to western Missouri.

On May seventh, they ransacked the town of Holden, forty miles from Independence, robbing the stores and killing one man. An hour later, the bushwhackers descended on another town, burning five homes and killing eight men. They made their way back to their sanctuary in the Sni-A-Bar, and along the ride they killed fifteen more. They told everyone they met that they did not believe Lee had surrendered. It was just another Yankee lie.

On May eleventh, Archie Clements sent a message to the commander of the 180-man federal garrison at Lexington, Missouri, demanding the town's surrender.

> *SIX MILES OUT THE FIELD*, *May 11, 1865*
> *Major Davis, Lexington, Mo.*
> *SIR: This is to notify you that I will give you until Friday morning, May 12, 1865, to surrender the town of Lexington. If you surrender we will treat you and all taken as prisoners of war. If we have to take it by storm we will burn the town and kill the soldiers. We have the force, and are determined to have it.*
> *I am, sir, your obedient servant,*
>
> A. CLEMENTS

Major Davis ignored the threat, and Clements, wisely, did not attack. Not long thereafter, however, the situation changed. Davis and other Union officers in western Missouri began to receive messages from bushwhackers, asking about terms for *their* surrender. The guerrillas were convinced by then that the war was truly over and the South had lost.

On May seventeenth, Dave Pool met with Major Davis. Davis told Pool that Maj. Gen. Grenville Dodge, the new Union commander of Missouri, had authorized the granting of full amnesty to all guerrillas who surrendered. There would be no punishment for past crimes. That was what the bushwhackers had been waiting to hear. Four days later, Pool led 85 men into Lexington, past a line of curious spectators and 180 Union troops ready for action. The guerrillas surrendered peacefully, took the oath of allegiance to the United States, and were granted paroles.

By the end of May, more than two hundred bushwhackers had surrendered. Dave Pool volunteered to locate those still in hiding and persuade them to turn themselves in. The local citizens, however, who had suffered grievously from the activities of these men, were irate at the government's leniency. Col. Chester Harding, commander of the district that included Lexington, wrote that the people were "vexed at the course pursued. They think we should meet these fellows in the brush and kill them, or else violate our plighted faith when they are in our power."

Although Colonel Harding was not about to violate the terms of the surrender agreements, he made it clear to the bushwhackers the consequences of failing to abide by the agreement. "I have notified the bushwhackers that the mercy extended to them is unparalleled, and that we expect them to keep the same good faith which we show them. If they step over the line of their obligations they will be arrested and shot without trial."

Colonel Harding also instructed his subordinates to take harsh measures with bushwhackers who failed to honor the surrender terms. "If any one of the surrendering bushwhackers violates the oath he has taken, shoot him. Inform all who are now in your sub-district, and those who may hereafter come, that we keep our word sacred and that if they do not honorably stand by their obligations they can expect no mercy."

There is no record of any former guerrillas being shot by federal soldiers, though it could easily have occurred and not been reported. Some of Quantrill's men were harassed and chased from the state. A few were killed by pro-Union men in Missouri who believed strongly that bushwhackers should be punished, not pardoned.

Archie Clements refused to surrender. When he accepted the fact that the Confederacy had been defeated, he returned to Texas. In the summer of 1866, he went back to Missouri, even though there was a price on his head. Being a wanted man did not force Clements to stay in hiding. He was often seen in Lexington, visiting his old friend Dave Pool, drinking and riding about as though daring Union authorities to take him.

In December 1866, a new state law required all men over the age of eighteen to register for service in the state militia. Those who did not register were subject to a twenty-five-dollar fine. Clements thought it would be a lark to register for the militia that had once tried to hunt him down. He sent word to the commander in Lexington that he would do so if he was assured that he would not be arrested or harassed while he was in town. The commander sent Dave Pool to tell Clements he would be safe.

On December thirteenth, Clements led a column of twenty-six armed men into Lexington. They had drinks and dinner at the City Hotel, then went to the courthouse to register for the militia. The military commander, Major Montgomery, considered them dangerous and warned them to leave town. They rode out of town, but Clements and another man returned to the hotel bar. As soon as Major Montgomery heard the news, he sent three soldiers to arrest Clements, and he positioned others at the courthouse windows overlooking the main street.

When the soldiers entered the bar, Clements pulled out his gun and started shooting. He ran out the side door to where his horse was tied. He mounted, wheeled around, and rode off down the main street, just as Major Montgomery thought he would. The soldiers opened fire from the windows. Clements's horse "slowed to a walk. A short distance down the block, Archie fell off his horse face first. When townspeople reached him, he was dead."

After the war, some of Quantrill's men continued their life of crime. Having seen how profitable robbing banks could be, it was inevitable that some would choose to rob again. The first recorded incident occurred on February 13, 1866, in Liberty, Missouri. A dozen men stole nearly sixty thousand dollars from the Clay County Savings Bank, shot up the town, and killed one man.

The raid had been Jesse James's idea. Badly wounded in the closing days of the war, he decided, while recuperating, that the best way to take revenge against the Yankees was to rob their banks. Frank James also liked the idea. He had surrendered to Union forces in July 1865, three months after Lee's surrender. He had turned himself in at Louisville and was paroled immediately, along with a dozen others who had been with Quantrill to the end. Frank James persuaded Cole Younger, recently returned from his uncle's place in California, to join them. Other old bushwhackers went along, including Cole's brother-in-law, John Jarrette.

Other bands of Quantrill's men went into the bank-robbing business. In October 1866, four men robbed a bank in Lexington. A posse was formed to go after them; it was led by Dave Pool, who reported that somehow he was unable to track down his one-time buddies.

Frank and Jesse James and their gang embarked on a crime spree that made them the most famous and feared outlaws in the West. They robbed banks and trains and became celebrities to a large segment of the American public, who saw them as good men gone wrong, driven by the injustice they had suffered at the hands of Unionists during the war. In sensational, often fictional journalistic accounts of their exploits, they were presented as heroes who stole from the rich to help the poor. In reality, they stole only to help themselves.

Sympathy for the James boys peaked in 1875 when Pinkerton detectives, who had been pursuing them for years, threw a bomb through a window of the family home. The blast killed their nine-year-old half brother and severed the right arm of their mother. In 1882, thirty-four-year-old Jesse James was killed at his home in St. Joseph, Missouri, while standing on a chair to dust a picture. Bob Ford, a member of his gang, tempted by a ten-thousand-dollar reward and a promise of immunity from prosecution for past crimes, shot him with a revolver Jesse had given him the day before.

For many years, admirers of Jesse James maintained he had not been killed by Bob Ford but had lived peacefully to a ripe old age. In late 1995, the remains buried in James's grave were exhumed and the bones and hair underwent DNA analysis. The tests confirmed that the remains were those of James, and he was reburied in a closed casket draped in a Confederate flag. A crowd of six hundred attended the funeral, which featured an honor guard of a dozen men in Confederate uniforms.

The year after Jesse James was gunned down, Frank James turned himself in to the governor of Missouri. "I'm tired of running," James said. "Tired of waiting for a ball in the back. Tired of looking into the faces of friends and seeing a Judas." Twice he was tried for his crimes and acquitted for lack of evidence.

He took a variety of odd jobs over the years, as shoe salesman, cowboy, livestock importer, doorman at a St. Louis burlesque house, and bit actor in a traveling theater company. In 1903, Frank James and Cole Younger started a Wild West show, but James left after a year to buy a ranch in Oklahoma. In 1911, he returned to his boyhood home in Missouri to give guided tours of the house to people who wanted to see a living legend.

Frank James died peacefully in 1915 at the age of seventy-one. Perhaps he was still asking the question he had put to the reporter in 1897, when he wandered over the hillside at Centralia where he and Bloody Bill Anderson had killed so many Yankee soldiers. "What have I been spared for when so many of my comrades were taken?"

Cole Younger was captured in 1876, with his brothers Jim and Bob, following a botched bank robbery in Northfield, Minnesota. Given long sentences, they became model prisoners. Cole was a jailhouse celebrity; his cell (with him in it) was open to public view. In his first three days in prison, more than four thousand sightseers filed past to see the famous outlaw. Cole was a gracious host, chatting amiably with one and all.

Bob Younger died of tuberculosis in prison in 1899. Jim committed suicide in 1902, a year after his release. Cole was released in 1901. He never spoke publicly about his days as a criminal. While in prison, he told a reporter: "I am aware that my name has been connected with all the bank robberies in the country; but positively I had nothing to do with any of them. I look upon my life since the war as a blank, and will never say anything to make it appear otherwise. The world may believe as it pleases."

After Cole left prison and teamed up with Frank James in their Wild West show, they brought their troupe to Boonville, Missouri, for a performance. On the buggy ride from the railroad station, they drove past the bank.

"Frank," Cole said, "we ought to get our big bills changed into small money. Come on, we'll go in and do that."

Frank thought it over for a moment and smiled.

"If Cole Younger and Frank James walk into that bank together," he said, "they'll slam the vault door and begin shooting."

They decided to send their driver to get the money changed.

After he gave up the show, Cole Younger spent several years on a lecture tour, talking about his wartime experiences and his days in jail. He concluded every speech with a moral: Crime does not pay. With the money from these popular and profitable lectures, he bought a home and settled down with his niece, Nora Hall, in Lee's Summit, Missouri, where he had roamed with Quantrill in the old days. He liked to sit on the front porch and visit with the people who stopped to see him. Friends from bushwhacking and bank-robbing days came to relive the past. He particularly enjoyed visits from Frank James; the pair could talk and laugh for hours. When he learned of Frank's death, Cole went upstairs to his room and sat quietly alone for the rest of the day.

On August 21, 1913, fifty years to the day after the Lawrence raid, Cole and Nora attended a revival meeting. Cole listened attentively to the evangelist Orville Hamilton.

> [Hamilton was pleading] for all sinners to come forward and embrace the opportunity to begin life anew. As the congregation sang the hymn "Just As I Am," Cole Younger kissed his niece on the cheek and rose. As the immense group crowded within the tent watched in astonishment and whispered his name in hushed tones, Cole slowly walked to the front of the congregation and offered his hand to Reverend Hamilton.

> "I want to repent my sins and join the church," Cole said.

Cole Younger died in 1916 at the age of seventy-two. He carried fourteen bullets in his body from the wild days of his youth. He once quipped, "I guess you could strike lead in me almost any place you drilled." Among his pallbearers were the sons of Frank and Jesse James.

In 1889, twenty-four years after the end of the war, Quantrill's boys began holding annual reunions, which by 1905 had grown into elaborate two-day affairs. Up to forty men could be counted on to attend. The men met in Independence or Blue Springs and always displayed a large framed painting of Quantrill. As a joke, someone liked to yell, "Blue coats!" and the men would jump and laugh, pretending the Yankees were bearing down on them again.

Cole Younger was a favorite at the reunions. The men would gather around him and exchange tall tales, which tended to get taller as the years rolled by. Cole always spoke of "Captain Quantrill" with nothing but respect; no one talked about the butchery at Lawrence and other places. On one occasion, Cole gave his "crime does not pay" lecture, which met with an enthusiastic reception. Cole led the men in a spirited rebel yell, after which they hobbled off, arms around one another's shoulders, to the picnic tables. The reunions continued for forty years; the last was held in 1929.

Kate King Quantrill married twice more. She died in 1930 at the age of eighty-two at the Jackson County Old Folks Home near Kansas City, Kansas. She never spoke publicly about her days with Quantrill.

A final tale remains to be told: the strange odyssey of Quantrill's bones, occasioned by the efforts of his mother to bring her son home. For years, she refused to believe that her Bill could be the man Northern newspapers described as such a fiend and monster. It was a schoolmate of Quantrill's, searching for material for a biography, who finally persuaded her of his true nature.

William W. Scott collected a vast amount of information about his boyhood friend. In 1887, at Mrs. Quantrill's request, he exhumed Quantrill's remains so his mother could take them home to Canal Dover. When Scott showed Mrs. Quantrill the skull, she identified it as that of her son. She told Scott she recognized the chipped tooth on the lower jaw.

Scott packed the bones in a box, and Mrs. Quantrill transported them to Canal Dover. The city fathers were outraged and refused to allow the notorious bushwhacker to be buried within the town limits. Finally, they relented and agreed to the burial, but only if the location of the grave site was kept secret.

Unbeknownst to Quantrill's mother, Scott had reserved the skull and a couple of the bones for himself. He kept the skull and a bone from Quantrill's right arm and gave Quantrill's shinbone to the Kansas State Historical Society. A later biographer, William Connelley, obtained the arm bone from Scott and donated it to the same historical society.

When Scott died in 1902, his son inherited Quantrill's skull. Legend has it that the skull was used until 1941 as part of the initiation ceremonies at a college fraternity.

ACKNOWLEDGMENTS

A NYONE ATTEMPTING to tell the story of a period or person in history owes a debt of gratitude to many individuals and organizations. For me, the list includes the people who lived during the period in question and left behind written records of their experiences, the dedicated archivists and librarians who preserved and cataloged those records, and past authors who worked with this material to present their views of Quantrill's life and times.

It is a pleasure to acknowledge the help of Cindy Stewart, senior manuscript specialist with the Western Historical Manuscript Collection, a joint collection of the University of Missouri at Columbia and the State Historical Society of Missouri; Kathy A. Lafferty, of the Kansas Collection, University of Kansas Libraries, Lawrence; and the staff of the Center for Historical Research, Kansas State Historical Society, Topeka, for their patience and support in responding so thoroughly and rapidly to my many requests for material. I am also grateful to the reference and interlibrary loan staff at the Clearwater (Florida) Public Library, especially Candace McDaniel, for cheerfully filling my requests, many of which were for nineteenth-century books long out of print. Historians would not be able to function without the assistance of such concerned and committed archivists and librarians as those with whom I was fortunate to work.

Most of what is known about the early life of William Clarke Quantrill has come to us through the efforts of W. W. Scott and William Elsey Connelley. Scott, who grew up with Quantrill, spent many years gathering source material for a biography he planned to write. When he died, his data went to Connelley, then secretary of the Kansas State Historical Society.

Connelley interviewed many people who knew Quantrill, including several men who rode with him during the Civil War and who accompanied him on the raid on Lawrence, Kansas. Connelley also collected documents, newspapers, and other printed material relevant to Quantrill and his times. In 1910, Connelley published the results of this comprehensive research in a book entitled *Quantrill and the Border Wars*.

Other authors have given us their impressions of Quantrill and his activities, notably Carl Breihan (*Quantrill and His Civil War Guerrillas*, 1959); Albert Castel (*William Clarke Quantrill: His Life and Times*, 1962); and Thomas Goodrich (*Bloody Dawn: The Story of the Lawrence Massacre*, 1991). These and additional books that proved helpful, as well as the official records of the Union and Confederate armies (*The War of the Rebellion*), are cited in the bibliography and chapter notes.

My greatest debt is to my wife, Sydney Ellen—librarian, researcher, and editor. Her impact on this book is clear on every page and in every step of the writing and production process. Her attentiveness, cheerfulness, and support after so many books are qualities I continue to find amazing.

Finally, history is, ultimately and intimately, interpretative and subjective. It does not—indeed, cannot—provide as objective a record of an event as, for example, a photograph. Writing about history is more like offering a painting—an impression, not a reproduction; a likeness, not a replica.

Historians do not have access to all the details of an event. Unlike a scientific experiment, a historical event cannot be replicated in its entirety. Only some of the details may be available for study in the form of fragments such as diaries and letters, photographs, interviews, and official reports. And it is from such fragments that we attempt to re-create the past. Thus, the historian functions much like an archaeologist, who uses fragments of past civilizations—shards of clay pots, arrowheads, human bones—to reconstruct, as carefully and accurately as possible, the nature of that time and place. In reassembling fragments, the historian, like the archaeologist, must work with pieces that may be incomplete or misleading, requiring subjective judgments as to how they best fit together to reconstruct a city or re-create a historical event. Because historical judgments are subjective, different writers may organize the pieces in different ways.

As Barbara Tuchman noted, the historian "discovers that truth is subjective and separate, made up of little bits seen, experienced, and recorded by different people. It is like a design seen through a kaleidoscope; when the cylinder is shaken the countless colored fragments form a new picture. Yet they are the same fragments that made a different picture a moment earlier."

This is my picture, my impression of the life and times of William Clarke Quantrill, my way of putting the fragments together.

NOTES

1. HE BORE MALICE

"bloodiest man": Castel, *William Clarke Quantrill,* p. 22. "a sort of gay, nervous chuckle": manuscript memoirs of Frank Smith quoted in Castel, p. 86. "He brooded over imagined insults": Breihan, *Quantrill and His Civil War Guerrillas,* p. 26.

2. I ALONE AM MISERABLE

"Her temperament was brooding": Connelley, *Quantrill and the Border Wars,* p. 34. "a vile . . . scoundrel": Connelley, p. 30. "Well I must tell you": Quantrill's letter of November 17, 1855, Kansas Collection, University of Kansas Libraries. "I suppose you think": Quantrill's letter of February 21, 1856, Kansas Collection, University of Kansas Libraries. "Well, mother": Quantrill's letter of July 14, 1856, Kansas Collection, University of Kansas Libraries. "[His] venture into the world": Castel, *William Clarke Quantrill,* p. 25. "If you can do this": Quantrill's letter of May 16, 1857, Kansas Collection, University of Kansas Libraries. "Bill, I hated to give you," "I'm glad to be rid of you," "Bill Quantrill, you're even worse": Breihan, *Quantrill and His Civil War Guerrillas,* pp. 28–29. "Bill, stop!" and "Lay your gun down": Connelley, p. 68, quoting Andreas, *History of*

Kansas, p. 877. "I have but one wish": Quantrill's letter of July 9, 1857, Kansas Collection, University of Kansas Libraries. "About the girls": Quantrill's letter quoted in Connelley, pp. 73, 74. "A pair of high-heeled calfskin boots": R. M. Peck quoted in Connelley, p. 75. "You need not expect me home": Quantrill's letter of October 15, 1858, Kansas Collection, University of Kansas Libraries. "I hardly know what to do": Quantrill's letter of July 30, 1859, Kansas Collection, University of Kansas Libraries. "Still, I have been taught": Quantrill's letter of January 26, 1860, Kansas Collection, University of Kansas Libraries. "I can now see more clearly": Quantrill's letter of February 8, 1860, Kansas Collection, University of Kansas Libraries. "I have not enjoyed": Quantrill's letter quoted in Connelley, p. 97. "I think everything": Quantrill's letter of March 25, 1860, Kansas Collection, University of Kansas Libraries.

3. A RIFLE IN ONE HAND AND A BIBLE IN THE OTHER

"most important single event": McPherson, *Battle Cry of Freedom,* p. 121. "the side that got there first": Nichols, *Bleeding Kansas,* p. 8. "Come on then": Nichols, p. 12. "at whatever sacrifice": McPherson, p. 122. "The storm that is rising": Boyer, *Legend of John Brown,* p. 108. John Greenleaf Whittier poem: quoted in Boyer, pp. 110–111; this version differs slightly from the original but represents John Brown's use of the work. "Church of the Holy Rifles": Boyer, p. 505. "Shall we allow the cutthroats": Castel, *William Clarke Quantrill,* p. 2, quoting the Liberty, Missouri, *Democratic Platform* newspaper. "We are organizing": McPherson, p. 146. "Mark every scoundrel": McPherson, pp. 146–147. "Men on horses": Nichols, p. 28. "We mean to have Kansas": Castel, p. 6. "You cannot now destroy these people": McPherson, p. 148. "just as soon buy a nigger as a mule": Nichols, p. 42. "He burst with vitality": Boyer, p. 566. "He talked like none of the others": Monaghan, *Civil War on the Western Border,* p. 31. "Jim Lane had only to rise": Nichols, p. 43. "as good a man as we have": Fellman, *Inside War,* p. 140. "Here's Brown": Nevins, *Ordeal of the Union,* vol. 2, p. 432. "I believe that was intended for me": Castel, p. 8. "Imagine a man standing": Castel, p. 9. "This day we have entered Lawrence": Monaghan, p. 58. "watched from windows and sidewalks": Monaghan, p. 59. "My soul is wrung by this outrage": McPherson, p. 149. "A crime has been committed": Donald, *Charles Sumner,* p. 283. "hirelings": Nevins, p. 440. "The senator from South Carolina": Monaghan, p. 55; Donald, p. 285. "The senator touches nothing": Donald, p. 286. Sumner-Brooks confrontation: Donald, pp. 294–295. "Every Southern man sustains me": Donald, p. 304. "He was ignorant": Nevins, p. 473. "Something must be done": McPherson, p. 152. "It has been ordained": Nichols, p. 113. "I begged them": Nichols, p. 114. "I believe that I did" and "committed murder": Oates, *To Purge This Land with Blood,* p. 147. "seething hell": Castel, p. 12. "weary of war": Cordley, *A History of Lawrence, Kansas,* p. 140. "everything they wanted": Castel, p. 17. Charles Hamilton incident: Castel, p. 18. "barbarous in origin" and "no personal griefs": Donald, p. 354.

4. I Don't Expect to See Any of You Alive Again

"a holy terror": Connelley, *Quantrill and the Border Wars,* p. 109. "He could not be true": Connelley, p. 114. "I was Badly impressed with him": Connelley, p. 119. Quantrill's letter of June 23, 1860: Kansas Collection, University of Kansas Libraries. "I don't expect to see any of you alive again": Snyder quoted in Castel, *William Clarke Quantrill,* p. 36. Morgan Walker incident: Castel, p. 37. "badly lamed": Elliott, "The Quantrill Raid," *Kansas Historical Collections,* 1920, vol. 2, p. 181. "He seemed to be a very pleasant sort of fellow": Frank Smith quoted in Castel, pp. 39–40. "with that brazen assurance": Connelley, p. 187. "strew the road": Connelley, p. 189. "I told him in case": Connelley, p. 191.

5. In the Name of God and Devil

"I had, in obedience to the advice of my father": Connelley, *Quantrill and the Border Wars,* p. 203. "fight or frolic": McCorkle, *Three Years with Quantrill,* pp. 9–10. "some of the most psychopathic killers": McPherson, *Battle Cry of Freedom,* p. 785. "a maniac in battle": Hale, *They Called Him Bloody Bill,* p. 1. "If I cared for my life": Breihan, *Quantrill and His Civil War Guerrillas,* p. 58. "To kill, steal and plunder": Hale, p. 5. "a sort of a cross between an eagle and a snake" and "Over his features": Cordley, *A History of Lawrence, Kansas,* p. 199. "blood thirsty cuss": Goodrich, *Bloody Dawn,* p. 12. "An unfeeling savage": Brownlee, *Gray Ghost of the Confederacy,* p. 138. Younger-Walley incident: Breihan, *Younger Brothers,* p. 7. "Little Riley Crawford": Brownlee, p. 62. "If you ever want to pick a company": James quoted in Horan, *Authentic Wild West: The Outlaws,* pp.

125–126. "The Federals' pistols": Castel, *William Clarke Quantrill,* p. 114. "When the soldiers drew close": Castel, p. 114. "[H]e would wake up in the night": Croy, *Last of the Great Outlaws,* p. 9. Annie Fickle story and Black Oath story: Breihan, *Quantrill and His Civil War Guerrillas,* pp. 43–44; Breihan, *Younger Brothers,* p. 188. "I never saw it": Breihan, *Ride the Razor's Edge,* p. 238. General Orders Number 32: *War of the Rebellion: Official Records,* series 1, vol. 8, p. 464.

6. WE DRAW THE FIRST BLOOD

Captain Oliver's letter to General Pope: *War of the Rebellion: Official Records,* series 1, vol. 8, p. 57. Riley Alley song: Frank Smith quoted in Castel, *William Clarke Quantrill,* p. 69. "proceeded to belabor me with his saber": Gregg, "A Little Dab of History Without Embellishment," Western Historical Manuscript Collection, University of Missouri at Columbia, p. 11. "screaming and sweating like devils" and "damn good shot": Castel, p. 70. Ellis incident and quotations: Connelley, *Quantrill and the Border Wars,* p. 227–229. "Ellis, I am damned sorry," Castel, p. 71. "Where at first there was only killing": Breihan, *Ride the Razor's Edge,* p. 237. "Now, boys, I accept the challenge": Castel, p. 73. "They were disgusted at the idea": Gregg, p. 10. "Boys, Halleck issued the order": Connelley, p. 238. "Steady, boys": Castel, p. 76. "Cole Younger suffered": McCorkle, *Three Years With Quantrill,* pp. 40–41. "The Tate House fight": Castel, p. 76. "[I was] acting barber," and log house and Lowe house incidents: Gregg, pp. 5–6 (supplement). "before we had accomplished anything": Gregg, pp. 6–7 (supplement). "set upon a stump": Gregg, p. 2 (supplement). "Little wonder": Castel, pp. 79–80.

7. THEY COULD NOT STAND OUR ONSLAUGHT

General Totten's special order of April 21, 1862: *War of the Rebellion: Official Records,* series 2, vol. 3, p. 468. Gregg's account of Quantrill-Gower battle: Gregg, "A Little Dab of History Without Embellishment," Western Historical Manuscript Collection, University of Missouri at Columbia, pp. 15–21. Cole Younger posing as a spy in Independence: Croy, *Last of the Great Outlaws,* p. 19. "You will be well supported": Connelley, *Quantrill and the Border Wars,* p. 262. "For God's sake don't fire": Connelley, p. 263. "an expression of fiendish glee": Castel, *William Clarke Quantrill,* p. 90. "Surrender or roast!": Castel, p. 91. "From the fifteenth day of August": Connelley, p. 269. "Halloo and be damned": Castel, p. 94. "I want you to promise me": Croy, p. 21. "[that he] decided to let these 'big guns' ": Connelley, p. 270. "[S]uddenly I saw a change" and "Take Lieutenant Copeland": Gregg, p. 27. "We are going to Kansas": Castel, p. 96. "We had killed fourteen men": Gregg, p. 31. "He very politely": Connelley, p. 272. "with the admonition": Castel, p. 97. "As usual, they could not stand our onslaught": Gregg, p. 32. "No, I do not know you" and "You must obey these orders": Gregg, p. 35. "Settlers living in the Kansas border": Castel, p. 98. "extremely zealous and useful": *War of the Rebellion,* series 1, vol. 13, p. 33.

8. I SAY SACK THE TOWN

"gaunt and emaciated": Foote, *The Civil War,* vol. 1, p. 787. "extravagantly romantic": Castel, *William Clarke Quantrill,* p. 40. Quantrill-Seddon meeting: Maj. John Edwards quoted in Connelley, *Quantrill and the Border Wars,* pp. 278–281. "was the worst possible course": Connelley, p. 182. "On Quantrill's return": Gregg, "A Little Dab of History Without Embellishment," Western Historical Manuscript Collection, University of Missouri at Columbia, pp. 44–45. "This method of protecting burned towns": Goodrich, *Bloody Dawn,* p. 20. "We can be killed": Goodrich, *Bloody Dawn,* p. 77. "Remember the dying words": McCorkle, *Three Years with Quantrill,* pp. 68–69. "Most of her time with Quantrill": Breihan, *Ride the Razor's Edge,* p. 141. "the monster of monsters": Gregg, p. 74. "I hope soon to have troops enough": Ewing quoted in Goodrich, *Bloody Dawn,* p. 21. "About two-thirds": *War of the Rebellion: Official Records,* series 1, vol. 22, part 2, p. 428. General Orders Number 10, *War of the Rebellion,* pp. 460–461. Women's prison collapse: Goodrich, *Bloody Dawn,* p. 8. "Vengeance is in my heart": Goodrich, *Bloody Dawn,* p. 78. "He raged against Kansas": Connelley, pp. 298, 308. "Let's go to Lawrence" and "I know": Gregg, p. 47. "I consider it almost a forlorn hope": Goodrich, *Black Flag,* p. 75. "The march to Lawrence is a long one" and the questioning of the guerrillas: Breihan, *Younger Brothers,* pp. 39–40; Maj. John Edwards quoted in Connelley, p. 311; Croy, *Last of the Great Outlaws,* p. 32.

9. KILL EVERY MAN BIG ENOUGH TO CARRY A GUN

Eldridge House as "magnificent": Goodrich, *Bloody Dawn,* p. 52. "They had been dressed up": Lowman, *Narrative of the Lawrence Mas-*

sacre, p. 51. "Quantrill is coming": Robinson, "Sara Tappan Doolittle Robinson's Personal Recollections of Quantrill's Raid," Kansas Collection, University of Kansas Libraries, p. 1. "They could not have been posted anywhere": Lowman, p. 35. "the beginning of the end": Goodrich, p. 44. "If I ever hear of you talking": Castel, *William Clarke Quantrill,* p. 124. "You, one and all" and "The Kansan has been murdering": Larkin, *Fighting Artist,* pp. 155–156. "In the bright sunlight": Gregg, "A Little Dab of History Without Embellishment," Western Historical Manuscript Collection, University of Missouri at Columbia, p. 55. "He was so severely criticized": Pike, "Statement of Captain J. A. Pike Concerning the Quantrill Raid," Western Historical Manuscript Collection, University of Missouri at Columbia, pp. 5–6. "By Captain Pike's error of judgment": General Ewing, *War of the Rebellion: Official Records,* series 1, vol. 22, part 1, p. 580. "as empty handed as they came": Lowman, p. 43. "watch the enemy and report": *War of the Rebellion,* p. 585. "My force then consisted of about 180 men": Captain Coleman, *War of the Rebellion,* p. 590. "The night was very dark": Pike, p. 11. "Crouching low to the ground": Goodrich, p. 46. "In again finding [the trail]": Captain Coleman, *War of the Rebellion,* p. 590. "We had now arrived" and "Things went on this way": Gregg, p. 56. "Rush on, boys": Boughton, *Lawrence Massacre,* p. 5. "the horses were hurried to a long trot": Gregg, p. 57. "Her flanks heaved": Connelley, *Quantrill and the Border Wars,* p. 333. "Low-crowned, broad-brimmed hats": Connelley, p. 347. "Kill every man": Brownlee, *Gray Ghost of the Confederacy,* p. 123. "You can do as you please": Castel, *A Frontier State at War,* p. 126.

10. A TEMPEST OF FIRE AND DEATH

"For God's sake" and "No quarter": eyewitness Henry Clarke quoted in Goodrich, *Black Flag,* p. 78. "On to the hotel," "We'll surrender ourselves" and "All right": Breihan, *Younger Brothers,* p. 43. "Kill!": Gregg, "A Little Dab of History Without Embellishment," Western Historical Manuscript Collection, University of Missouri at Columbia, p. 59. "Upstairs, fine ladies and gentlemen": Goodrich, *Bloody Dawn,* p. 89. "Who sent for me?" and "What do you want": Lowman, *Narrative of the Lawrence Massacre,* p. 56. "I once boarded there": Breihan, *Younger Brothers,* p. 43. "A tempest of fire": Lowman, p. 58. "Hell let loose": Boughton, *Lawrence Massacre,* p. 10. "We are not so particular" and "We are fiends from Hell": Annie Laurie Quinby, sister of John and Will Laurie, quoted in Connelley, *Quantrill and the Border Wars,* p. 349. "Oh my God," "No, I won't let you," and "Getta wandered": Goodrich, *Bloody Dawn,* pp. 92, 94. "If they take Lawrence," "Where shall we meet?" and "Shoot him": Cordley, *A History of Lawrence, Kansas,* pp. 208–209. "We have killed your husband": Boughton, p. 12. "pounded his head": Lowman, p. 72. "weeping and wailing": Lowman, p. 49. "For God's sake do not go up there" and "she replied": Brown, "Quantrill Raid Account of William Brown," Western Historical Manuscript Collection, University of Missouri at Columbia, p. 3. "Every other house": Goodrich, *Bloody Dawn,* p. 102. "We have come," "If it is going to help," and "You have killed": Cordley, pp. 212, 213. "Fred, one of them damned nigger-thieving abolitionists" and "It was but a breath": Lowman, pp. 62–63. "they must bring him": Lowman, p. 82. "You want to know": *Lexington Herald* article quoted in Connelley, p. 353. "Quantrill has come!" "Oh! don't," and "There might have been": Robinson, "Sara Tappan Doolittle Robinson's Personal Recollections of Quantrill's Raid," Kansas Collection, University of Kansas Libraries, pp. 2, 6. "that a plantain leaf": Horton, "James C. Horton's Personal Narrative," *Kansas Historical Collections,* 1907–1908, vol. 10, p. 605. "they had been in Missouri": Lowman, p. 86. "Now is your time": Lowman, p. 70.

11. OH GOD, SAVE US!

"Along the walks": Lowman, *Narrative of the Lawrence Massacre,* p. 90. "Burn the God damn little brat": Goodrich, *Bloody Dawn,* p. 115. "his coolness and self-possession," "New York," "Oh it's you," "thrust his revolver," and "She then took her three little ones": Cordley, *A History of Lawrence, Kansas,* pp. 213–215. The Reverend Hugh Fisher incident: Fisher, *Gun and the Gospel,* pp. 196–204. "seized hold of the bridle rein": Boughton, *Lawrence Massacre,* p. 26. Cyclone cellar incident: Cordley, p. 222. Read family incident: Boughton, pp. 21–22. Bullene family incident: Cordley, p. 227. Allen incident: Boughton, p. 14. "He grasped the bridles": Lowman, p. 95. "I'll make you rue this": Goodrich, *Bloody Dawn,* p. 102. "Damn your Kansas hide": Breihan, *Younger Brothers,* p. 48. "We are old people": Cordley, p. 217. "Go and see": Cordley, p. 221. "Don't take on so": Boughton, p. 29. Asthma story: Croy, *Last of the Great Outlaws,* p. 35. "They told me": Cordley, p. 245. "Oh God": Lowman, p. 93. "He raised his hands": Connelley, *Quantrill and the Border Wars,* p. 380. "All you God damned": Goodrich, p. 117. "Him kill everybody": Connelley, p. 381. "Oh, we intend to kill": Connelley, p. 383.

12. LET US FOLLOW THEM, BOYS

"Down the Fort Scott Road": Goodrich, *Bloody Dawn*, p. 135. "Let us follow them": Cordley, *A History of Lawrence, Kansas*, p. 234. "Quantrill is in Lawrence": Connelley, *Quantrill and the Border Wars*, p. 398. "Tell Major Plumb": Cordley, p. 236. "Boys, let down these rail fences": Castel, *William Clarke Quantrill*, p. 137. "Throw the fence and charge": Cordley, p. 237. "waving their hats": Goodrich, p. 138. "The sweating bodies": Castel, p. 138. "It really looked as though," "Halt!" "Steady men," "his long hair," and "Some of the new": Gregg, "A Little Dab of History Without Embellishment," Western Historical Manuscript Collection, University of Missouri at Columbia, pp. 67–70. "Is that you, Plumb?": Goodrich, p. 143. "He was slow": General Ewing, *War of the Rebellion: Official Records*, series 1, vol. 22, part 1, p. 581. "I will just kill you": Connelley, pp. 412–413. "Boys, we are back home": Castel, p. 139. "The Kansans are coming . . . We will saddle up": Gregg, pp. 71–72. "Stop it!" and "Just take us out": Connelley, pp. 415–416. Pvt. Hervey Johnson's account: Unrau, "In Pursuit of Quantrill," *Kansas Historical Quarterly*, Autumn 1973, vol. 39, no. 3, pp. 386–388. "You are a dead dog": Connelley, p. 418.

13. THE HEATHEN ARE COME INTO THINE INHERITANCE

Reverend Cordley's account, including his wording of the Seventy-ninth Psalm: Cordley, *A History of Lawrence, Kansas*, pp. 239–249. "I want you to help me find my boy": Goodrich, *Bloody Dawn*, p. 122. Callew incident: Robinson, "Sara Tappan Doolittle Robinson's Personal Recollections of Quantrill's Raid," Kansas Collection, University of Kansas Libraries, p. 12. "Quantrill is coming" and spoons story: Allison, "Isadora Augusta Johnson Allison's Narrative: 'A Night of Terror'," Kansas Collection, University of Kansas Libraries, pp. 5–7. "They are coming again" and "reserves cracked": Goodrich, *Bloody Dawn*, p. 130. "Run for your life": Fisher, *Gun and the Gospel*, p. 213. "The horror of that Sunday": Cordley, p. 249. "Up to this morning": *Missouri Democrat* quoted in *War of the Rebellion: Official Records*, series 1, vol. 22, part 2, p. 487. Ridenour-Baker situation: Horton, "James C. Horton's Personal Narrative," *Kansas Historical Collections*, 1907–1908, vol. 10, p. 607. "The first week": Fisher,

p. 212. "The feeling among all classes": *The New York Times,* August 23, 1864. "Ewing is frightened": *Missouri Democrat* article quoted in *War of the Rebellion,* p. 487. "The feeling among": *The New York Times,* August 23, 1864. "horrors of the massacre," "My political enemies," "I have not the slightest doubt," and "pretty much convinced": *War of the Rebellion,* pp. 471–473. "I must hold Missouri": *War of the Rebellion,* series 1, vol. 22, part 1, p. 576. "The harshest military measure": Castel, *William Clarke Quantrill,* p. 145. "Perhaps the harshest act": Goodrich, *Black Flag,* p. 100. "Barefooted and bareheaded": Breihan, *Quantrill and His Civil War Guerrillas,* p. 139. "poor people": Castel, p. 145. Cole Younger's recollections of the Younger family evacuation: Brant, *Outlaw Youngers,* p. 52. "It is heart-sickening": Colonel Lazear quoted in Brownlee, *Gray Ghost of the Confederacy,* pp. 126–127. Bingham-Ewing confrontation: Larkin: *Fighting Artist,* pp. 201–206, 327–328. "Mediocre art": Castel, p. 147. "It was a pardon": Goodrich, *Bloody Dawn,* p. 153. "If I decided," "I, of course, would be held," "No armed bodies of men": *War of the Rebellion,* pp. 573–575. Jim Lane's last days: Fisher, p. 43; Speer, *Life of Gen. James H. Lane,* p. 315.

14. IT WAS A FEARFUL SIGHT

"those whom his order was designed to destroy": Castel, *William Clarke Quantrill,* p. 148. John McCorkle's account, including the drummer boy incident and the freed black man incident: McCorkle, *Three Years with Quantrill,* p. 89–95. "Oh, it is just a few of Jackman's guerrillas": Castel, p. 151. General Blunt; Colonel Blair; Major Henning; and Sergeant Splane: *War of the Rebellion: Official Records,* series 1, vol. 22, part 1, pp. 689–697. "Get up, you Federal son of a bitch": Connelley, *Quantrill and the Border Wars,* p. 430. "By God, Shelby could not whip Blunt": Steele and Cottrell, *Civil War in the Ozarks,* p. 83. Quantrill-McCorkle conversation: McCorkle, p. 93. "No, there is nothing to be gained": Gregg, "A Little Dab of History Without Embellishment," Western Historical Manuscript Collection, University of Missouri at Columbia, p. 86. "In a short time": McCorkle, p. 95. Quantrill's report to General Price: *War of the Rebellion,* p. 701. "it was not a pleasant winter": Hale, *They Called Him Bloody Bill,* p. 11. "A fairly good-looking girl": Croy, *Last of the Great Outlaws,* p. 40. General Price's letter to Governor Reynolds: *War of the Rebellion: Official Records,* series 1, vol. 53, pp. 907–908. "gallant command": *War of the Rebellion,* p. 908. McCulloch-Smith correspondence: *War of the Rebellion: Official Records,* series 1, vol. 26, part 2, pp. 348, 379, 383. "Regular Army to the shoesoles": Foote, *The Civil War,* vol. 1, p. 208. "brush crowd": Fellman, *Inside War,* p. 105. McCulloch-Magruder, McCulloch-Smith, and McCulloch-Bee correspondence: *War of the Rebellion: Official Records,* series 1, vol. 34, part 2, pp. 942, 945, 958. "No, sir, I will not go to dinner": Connelley, p. 441. "Boys . . . the outfit is under arrest!" and "Well, don't you know": Castel, pp. 166–167.

15. DEATH IS COMING

"This wholesale killing" and "I want to compensate": Gregg, "A Little Dab of History Without Embellishment," Western Historical Manuscript Collection, University of Missouri at Columbia, pp. 62, 76. "There goes," "I will not kill Gregg," "How about me?" "Oh, well," and "You're the only damned man I ever was afraid of": Connelley, *Quantrill and the Border Wars,* pp. 447–448. "subservient, conciliatory": Connelley, p. 437. "You are afraid of me" and "Yes . . . I'm afraid": Castel, *William Clarke Quantrill,* p. 170. "We are going into Fayette": Castel, p. 185. "Now began the wild . . . assault": Hale, *They Called Him Bloody Bill,* p. 38. "like charging a stone wall": Horan, *Authentic Wild West,* p. 127. Stagecoach and train incidents: Hale, pp. 46–47. Confrontation with Major Johnson's forces: Hale, pp. 51, 60; Horan, pp. 123, 126; McCorkle, *Three Years with Quantrill,* p. 115. On Anderson's body: *War of the Rebellion: Official Records,* series 1, vol. 41, part 4, p. 354. Younger's service for Anderson: *Richmond Missourian* article, June 11, 1908, quoted in Breihan, *Quantrill and His Civil War Guerrillas,* pp. 160–161. Anderson's grave site marker: Hale, p. 118. Todd-McCorkle conversation: McCorkle, p. 122. "I want no such riffraff" and "If you dare": Breihan, pp. 158–159. "It is certain": *War of the Rebellion,* p. 190. "35 guerrillas," "Captain Clarke escaped," "Order your men," and "I chased Quantrill": *War of the Rebellion: Official Records,* series 1, vol. 49, part 1, pp. 17–18, 35–36, 612, 625. Quantrill's poem of February 26, 1865: Kansas Collection, University of Kansas Libraries. "Now I am saved the trouble!": Breihan, p. 162. "Excuse us, ladies" and "Here's to the death of Abraham Lincoln": Connelley, p. 465. "That means my work is done": Connelley, p. 467. "It is useless" and "It is impossible": McCorkle, p. 151.

16. I'M TIRED OF RUNNING

Clements message to Major Davis: Hale, *They Called Him Bloody Bill*, p. 86. Colonel Harding's quotes: *War of the Rebellion: Official Records*, series 1, vol. 48, part 2, pp. 705–706. "slowed to a walk": Hale, p. 110. "I'm tired of running": Horan, *Authentic Wild West*, p. 1. "What have I been spared for": Horan, p. 124. "I am aware that my name": Breihan, *Younger Brothers*, p. 178. "Frank, we ought" and "If Cole Younger and Frank James": Croy, *Last of the Great Outlaws*, p. 193. "[Hamilton was pleading] for all sinners": Brant, *Outlaw Youngers*, pp. 309–310. "I want to repent": Croy, p. 194. "I guess you could strike lead": Croy, p. ix.

BIBLIOGRAPHY

Allison, Isadora Augusta Johnson. "A Night of Terror." Manuscript, Kansas Collection, University of Kansas Libraries.

Bidlack, Russell E. "Erastus D. Ladd's Description of the Lawrence Massacre." *Kansas Historical Quarterly* (Summer 1963): vol. 29, no. 2, pp. 113–121.

Boughton, J. S. *The Lawrence Massacre by Quantrell, August 21, 1863, As Given By Eye Witnesses of the Barbarous Scene Unparalleled in the History of Civilized Warfare.* Lawrence, Kansas: J. S. Boughton, Publisher, 1880.

Boyer, Richard O. *The Legend of John Brown: A Biography and a History.* New York: Alfred A. Knopf, 1973.

Brant, Marley. *The Outlaw Youngers: A Confederate Brotherhood.* Lanham: Madison Books, 1992.

Breihan, Carl W. *Quantrill and His Civil War Guerrillas.* New York: Promontory Press, 1959.

Breihan, Carl W. *Ride the Razor's Edge: The Younger Brothers Story.* Gretna, Louisiana: Pelican Publishing Company, 1992.

Breihan, Carl W. Younger Brothers. San Antonio: Naylor, no date.

Brown, William. "Quantrill Raid Account of William Brown." Manuscript, Western Historical Manuscript Collection, University of Missouri at Columbia.

Brownlee, Richard S. *Gray Ghost of the Confederacy: Guerrilla Warfare in the West, 1861–1865*. Baton Rouge: Louisiana State University Press, 1958.

Caldwell, Martha B. "The Eldridge House." *Kansas Historical Quarterly* (November 1940): vol. 9, no. 4, pp. 347–370.

Castel, Albert. *A Frontier State at War: Kansas, 1861–1865*. Ithaca, New York: Cornell University Press for the American Historical Association, 1958.

Castel, Albert. "The Guerrilla War, 1861–1865." *Civil War Times Illustrated*, 1974 (special issue).

Castel, Albert. *William Clarke Quantrill: His Life and Times*. New York: Frederick Fell, 1962.

Connelley, William Elsey. *Quantrill and the Border Wars*. Cedar Rapids, Iowa: Torch Press, 1910; New York: Pageant Book Company, 1956.

Conway, Alan. "The Sacking of Lawrence." *Kansas Historical Quarterly* (Summer 1958): vol. 24, no. 2, pp. 144–150.

Cordley, Richard. *A History of Lawrence, Kansas*. Lawrence: E. F. Caldwell, Lawrence Journal Press, 1895.

Croy, Homer. *Last of the Great Outlaws: The Story of Cole Younger*. New York: Duell, Sloan and Pearce, 1956.

Donald, David. *Charles Sumner and the Coming of the Civil War*. New York: Alfred A. Knopf, 1960.

Edwards, John. *Noted Guerrillas*. St. Louis: 1877.

Elliott, R. G. "The Quantrill Raid as Seen from the Eldridge House." *Kansas Historical Collections* (1920): vol. 2, pp. 179–196.

Fellman, Michael. *Inside War: The Guerrilla Conflict in Missouri During the American Civil War*. New York: Oxford University Press, 1989.

Fisher, Hugh D. *The Gun and the Gospel: Early Kansas and Chaplain Fisher* (2nd ed.). Chicago: Medical Century Company, 1899.

Foote, Shelby. *The Civil War*, vol. 1: *Fort Sumter to Perryville*. New York: Random House, 1958.

Goodrich, Thomas. *Black Flag: Guerrilla Warfare on the Western Border, 1861–1865*. Bloomington: Indiana University Press, 1995.

Goodrich, Thomas. *Bloody Dawn: The Story of the Lawrence Massacre.* Kent, Ohio: Kent State University Press, 1991.

Gregg, William H. "A Little Dab of History Without Embellishment." Manuscript, Western Historical Manuscript Collection, University of Missouri at Columbia.

Hale, Donald R. *They Called Him Bloody Bill: The Life of William Anderson, Missouri Guerrilla.* Clinton, Missouri: The Printery, 1992.

Horan, James D. *The Authentic Wild West: The Outlaws.* New York: Crown, 1977.

Horton, James C. "Personal Narrative: Peter D. Ridenour and Harlow W. Baker, Two Pioneer Kansas Merchants." *Kansas Historical Collections* (1907–1908): vol. 10, pp. 589–621.

Larkin, Lew. *Bingham: Fighting Artist: The Story of Missouri's Immortal Painter, Patriot, Soldier and Statesman.* Kansas City: Burton Publishing Company, 1954.

Lowman, H. E. *Narrative of the Lawrence Massacre on the Morning of the 21st of August, 1863.* Lawrence: State Journal Steam Press, 1864.

McCorkle, John. *Three Years with Quantrill: A True Story Told by his Scout.* Armstrong, Missouri: Armstrong Herald Printers, 1914; Norman: University of Oklahoma Press, 1992.

McPherson, James M. *Battle Cry of Freedom: The Civil War Era.* New York: Oxford University Press, 1988.

Monaghan, Jay. *Civil War on the Western Border, 1854–1865.* Boston: Little, Brown, 1955.

Nevins, Allan. *Ordeal of the Union,* vol. 2: *A House Dividing, 1852–1857.* New York: Charles Scribner's Sons, 1947.

Nichols, Alice. *Bleeding Kansas.* New York: Oxford University Press, 1954.

Oates, Stephen B. *To Purge This Land with Blood: A Biography of John Brown.* New York: Harper and Row, 1970.

Pike, Joshua A. "Statement of Captain J. A. Pike Concerning the Quantrill Raid." Manuscript, Western Historical Manuscript Collection, University of Missouri at Columbia.

Quantrill, William Clarke. Letters, Kansas Collection, University of Kansas Libraries, various dates.

Robinson, Sara Tappan Doolittle. "Personal Recollections of Quantrill's Raid." Manuscript, Kansas Collection, University of Kansas Libraries.

Speer, John. *Life of General James H. Lane, "The Liberator of Kansas,"
with Corroborative Incidents of Pioneer History.* Garden City,
Kansas: John Speer, Printer, 1896.

Steele, Phillip W., and Cottrell, Steve. *Civil War in the Ozarks.* Gretna,
Louisiana: Pelican Publishing Company, 1993.

Unrau, William E. (Ed.). "In Pursuit of Quantrill: An Enlisted Man's
Response." *Kansas Historical Quarterly* (Autumn 1973): vol. 39,
no. 3, pp. 379–391.

U.S. War Department. *War of the Rebellion: A Compilation of the Official Records of the Union and Confederate Armies.* Washington,
DC: Government Printing Office.

Williams, Burton J. "Quantrill's Raid on Lawrence: A Question of
Complicity." *Kansas Historical Quarterly* (Summer 1968): vol.
34, no. 2, pp. 143–149.

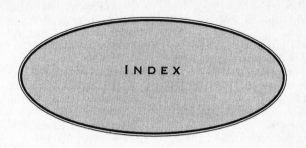

INDEX

Doyle, James & Mahala, 40
Dry Wood Creek battle, 69, 77

Edwards, John, 130, 145
Eldridge, James, 192–193
Eldridge House, 149, 171–174,
181, 191
Ellis, Abraham, 89–91
Ellis, Lt., 187–188, 204–205
Ewing, Thomas, Jr., 142, 150, 152,
156, 160, 223, 228–230,
241–244, 253, 281
background, 136–137
confrontation with Bingham,
246– 248
confrontation with Lane, 230
establishes border outposts,
138–139
issues depopulation order, 243–
244

Fayette raid, 283–284
Fickle, Annie, 82–83
Fillmore, Lemuel, 190
Finley, James B., 176
Fisher, Elizabeth, 196–199
Fisher, Hugh, 196–199, 237, 240–
241, 252
Fitch, Edward & Sarah, 195, 233
Ford, Bob, 305
Ford, Mr., 192
Fort Baxter battle, 255–256
Fort Bridger, 15
Fort Gibson, 257
Fort Leavenworth, 15, 92–93, 120,
152
Fort Scott Road, 214–218, 256
Fort Sumter, 66
Foster, Emory, 118, 119
Frank Leslie's Weekly correspon
dent, 259
Free-Soilers, 27–30, 32, 36, 42, 44,
45, 55
Free State, 32
Free State Hotel, 32, 34, 149
Free-state movement, 21–46
Fugitive slaves, 48–52, 54–56
Full moon scare, 151–152

Gates, Levi, 179–180
General Orders:
No. 10, 140
No. 11, 230, 242–251, 253, 265,
281
No. 32, 85, 94
No. 92, 250
George, Hicks, 108
Gilchrist, Joe, 101
Glassock, Dick, 299
Goodman, Thomas, 286–287
Gower, James, 106–107, 109, 110
Greeley, Horace, 149
Gregg, Bill (William H.), 88–90,
94, 98–99, 101, 116, 119, 121,
122, 124–127, 132, 145, 155–
156, 161–163, 167, 169, 170,
212, 214, 220, 226, 227,
255–256
elected third lieutenant, 117
leaves bushwhackers, 276–278
on Quantrill's leadership, 133
on Sugar Creek battle, 107–110
Griswold, Jerome F., 181–182,
192
Grovenor, Gordon, 210
Guest, William, 164

Hadley, T. J., 150–152, 187
Hale, Donald, 290
Hall, Nora, 307
Hallar, William, 117, 118, 120
Halleck, Henry W., 85, 94
Hamilton, Charles, 45
Hamilton, Orville, 307
Hampson, John F., 176–177
Harding, Chester, 302–303
Hart, Charley, see Quantrill,
William Clarke
Hayes, Upton, 106, 111, 112, 116,
118–121
Hazeltine, William, 192
Henning, Benjamin, 259
Herald of Freedom, 32
Herald Tribune, 149
Herd, Jake, 47–49, 51–52, 54
Higbee, Charles, 130
Hindman, Thomas, 128, 129, 132